Barbie's Queer Accessories

Erica Rand

Duke University Press

Durham and London

1995

© 1995 Duke University Press   All rights reserved
Fourth printing, 2003
Printed in the United States of America on acid-free paper ∞
Typeset in Century Oldstyle by Tseng Information Systems, Inc.
Library of Congress Cataloging-in-Publication Data appear on
the last printed page of this book.
"Homocide" and "Soft Targets" from *Ceremonies* by Essex Hemphill,
copyright (©) 1992 by Essex Hemphill. Used by permission of
Dutton Signet, a division of Penguin Books USA Inc.

Barbie is a registered trademark of the Mattel Corporation, and
Barbie images and material are protected under copyrights of the
Mattel Corporation. The references to Barbie material and the
use of Barbie images in this book are made under the fair use
provisions of U.S. copyright law, which protect the reproduction of
a work "for purposes such as criticism, comment, news reporting,
teaching, scholarship, or research." This book is not authorized
by the Mattel Corporation.

Contents

To Marilyn Graton

Acknowledgments

In 1992, when Kelly McCullough asked for a summer research job, I had no idea what an undergraduate assistant could do that would take a whole summer. My imagination turned out to be as limited as her contribution, which began with getting the job funded, was stupendous. I assigned her little beyond the drudge work of bibliographic retrieval. She did much more: she figured out things I needed, like annual reports, before I did; decoded Mattel's phone system to get beyond low-level triage; coaxed out much more material than Mattel ordinarily dispenses; tracked down and interviewed interesting people, including a person she read about in passing whom Mattel hired to play Barbie in shopping-mall fashion shows. Everyone she contacted, it seems, was willing to speak to her for hours and often volunteered to send helpful material, like 120 newspaper articles on Barbie's thirtieth birthday. During the next summer, Kelly conducted great consumer interviews. Virtually every section in this book owes much to her creative research and remarkable talent as an interviewer. I thank, too, Elise Greven, who did a lot of early groundwork at a time when Bates College still thought that primary compensation for student assistants should be the "honor" of working for a faculty member.

To many others, too, I owe gratitude. My Barbie writing began with an essay for Laura Doan's *The Lesbian Postmodern* (1994, Columbia University Press); Laura accepted my project despite her initial invitation to write about something else and gave helpful comments at this early stage. Ken Wissoker suggested that I write the book and has been a dream editor throughout. It is often said that it took a doll named Ken for Barbie to really get a life. While this is hardly true about Barbie, not the least because Midge came later, it is certainly true of *Barbie's Queer Accessories*. Georgia Nigro shared her expertise in child psychology. Charles Nero and William Pope.L, two incredible culture guys to have down the block and down the stairs, let me accost them repeatedly when I needed someone to work through my thoughts with. While they are cited only a few times, their insights are everywhere influential. So, too, are those of Bee Bell, whose fierce activist and critical talents, among many others, have abetted my survival and pleasure, and those of Annette Dragon, whose photographic assistance represents only one of the top skills that have taken me through many pains and many delights.

I presented material in progress at Wayne State University, the Pennsylvania State University, the University of Missouri, and the University of Southern Maine, and in a panel sponsored by the Gay and Lesbian Caucus of the College Art Association. Comments on each occasion were invaluable, as were close readings of the manuscript by Lynn Spigel, Michèle Barale, and Michael Moon. Countless people shared Barbie clippings, videos, creations, objects, and stories. I am grateful to the adults who were willing to share their sometimes difficult memories and to the girls, especially Hannah and Kathryn, who led me candidly into their own current, complicated, and compellingly theorized imaginative worlds.

I was helped at Bates College by a Roger C. Schmutz faculty research grant, by a one-semester pretenure leave, and by many people: Rebecca Corrie, Don Lent, Bill Matthews, Jim Parakilas, and Martha Crunkleton, who got me out of trouble repeatedly, or, more precisely, helped me remain simultaneously in trouble and employed; everyone who fed my research via interdepartment mail, especially Dennis Grafflin, Anne Williams, Bob Branham, and Marcy Plavin; Sheila Sylvester, Ann Darby, Joyce Caron, Sylvia Deschaine, Sylvia Hawks, and Sandra Groleau, who make it possible for me to retain time and energy to write; inspired and inspiring students; the Gay-Lesbian-Bisexual Alliance; Paula Matthews, Paul Heroux, Ned Harwood, Christina Brinkley, and Robert Feintuch; and Paqui Lopez, Avi Chomski, and Kirk Read (if Barbie ever goes tenure track, Barbie's Dream Cohort ought to look a lot like mine). I thank also my aerobics classmates and teachers at the Auburn, Maine, YMCA, the one place where no one ever treats me like a scandal and where, consequently, I found unexpected haven. Ana R. Kissed, Rose Marasco, Elspeth Brown, Ray Gagnon, Kevin Gagnon, and the people in ACT UP/Portland are great allies with whom I have been privileged to hook up since moving to Lewiston. People who think that good politics happen only in big cities need to learn otherwise. And all should have met Don Plourde. An inspiring advocate for educational access, queer rights, and universal health care, he could speak the politics of social justice in a language accessible to virtually everyone who heard him, which he compelled many people to do. I miss him.

These people represent only some of many who, directly or indirectly, have, over many years, contributed to my thinking about the stuff of Barbie consumption—sex and passion, friends and lovers, power and politics, past and present, people and objects. I thank also Beth Helsinger, Kelly Hensen, Susan Hill, Joanne Kalogeras, Jonathan Katz, David Keer, Lise Kildegaard, Sura Levine, Sallie McCorkle, Nadine McGann, Susan Miller, Andrew Parker, Mary Patten, Linda Seidel, Mary Sheriff, and Maxine Wolfe. I owe much as well to my family: my siblings, Spencer Rand and Cynthia Barabas, who let me tell our stories; my late grandfathers, Bill Chananie and Irving Rand; my grandmothers, Sophie Chananie, Adele Rand, and Iola Graton; my stepfather, Waldo Graton, and everyone he brought with him—since my own Barbie story concerns family grief over the death of my biological father, Jack Rand, I want also to record here the subsequent pleasure of expanding the family portrait. I learned at home to be "out and proud" as a Jew and to take risks for social justice with attention to my own survival. While a book with *queer* in the title is not the outcome for which many in my family had hoped to take credit, they all stand by me anyway. Finally, this book is dedicated to my mother, Marilyn Graton, who taught me when I was nine that every historical narrative is invested with the politics of the teller. All my work since has been based on this principle and emboldened by her love and support. Barbie's life, rumor has it, has been greatly enhanced by having no visible parentage. I doubt it.

Introduction:

On Our Backs,

in Our Attics,

on Our Minds

Like Barbie, who comes with several conflicting myths of origin that seem at once to explain everything and nothing—The Devoted Mom Who Wanted a Fashion Doll for Her Daughter, The Inventor Who Also Helped Design the Sparrow and Hawk Missiles and Later Married Zsa Zsa Gabor, and The U.S. Entrepreneurs Who Realized They Could Market a German Sex-Symbol Doll to Children—this book has several telling, if partial, founding tales.

Founding Tale 1: In the fall of 1989, when I was teaching at Northeastern Illinois University, my friend Joanne Kalogeras sent me a recent issue of the lesbian sex magazine *On Our Backs* because it contained a photo-essay called "Gals and Dolls" that features a woman inserting a Barbie (feet first) into her vagina.[1] I loved it, and I immediately wanted to teach it in my art history/women's studies class. I had scheduled a unit on popular culture, and the photographs seemed like a refreshingly direct response to the often-asked feminist query, how can pop culture be subversively refunctioned for women's pleasure?

Besides, Barbie seemed like a great takeoff point for considering cultural appropriation in general. Barbie has been ubiquitous now for three decades. Surely Barbie was a cultural icon whom virtually all my students, who varied widely in age and social background, could identify. Many, I speculated, might also remember having positioned themselves, as children or as mothers, in relation to Barbie. Barbie also has some features particularly conducive to lesbian reappropriation: the nifty Barbie-of-the-eighties slogan "We girls can do anything" (or "Go Girl" as Queer Nation Barbie might put it) and a series of wardrobe-crafted identities to pull out of her closet. Like Madonna, then approaching her peak of popularity in lesbian subculture, Barbie suggests that roles are only as fixed as costumes. I was also interested in the Barbie features that make her seem to resist the free play of accessorizing signifiers. One potential limit to Lesbian Barbie obsessed me: Barbie's closet may be diversely stocked, assuming one can make what one can't buy, but her body, with its permanently pointed breasts and feet, seemed unalterably fem. Could Barbie, firmly premolded by Mattel, really be liberated from it? Barbie seemed like a great tool for discussing the difficulties as well as the subversive potential of cultural subversion.

Yet I worried about inserting a Barbie dildo into the heterosexist context of the university classroom. My job situation was precarious; what would my colleagues think about me teaching, or owning, lesbian porn? Could I maintain spin control in the classroom? Could I frame the images discursively so as to be more than scandalous, so as to avoid merely reinforcing stereotypes about lesbian perversity? Assuming that most of my students had a quite limited mental stockpile of lesbian images, could any discursive frame prevent them from thinking that these photographs typified lesbian practice? I didn't want them to think that all lesbians lived in pairs with two children, many Birkenstocks, and a sex life characterized by nurturing sweetness, but I didn't necessarily want them to think of woman-with-Barbie-dildo as normative either.

I also worried about the ethics and politics of circulating lesbian erotica among nonlesbians. I knew I wouldn't be violating the wishes of the publishers; *On Our Backs,* which advertises in straight, if "alternative," publications such as the *Chicago Reader,* is hardly a separatist publication.[2] Nor did I ordinarily balk at showing images that generated discomfort. But I wondered how my dyke students would react. Would flashing our subcultural sex products on the screen or the predictable derisive class comments make any of them feel uncomfortable, unsafe, or violated? I wanted to ask them, but I couldn't. In a world where the closet prevails it is impossible to know exactly who the dykes in one's classroom are. Most of the dykes I could identify had come out to me, as often happens in the classroom and elsewhere, only through subtle hints offered up on the tacit condition that nothing would ever be explicitly articulated; to approach them on the subject might be more violatory than showing the images without their input.

Clearly, though, I needed advice. So I asked friends and colleagues, whose responses can be loosely coded by gender and sexual orientation. Liberal straight men (I encountered no gay men in my casual survey) said, "Show them—and I'd be happy to look at them first if you're unsure." Straight women got this sick, trapped look; they thought it might be a bad idea but feared giving the impression that they wanted to censure either the images or the acts depicted. The dykes first said, "Don't show them," but after further discussion advised me semiseriously to have the slides made, read my horoscope on the day of class, and go for it if the signs were favorable.

All this Barbie talk did little to help me solve my pedagogical dilemma, but it led to an interesting discovery. People were dying to play Barbie with me. They gave me Barbie presents: stickers; valentines; postcards from the Nostalgic Barbie series that make gentle Mattel-authorized fun of Barbie; a Barbie beanbag chair sized for children; a tiny Barbie personal computer that scrolls text (sort of); the most amazing official Barbie lingerie with thigh-high pink and black lace stockings and a matching strapless chemise that won't stay up over her breasts even if you pose Barbie, as I did, with her head down and her butt in the air; two Barbie lunch boxes, one with the Barbie thermos replaced by adult toys; and a Barbie reaccessorized to be Sex-Play Barbie, who comes with a little hand-carved dildo and grown-up handcuffs "just like Barbie's." I also got articles, student papers, newspaper clippings, and bibliographic citations, from which I learned about many things: the stripper duo Mattel sued for using Barbie and Ken as stage names; the woman who spent $50,000 on plastic surgery in order to look like Barbie; the recent fad among gay men for taking Barbie to the beach; the Barbie Round-Up in Nevada for adult Barbie collectors; and innumerable examples of Barbie art and Barbie play that will never wind up in a Saturday-morning commercial.

People also wanted to tell me Barbie stories. My friends told me about how they had loved or hated Barbie and about what they had done with and to her—how they had turned her punk, set her on fire, made her fuck Midge or Ken or G.I. Joe, or, on occasion, gotten the much advertised "hours of fun" by following Mattel's directions. People I hardly knew who heard of my interest were anxious to tell me their Barbie tales. More stories came in from friends who, unasked, had collected Barbie anecdotes from their friends and families for me.

These tales confirmed my initial speculation that many people remember positioning themselves in relation to Barbie. They also suggested, however, how much I had misimagined these positionings as involving a relatively simple decision about whether Barbie was cool or a bimbo. I began to see that

Barbie generated far more intense and complex reactions, partly because I had retrieved my own Barbie memory, which leads to the following.

Founding Tale 2: One reason that I loved the Barbie dildo, aside from its potential as a teaching tool, was that it gave me an opportunity to extract Barbie from a context of painful childhood memories. My mother, like many, disapproved of Barbie and did not want me to have the pointy-breasted teenager who literally couldn't stand on her own two feet; she also disdained the military-glamourizing G.I. Joe. But after my father died, when I was six, the influx of toys for the children, from people who didn't know how else to show support, included a Barbie doll and a Barbie Queen-of-the-Prom game for me and a G.I. Joe for my three-year-old brother. While my brother adored his G.I. Joe—failing, as I noted with some sibling-rivalry satisfaction, to understand its political retroness—I followed my mother's lead and determined to show little interest in Barbie. I remember my junior feminist analysis (or memorization) of Barbie's dubious value as a role model and my childlike socioeconomic analysis of why I'd never have more Barbie clothes than the outfit Barbie came with: only girls with rich mothers or with mothers who sewed had those. Mostly, however, I remember reciting to myself over and over a telling explanation of my mother's reluctance to separate my brother from his G.I. Joe: "Mom can't take it away from him because *he's* already lost too much." This construction of myself as a rational yet emotionally attuned grown-up caregiver (for those I labeled more bereaved than I) established a habit of dislocating my own grief that took several decades to unknot. For years, I thought that this was primarily a story about Barbie since it was she on whom I most consciously expended my emotional and intellectual labor; only recently did I realize that this was fundamentally a story about something else.

My Barbie story is relatively atypical in being a story about gender identity and death instead of gender identity and sex, but my understanding of a childhood relation to Barbie as a revelatory feature of my psychological, ideological, and political development is fairly common. In many stories I heard or read, people either saw their childhood disinterest in Barbie as an early herald of their adult status as a gender-role outlaw or had some similarly intense story to tell about Barbie play that seemed as self-illuminating to them as my Barbie story seems to me: I must have been a dyke at age five because, I knew I understood white-girl privilege because, I made Ken a rapist because—and so on.

Barbie's Queer Accessories concerns the use and circulation of Barbie: what you can, and could formerly, buy from Mattel; what Mattel tells you to do, and not to do, with Barbie; what people have done with Barbie as adults and as kids; what Barbie play suggests about the place of the consumer in cultural studies, about the place of queerness in relation to mainstream and margin, about the effects of cultural products on ideology, and about the limits and possibilities of cultural subversion as a strategy of political activism. As this list of topics suggests, I approach this project both as a political activist and as a cultural critic and theorist (not that politics, theory, and criticism can be separated) and from a particular interest in doing dyke, feminist, and queer work both within and outside academics. Since my perspective has determined the content of this book, and since there are many other voices and goals from which a study of Barbie might well proceed, some discussion of my focus and omissions is in order.

In stating that I undertake the study of Barbie as a political project, I do not intend to suggest that a book about Barbie can provide a textbook for social and economic justice. Such a claim would be as ludicrous as it would be self-aggrandizing; justice requires redistribution of resources and power, which neither studying nor subverting Barbie can effect. Yet cultural products need political attention. Political battles are fought over and through the manipulation of cultural symbols. People use them to signal political identities, to effect political coalitions, to disrupt and challenge beliefs and connections that have come to seem natural. People also glean their sense of possibility and self-worth partly from available cultural products—objects, narratives, interpretations. Surely, for instance, the feelings of despair, self-loathing, and helplessness that often attend coming out to oneself stem partly from living in an environment filled with pop songs, music videos, movies, books, television shows, and ads that presume or articulate the naturalness and greater value of heterosexual desire. The world will not change if Brandon and Dylan become lovers and join ACT UP 90210, but it matters that we already know that they won't, no matter how often they looked soulfully into each other's eyes during the first few seasons. It also matters that Mattel chose these white, rich, and heterosexual characters to turn into dolls and that they made dolls out of all the main teen characters except the Jewish ones.

Joseph Beam eloquently describes the political toll of living in a hostile cultural world:

> On the walls surrounding me are pictures of powerful people, mentors if you will. Among them are: Audre Lorde, James Baldwin, John Edgar Wideman, Essex Hemphill, Lamont Steptoe, Judy Grahn, Tommy Avicolli, Charles Fuller, Toni Morrison, and Barbara Smith. These writers,

of local and international fame, are connected by their desire to create images by which they could survive as gays and lesbians, as blacks, and as poor people. Their presence in my writing space bespeaks what another writer, Samuel Delany, calls "the possibility of possibilities."

But it has not always been this way. In the winter of '79, in grad school, in the hinterlands of Iowa, I thought I was the first black gay man to have ever lived. I knew not how to live my life as a man who desired emotional, physical, and spiritual fulfillment from other men. I lived a guarded existence: I watched how I crossed my legs, held my cigarettes, the brightness of the colors I wore. I was sure that some effeminate action would alert the world to my homosexuality. I spent so much energy in self-observation that little was left for classwork and still less to challenge the institutionalized racism I found there. . . .

Several years passed before I realized that my burden of shame could be a source of strength. It was imperative for my survival that I did not attend to or believe the images that were presented of black people or of gay people. Perhaps that was the beginning of my passage from passivism to activism, that I needed to create my reality, that I needed to create images by which I, and other black gay men to follow, could live this life.[3]

Political struggle demands attention to culture—understanding what's out there, resisting cultural messages that disempower us, creating and circulating alternative visions.

Barbie already looms large on the battlefield of cultural politics. Feminists and antiracists debate Barbie's effects on little girls. Queer activists wear "I cross-dressed my Barbie" T-shirts. Loggers accuse Mattel of promoting leftist eco-values when a commercial shows children at the Barbie Children's Summit singing about saving the trees. Mattel tries to cash in on political trends ranging from liberation discourse (thus Doctor Barbie and a new line of African American fashion dolls who "proudly" wear "ethnic print" clothing) to pro-military patriotism (thus Barbie's appearance annually since 1989 in a different military costume). And Barbie consumers have told enough childhood stories of forming their political, sexual, and gender identities in reaction to Barbie, and, conversely, of transforming or discarding Barbie to suit those identities, to indicate that Mattel and its critics have good reason to be concerned about the politics of Barbie.

The political battles over Barbie raise many questions about how culture affects politics. Why do particular cultural products become the bearers of so much meaning for so many people? What about Barbie, as opposed to other dolls, toys, books, or games, makes her so important? How much do (can) cultural producers direct consumption? How much do children follow cues from Mattel as they play with and think about Barbie? To what extent does Barbie's popularity come from the doll itself rather than from Mattel's successful marketing strategies—like the recently developed Wall of Pink, which entails packaging the dolls so that rows and rows of bright pink boxes attract the eye in toy stores?

How influential can individual products really be? Each of the many stories told by feminists about being oppressed by Barbie as a child at once testifies to Barbie's influence and provides evidence that it might be short-lived; after all, they have all been told by people who developed a stance of political consciousness from which they have rejected the Barbie ideal. There is also a chicken-and-egg issue about the causal relation between the popularity of Barbie and the continuing value placed on white, skinny, voluptuous, blue-eyed, blond females: Do people like Barbie because she reflects values acquired elsewhere, or do they learn first to value Barbie and then to value what she represents?

To what extent do people's narratives and memories about individual cultural products provide an accurate index of their influence? Many Barbie "survivor" stories occur in the context of political coming-to-consciousness tales or narratives of identity formation. How much does the desire to fashion an autobiography—to find in the past an explanation for the present—create or enhance the perception of Barbie's significance? Why have Barbie stories burgeoned recently? Have new social/political/cultural circumstances, or new habits of cultural criticism, or the proliferation of Barbie articles around Barbie's thirtieth birthday in 1989, triggered either people's memories or the desire to relate them? Given that memories rarely survive through decades as anything close to accurate transcriptions of events, is there any way to strip away distortions or to generalize about where and when they operate?

Conversely, what index of cultural affect do memories of noninfluence provide? Did Barbie actually fail to influence people who don't remember being transformed by Barbie, or do those people fail to recognize that influence? It could certainly be argued that one of the most pernicious effects of dubious cultural products is that they implant their values so subtly that few people will realize that they have a tale of value acquisition to tell. How many people, for instance, will come to wonder where they got the idea that God has no material form and simultaneously looks like an old white guy with a beard? Yet it's condescending and presumptuous to view as duped every consumer who doesn't remember having been affected by Barbie. When do nonmemories indicate nothing to remember, and when do they indicate the acquisition of values that are experienced as innate?

These are all questions of political as well as academic interest: we need to determine why and how much products transmit value in order to design effective strategies of cultural activism and to gauge the effort that should be devoted to cultural activism in political work. It is from this perspective that I conceive of this book as a political project and with this political goal in mind that I have chosen the issues on which to focus.

Chapter 1 concerns the history of Barbie and the Barbie meanings promoted by Mattel. Barbie provides a great opportunity to study the role of "artistic intention" in the creation of meaning because, unlike many cultural producers, Mattel is quite anxious to spread the word about what it wants its product to signify. Mattel's Barbie strategies also yield insight about two features of cultural value management that have received much attention: consent and incorporation. Many scholars have persuasively argued, following Antonio Gramsci's theory of hegemony, that dominant social groups achieve their dominance over subordinate groups, not just by imposing rules, but also, and sometimes more effectively, by promoting a belief system, or a dominant ideology, that both induces subordinated people to perceive their subordinate status as natural or commonsensical and is flexible enough to incorporate resistance to it. We are more likely to behave and think in ways that support our dominators rather than ourselves if we believe that we are choosing these behaviors and values freely—if we believe, for instance, that men should run governments and households because they are more rational than women. We are less likely to threaten the social order if we can be guided to channel antiestablishment anger into actions that only signal breaking the rules, like wearing a leather jacket (now available at fine department stores everywhere), or that break rules to no political benefit, like trashing your hotel room on tour.[4]

Mattel cannot be described as a social group, but it is certainly in the business of trying to shape the opinions and actions of many people for its own benefit, and it does so precisely by manipulating the concept of freedom so that consumers will embrace a very limited series of actions that will seem to have been chosen from an infinite range of possibilities. That is, Mattel touts Barbie as a catalyst for fantasy and since the 1960s has deliberately refrained from circulating certain Barbie biographical details or narratives—such as an age, a geographic location, or a wedding—that might foreclose fantasy options. Yet Mattel obviously wants children to decide that their fantasies would be aided by owning the limited and specific goods that Mattel is selling—Barbie can be anything, but wouldn't it be especially fun to make her a rock star with this Lights 'N Lace outfit and stage that you can buy?

Mattel, which sold $870 million of Barbie products in 1991 and was poised to top the $1 billion mark in 1993, thus merits study as an exemplar of successful hegemonic discourse. Mattel also merits study for its role in perpetuating other hegemonic discourses, and thereby the dominance of those served by these discourses, in the process of promoting itself. To name but a few such dubious ideological effects: Mattel promotes compulsory heterosexuality by making it look like the most natural and attractive choice; it promotes capitalism and the unequal distribution of resources by glamourizing a character with a huge amount of apparently unearned disposable cash and, to understate grossly, a disproportionate amount of luxury items; it promotes ageism and sexism by suggesting that a beautiful young body is a woman's most valuable commodity; it promotes racism by making "white" Barbie the standard (although it recently embraced a superficial multiculturalism in order to attract more ethnicity-conscious consumers, "Hispanic Barbie" remains a Hispanic version of Barbie).

Mattel's huge financial success testifies both to the power of hegemonic discourse in general and to Mattel's mastery of it. Consumer stories, however, suggest a somewhat different conclusion about both Mattel's mastery of hegemonic discourse and the capacity of hegemonic-discourse theory to explain cultural consumption. In chapter 2, I discuss adults' testimony about what they did with and thought about Barbie as children. Their stories indicate that, although Mattel has been incredibly successful in disseminating a sense of Barbie's desirability, both as an object and as a representation of socially desired characteristics, it has by no means sold all Barbie's consumers on the kind of play seen in commercials. To name but one commonly reinterpreted feature, as Teresa Ortega queries, "If Barbie has so many clothes, why is she always naked?"

Yet the countless examples of consumers reinterpreting Barbie do not necessarily signal Mattel's failure to inscribe meaning. Consumers who reinterpret Barbie's dressability as undressability may still think Barbie is the most beautiful doll in the world. And some people, such as Hayley Spicer, who won a national contest to find a "real-life" Barbie, seem to have bought the whole ideological line: "I am Barbie. My lifestyle is the same as hers. I like fast cars and horseback riding. My friends' daughters even call their Barbie dolls Hayley." While Spicer must certainly have tailored the Hayley/Barbie fit for public-relations reasons—she later modified it to the slightly better sounding, "I'm just like Barbie. I'm beautiful, ambitious, intelligent and aware of the environment and world problems"[5]—her desire to represent Barbie, along with evidence from other consumers, testifies to Mattel's influence.

Overall, the degree of fit, or lack thereof, between Mattel-generated meaning and consumer-generated interpretation varies considerably. So, too, does the apparent correlation between resistance to Mattel and resistance to social circumstances. Many of the oppositions that we often use to map cultural products—such as imitation versus subversion, dominant versus emergent, hegemonic versus counterhegemonic—tend to imply that we can judge resistance by whether the consumer of a product rejects or reauthorizes intended meanings. But Barbie consumption suggests that these oppositions do not suffice. One consumer might dress Barbie in Ken's clothes to protest repressive gender stereotyping. Another might do it because she thinks that girls should be girls and wants to make Barbie look like the kids she tortures on the playground. Still others seem to have expressed resistance through games that seem to follow Mattel's directions, using Barbie's glamourous careers, for instance, to imagine themselves out of difficult circumstances. This chapter looks at a broad, if not systematically diversified, range of consumers, in an attempt to discern who transforms meaning, how different factors contribute to meaning production—the products themselves, Mattel promotions, the influence of parents and peers, personal history, and matters of individual identity such as class, gender, sexuality, race, and economic status—and how the meanings produced bear on the relation between intention, reception, and resistance.

Chapter 3 examines adult subversions of Barbie pursued for pleasure, profit, and/or social criticism. Subversive reposings of Barbie occur in art, film, fiction, poetry, 'zines etc.; their number has grown exponentially in the past few years. I return here to the political and pedagogical issues that first interested me in Barbie via "Gals and Dolls": Can you steal Barbie from Mattel and circulate her with liberatory readings intact? I argue that, although Subversive Barbies wind up replicating in circulation a huge number of Mattel-generated Barbie features, it is nonetheless possible to steal this doll for political and pedagogical gain. Subversive Barbies in circulation also raise some broader issues about outing and the relation between academics and activism, which I discuss at the end of the chapter.

These chapters, then, explore from different angles what Iain Chambers calls "the flexible dialogue between the given and the possible" in consumer culture,[6] using Barbie consumption to examine the limits of both: what has been given, what has been possible, and what may be possible in the future. Throughout them runs another issue to which the title of the book refers: queerness. As the productions and consumptions that I discuss reveal, Barbie interpreters often function as Barbie's queer accessories. I am concerned here with *queerness* in two different common senses of which one, the other, or both may apply to a given interpreter: the narrow sex/gender sense of lesbian, gay, bisexual, and transgender and the broader sense of odd, irregular, and idiosyncratic. Since working this term from two angles is a complicated endeavor, I want to preface my discussion of what makes consumers queer accessories with some comment about what I do and don't intend to signify through this double use.

These two senses of *queer*, of course, are entangled historically and allusively (each use of *queer* calls to mind the other), and I have chosen to use *queer* partly for this entanglement, which lends to each sense a charge appropriate to the subject of Barbie consumption. The allusion to sex/gender queerness contained within *queer* used more broadly amplifies and invokes the perceived illicitness of deviant Barbie readings and uses of all sorts. The broader reference within the narrower reference helps to situate sex/gender queerings, which, generally, are queer in both senses, within a broader context of deviations. By taking advantage of this interallusiveness, however, I risk contributing to three dubious effects that run directly counter to my intentions. The first effect is the despecification of *queer* in the narrow sense: I don't want to steal from *queer* its potential to refer specifically to sex/gender queerness. The second is the despecification of forms of deviation and resistance that do not concern primarily or only sex/gender queering by applying to them a label that has sex/gender buzz: I don't want to hide issues of class or ethnicity, for example, under a blanket label queer. The third, which relates to the second, is the implication that sex/gender queerness or queer studies is the be-all-and-end-all of deviance and resistance, so that *queer* becomes a gold star to be applied to every manifestation of either. It shouldn't be: the antiracist subversive Barbies I discuss, for instance, need to be valued as antiracist, not because they can be subsumed under the label *queer—which they absolutely cannot be—*for having queered Barbie's meaning. Throughout the text, I have tried to minimize these negative effects by specifying the particular use of *queer* to which I refer and the particular contents of queerings that are not sex/gender focused.

This said, Barbie interpreters often function as Barbie's queer accessories, in either or both senses, in two ways. They act as accessories to the crime of helping Barbie escape from the straight world in which Mattel has tried to

enclose her; they queer Barbie's intended meanings by giving her queer artifactual and narrative accessories. Alternately, or sometimes simultaneously,
they act as queer accessories in the sense of unlikely allies; in the process
of queering Barbie, they sometimes become unwitting allies in Mattel's attempt to make her go straight. I study here relations between queerness
and straightness suggested by consumer narratives and productions, which
vary considerably. Sometimes, queerness looks like the dominant feature and
underlying truth behind straight facades. At other times, consumers seem to
be queer acting rather than straight acting, to be queering stories that seem
straighter below the surface than on it. All told, however, Barbie consumption confirms what theorists of queerness, resistance, and nonconformity
have been saying for some time now: queerness and resistant readings occur
at the center as well as at the margins of dominant culture. Where and how
they reside is another subject of this book.

This is what the book includes. What it excludes, and the reasons behind
my inclusions, exclusions, and methodological choices, I discuss by way of
an account of my extended Barbie interaction over three years with one consumer, Hannah. I met Hannah, then three years old, in the fall of 1990 when I
began teaching at Bates College in Lewiston, Maine, where Hannah has lived
all her life, and became friends with her parents, both of whom are on the faculty: her father, a composer, teaches music; her mother is a librarian whose
job includes being the audio librarian. We adults are all transplants to Lewiston, a small industrial city of thirty-nine thousand residents, many hard hit
by difficult economic times. The residents are predominantly white (over 95
percent). Franco-Americans of French Canadian ancestry, the largest ethnic
group, constitute the majority of the population and have also suffered a long
history of prejudice; *French* is often a derogatory appellation.

My first Barbie-related encounter with Hannah came in December 1990,
when she showed me a doll she was playing with in the bathtub. This was
a "fake" Barbie, which she knew; as I learned from her parents, she was
asking for a real one. Our second encounter occurred the next summer, by
which time she had a real Barbie, during a surprise birthday party for me at
her house. One gift was Western Fun Nia, from the Barbie line, which came
from my department chair's ten-year-old daughter, who knew I had only one
Barbie and insisted that her mother buy me another. Hannah took one look
and said, "What color is her skin?"

This question caught my ear because Hannah, who is white and blond, had
recently asked a similar question of an African American friend I brought to
her house:

"What color is your skin?"

"Brown," the woman replied. "What color is yours?"

"Beige," Hannah answered.

Since "beige" is the predominant skin color in Lewiston, and since I had never heard Hannah take particular note of "beige" skin color, I suspected at the time that Hannah had already acquired the habit of thinking in dominant white-centered terms, if not yet in the dominant vocabulary of *white* and *black:* "beige" people were "regular," the norm; everyone else was "different" or "other," a deviation from the standard. The conversation about Western Fun Nia seemed to confirm this hypothesis since "beige" Barbie is the norm, too—especially on the toy shelves in Lewiston, which display less Barbie "diversity" than toy-store shelves in more multiracial locations. It also suggested the complex interplay of factors in both ideological development and Barbie interpretation: Was Mattel backing up or helping generate Hannah's recognition of beige as the norm? Whatever Mattel's responsibility for Hannah's take on race, however, it had certainly presented Hannah with a readable code for "beige," which, like the difference between real and imitation Barbies, she had mastered before the age of four. The color of Western Fun Nia's body might well be taken to designate "beige" by itself. In fact, most of the adults in the room needed Hannah to clue us in that Nia wasn't merely a white Barbie with dark hair; Hannah knew it designated a doll of color because she, unlike the adults, was familiar with the predominant paler color that signaled "beige." (We adults then speculated that Nia was supposed to be Chicana; a product list, however, reveals that the color is meant to designate "American Indian.")

Of our many subsequent Barbie interactions, two stand out. One occurred in the summer of 1992. It began when Hannah asked me to play Barbie with her, right after asking me, for the nth time, to sleep over. Our props were a grown-up size picnic table, a naked Barbie for me, which she called Erica, and her Barbie in panties called Melissa—she insisted that she couldn't find any more Barbie clothes, but I have my doubts. Under her direction, we (Melissa and Erica) went first to the beach and then to Melissa's nephew's house, described in response to my query as a very big house with many bedrooms, a playroom, a computer room, and a music room. There, servants fed Melissa and Erica dinner, including a special prenatal vitamin for Melissa. Then the two dolls went upstairs in this house of many bedrooms and slept in the same bed, before getting up for another fun-filled day of activities that Melissa let Erica choose since Melissa had chosen the beach excursion.

The other was a conversation she initiated a year later, by which time she was almost six:

"Are you still writing about Barbies?"

"Yes. Are you still playing with Barbies?"

"Yes. I'm saving up so I can get Birthday Barbie."

"Why?"

"She comes with a fancy dress and a plastic birthday cake. I also want Skipper. She is a [music] conductor."

"Who do you like better, Barbie or Skipper?"

"Skipper."

"Why?"

"Skipper comes with blond hair or brown hair. Barbie only comes with blond hair."

"Barbie comes with brown hair, too. I gave you a Barbie with brown hair last year, remember?"

"Which one?"

"Totally Hair Barbie. But you're right. Barbies with brown hair are hard to find here in Lewiston. I had to go to Portland to get yours."

"Why did you do that?"

"Because I thought you might like a Barbie with brown hair since all the ones you had were blond."

"I really wanted a blond one."

"But you just said you like Skipper better because she comes in two colors, blond and brown."

"I do."

"But you really like blond hair better?"

"Yes."

"On people, too?"

"Yes."

"But you like Skipper better because you can choose between two colors?"

"Yes."

"So if you went into a store and you could pick either Skipper with blond hair or Skipper with brown hair, which would you pick?"

"First I'd get the one with blond hair and then later I'd get the one with brown hair."

"What if you could have a Barbie with a different skin color? Would you want one of those?"

"Oh, yes!"

Besides being illuminating about Hannah herself, these two incidents well illustrate both the payoffs and the limitations of studying Barbie through her consumers. I list below five points suggested by Hannah's story that I have found to be characteristic of Barbie-consumption evidence that issues from adults as well as children, followed by the decisions to which they have led me concerning the content, method, and language of this book.[7]

1. Consumer interpretation depends partly, but only partly, on what Mattel puts out. I argue in chapter 1 that Mattel makes Barbie products more attractive by emphasizing the consumer's ability to choose among many options while simultaneously casting one Barbie, the white, blond version, as the norm and investing it with the greatest apparent value. From the evidence of the Birthday Barbie conversation, Hannah seems to have been won over by both the strategy and the meaning construction that I attribute to Mattel. Hannah loves blond Barbie best. She thinks blondness looks even better when she can pick it from a range of choices. She likes blond hair best on people, too. And her excitement and awe over the possibility of owning a Barbie of color suggest that Hannah perceives them to be an exotic rarity, especially given her take on Nia two years earlier.

Yet I certainly couldn't have predicted Hannah's entire take on Barbie by analyzing Mattel's output. Hannah's world of Barbie contains objects and narratives that Mattel did not contribute, like the shared bed and prenatal vitamin. As important, her conception of what Mattel has to offer does not correspond to what's out there in general or what sells in Lewiston. Some perceptions, like her idea that Barbie comes in blond only, do not even accord with what she owns. Others simply cannot be discerned without her help, like the special appeal of the plastic cake or her reason for wanting the baton-toting Skipper, which turned out to be based on a misreading of Mattel's intention. When she told me that she wanted the conductor Skipper, her older brother Ben asked her how she knew Skipper was a music conductor rather than a train conductor. Hannah explained that Skipper had a baton. The next question should have been about why Hannah thought the wand signaled *conductor.* I discovered at Service Merchandise that the doll she wanted was actually Baton Twirling Skipper. Hannah's mistake is not surprising; she has more familiarity with conductors than twirlers.

2. Interacting with Barbie may involve, alternately or simultaneously, hard work or no work. Noting how often and easily lesbians and gays have transformed movies with heterosexual plots to suit their own fantasy scenarios, Deborah Bright argues that cultural appropriation is both more and less complicated than many have previously thought. On the one hand, "subject-identification in the movies is a slippery thing, more complicated than most

heterosexual feminist film theorists have acknowledged to date." On the other hand, "it is testimony to the vitality and fluidity of desire that it so easily appropriates whatever channels are available to it, and certainly without requiring the kind of elaborate psychic calisthenics that some film theorists assign to any female spectator who possesses a desiring look." [8]

Barbie hardly provides easy-access channels for everyone's desires; indeed, one of the most interesting things about Barbie is how many people have felt compelled to perform "psychic calisthenics" to accommodate Barbie in their imaginative lives. But Hannah's story, and the evidence of many other stories like hers, suggests that some Barbie play merits a similar conclusion about the mix of easy and hard features. From one angle, nothing is easy about Melissa and Erica's trip to the beach. The sheer number of difficult issues brought forth is remarkable: issues of class, work, and consumption; of gender, sexuality, and reproduction; of family relations and social etiquette. And the tale contains many clues that the process of constructing oneself in relation to one's desires entails troublesome identifications and objectifications. Especially noteworthy in this regard is the unnegotiable directive, in a tale that was obviously partly a story about Hannah and me, that my doll had to have my name while Hannah's had to have a different one—I am Barbie, I am not Barbie, I want Barbie, I want Barbie's temporary owner, someone else wants Barbie's temporary owner.

Yet, while the details of Hannah's tale certainly bespeak a narrator who has traveled difficult and labyrinthine psychic paths, with many oscillations between desire, identification, and rejection, her imaginative journey during the game seemed decidedly unarduous. I've seen Hannah spin out imaginative narratives under stress. One, told soon after her mother had undergone surgery, concerned a mother who had "lost her blood pressure" and a little girl who was rescued from her burning house by a fireman who'd had to choose between saving mother and saving daughter. Hannah told me that tale in visible distress; it was accompanied by equally agitated illustration. In contrast, the beach excursion had no signals of tone, gesture, or narrative rhythm to indicate that internal struggle was going on at the time of the telling or that Barbie was hard to appropriate. On the contrary, using Barbie to engage these difficult issues seemed incredibly easy; it was apparently nothing to give Barbie a female bedmate, a nephew, and a prenatal vitamin.

3. All consumer testimony about Barbie is marked by the particular circumstances of its creation and by the consumer's understanding of the people involved or addressed. Hannah did not give me the same rap that a child or another adult would get; what she tells me is shaped by the specifics of our

relationship.[9] I am an adult friend of the family who hangs around enough to have established a sustained relationship with Hannah, but not as much as she would like. Through the beach excursion she created a scenario in which Melissa, at least, got Erica to spend more time with her. She also knows me as a Barbie researcher—she initiated our Birthday Barbie conversation by asking if I was still writing about Barbie and presenting herself as a willing object of study—and as someone who has given her a Barbie in the past. Her careful description in the Birthday Barbie conversation of her favorite dolls on the toy shelves, her focus on the dolls she wants as opposed to the dolls that she owns already, might well have a strategic goal beyond having her views recorded for posterity.

My personal encounters with Barbie consumers are always structured by my participation in them. People I know address me as a writer and as something else—a friend, a teacher, a colleague, whatever. In these cases, our relationship beyond Barbie has some advantages. My ability to interpret Hannah's take on Nia and to recognize the signs of troubled imaginative work was greatly enhanced by incidental occurrences at social gatherings. Moreover, her very willingness to spin out difficult tales with me probably also depended on our sustained interaction over time.[10] Familiarity with my Barbie informants also has disadvantages: in exchange for a broader frame of reference, I lose access to accounts of Barbie that have nothing to do with the teller's relationship with me. No such relationship comes into play when I study material generated apart from me and produced by strangers. However, then I have no context except what that person provides. And artifacts unmarked by relationships with me are not thereby artifacts unmarked by relationships. I still have to presume that the tale has been shaped by the teller's relation to the original audience: editors and presumed readers, in the case of publications; other people, in the case of secondhand oral testimony.

4. Barbie accounts have also been shaped by the teller's own interpretations; they are products of interpretation rather than raw data awaiting a first interpretation by me. Both children and adults act as editors, cultural critics, theorists, and text makers. Sometimes Barbie narrators take on these roles consciously: "The Barbie company is trying to make Barbie a role model," Kathryn, my eight-year-old stepniece, told me. Sometimes these roles show themselves more subtly: in comments with manifest deductions and judgments (Barbie only comes in blond, and that's bad); in the use of the past to explain the present; in notable gaps or silences that suggest information withheld; in the visible use of narrative conventions, such as the telling of a story with a beginning, a middle, and an end. In every case, however, people

decide what to tell and how to tell it; I do not have access to what they don't tell.

5. It is impossible to learn everything about a consumer's view of and experience with Barbie from one encounter—or from many. In 1992, Hannah put two undressed Barbies in bed together. In 1993, she wanted a blond Barbie with a fancy dress and a plastic birthday cake. The first scenario is pretty queer in multiple senses; in the second, Hannah appears as Mattel's accessory to the production of Barbie's "straightest" meanings. Each alone gives a distorted picture of Hannah's take on Barbie. With the two together my picture is more accurate, yet still incomplete and somewhat opaque. Contextual information and relevant supplementary encounters make it less opaque than it would have been otherwise: they explain why Hannah saw a conductor instead of a twirler and why Barbies of color seem so exotic to her. But there's more that I want to know, and I can't either expect to happen upon every relevant conversation or simply ask her a lot of questions. For instance, when I asked Hannah why she preferred Skipper to Barbie, I was hoping that she would mention the difference between Barbie and Skipper that adults often remember as significant: Skipper has unpointed feet. Does Hannah notice or care about this? I couldn't find out without bringing up the subject myself, and then I wouldn't know whether I had put this feature into her mind.

And what would she tell me ten, twenty, or thirty years from now about how she viewed Barbie as a child? It's highly unlikely that she'll remember much of this. Six months after the Birthday Barbie conversation, she perceived the fact that I was writing about Barbie as new information. How much will be lost to memory? What will she deliberately edit out or discard as irrelevant? As I discuss in chapter 2, the evidence of adult memories suggests that much is lost over time and edited, retrieved (or misretrieved), and adapted to suit both narrative conventions and particular questions of interest to the teller.

The issues raised above determined both the content and the omissions here. I would have liked to present extensive ethnographic studies of three types of consumers: adults who remember Barbie's place in their childhood; adult Barbie collectors; and children today. Space permits me, however, to present only one type of consumer, and, after preliminary research, I decided to concentrate on the first, for several reasons. The huge Barbie collector's culture, complete with national and regional conferences, experts, dealers, reference guides, and publications, needs a book of its own, especially given the huge variety of people who collect Barbie. Collectors I encountered or read about include women who used Barbie collecting to fill a void resulting from geographic displacement undergone on behalf of a husband, a dyke whose long and continuing activist history includes co-founding an underground network to help women get abortions in the years before *Roe v. Wade,* gay men who view Barbie as high camp, and people who simply found the trade in Barbie to be a lucrative venture. Children, too, need a book, one grounded in an expertise in child psychology that I do not have.[11]

I also had to make a decision concerning how many adults with Barbie memories to discuss. The material that I presented about Hannah represents merely the beginning of an in-depth analysis of one consumer. I had to decide, then, whether to present, say, four adults in great depth or a greater number of consumers much less exhaustively. While the former approach has several advantages, it would have prevented me from addressing several crucial topics. Through no four consumers, for instance, could I convey the multiplicity of reactions to Barbie's perceived ethnicity (or lack thereof). A study of four obscures variety; it also, conversely, obscures some telling patterns. These patterns suggest that adult stories of childhood Barbie consumption have at least as much to do with dominant cultural habits of narration—or dominant subcultural narratives like the "coming-out" story—as with the psychological, biographical, and demographic histories of individual consumers. Moreover, the evidence of how much is lost or transformed in memory indicates that the reliability of individual memories cannot be judged against some "truth" about the time remembered; much of what happened, what was, or what was perceived during childhood simply cannot be accessed. Thus, assessing the roles of both convention and personal history in the construction of a particular narrative requires a study of that narrative in relation to other narratives as much as or more than in relation to other information about the narrator. In chapter 2, I have attempted to strike a balance by discussing enough consumers to indicate patterns while considering a few in the greater depth required to convey the dependence of Barbie interpretation on demographic and biographical specifics.

One other decision was determined partly by the limits of space: I have chosen to forgo some elegant content analyses and theoretical refinements—despite the pleasure it gives me to do them and the insights they offer—especially in places where they fail to abet the project of studying how Barbie signifies to her consumers. One relevant example here concerns a 1988 set of photographs by Rose Marasco of a ten-year-old girl in upstate New York. When Marasco asked "Jessica" if she could photograph her, the girl set up four dolls from the Barbie and the Rockers series on the base ledge of her family's trailer, positioned herself in front of them with plastic keyboards, and assumed a sequence of classic rock-musician poses. I first saw the photographs as testimonies to the validity of postmodern theories of gender and identity. They seemed to document the child's early sense that gender identities are matters of costume, performance, and posing as well as the importance of cultural products in identity construction. Also, since Jessica did not actually reproduce the Rockers' poses, they suggested Jessica's resistance to restrictive models of gender-appropriate behavior.

Marasco, however, has a different interpretation. She posited that Jessica deliberately declined to replicate the Rockers because she considered them her backup band; other poses, naturally, were appropriate for a lead singer. This assessment, which now seems obvious to me, does not by itself undermine my preliminary interpretation. Indeed, since Jessica probably gleaned these lead-musician poses from images of male rock stars—one photograph shows her rendition of the classic my-instrument-is-an-extension-of-my-penis posture—her resistance to given models of gender appropriation seems doubly articulated and the postmodernist insights suggested by the photographs doubly confirmed. But Marasco suggested, rightly, I believe, that Jessica was primarily constructing herself in resistance, not to dominant gender ideology, but to her own economic circumstances. With dolls who signified an economic status far above her own, Jessica turned her dingy surroundings into a stage on which she outshone the glamourous Rockers— a fantasy, Marasco sensed, that Jessica enacted often: "I felt that she had been doing this on her own for a long time; she knew exactly where the dolls should go."² From this angle, class rebellion outweighs gender rebellion, and resistance to cultural models exists alongside conformity; to use Barbie to imagine yourself in more glamourous circumstances is, in essence, to follow Mattel's directions.

I have tried to be sensitive to occasions when my interpretive instincts take me away from or obscure consumer interpretation. While I have no desire merely to transfer Barbie consumers into print unmediated by me and interpreted only by themselves—an impossible goal in any case—I do want to do everything possible to look at consumers' perceptions through their own lenses and to present interpretations that do not evacuate the consumer in the process of elaborating them. I refrain, then, from using consumers' narrative or artifactual Barbie products as catalysts for commentary that has little to do with what they perceived.

I have also chosen my vocabulary with an eye to keeping consumer experience in focus. I have tried to minimize my use of terms that have currency primarily within academe and to "do theory" with limited recourse to theoretical jargon. In part, this decision is a political one. At this time when coalition building must be a central political project of activists working against what is loosely termed *the Right,* it seems to me imperative not to produce texts ill-suited to circulation outside academe. I am equally motivated, however, by the requirements of the topic. While adopting a separate, academic vocabulary for my own analysis and theorizing would allow me to signal my own interpretive work clearly, it would also imply a contrast between the critic, who analyzes and does theory, and consumers, who merely relate experiences without having thought about them. This contrast is false; consumers analyze and do theory, too. It is also crucial to keep in focus that, while many Barbie stories bear on issues of central concern to postmodernist academics (the social construction of gender and sexuality, multiple subjectivities, the decentered and fragmented subject, etc.) and resemble the products of (particularly queer and transgender) subcultures, most Barbie play, subversive and otherwise, actually occurs far to the side of both postmodern theorizing and subcultural appropriation. I try to avoid, then, using a language, writing style, or interpretive emphasis that transfers consumer stories into a realm that their tellers do not inhabit or that lends to consumer struggle an aura of arduousness that may be undue: making it hard to recognize, for instance, that, despite the "psychic calisthenics" suggested by Melissa and Erica's trip to the beach, much of the excursion was a smooth sail.

One final methodological choice concerns my study of Barbie's history and Mattel artifacts in chapter 1. There is one other group of Barbie's queer accessories that I have not been able to include here: those who work for Mattel and for the makers of its licensed products. Some clearly must. It seems inconceivable, for instance, that the infamous Earring Magic Ken could have made it from conception through production and into stores in 1993 without many queer accessories on the inside: designing the product, perhaps; at the very least, deliberately failing to clue in the spin patrol about the cock ring reference of Ken's necklace or about how clearly Ken's outfit signals (slightly outdated) gay chic, thus rendering unconvincing those official protestations about how lots of men now wear earrings.

For the purposes of studying consumer interpretation, however, I am more interested in the circulating artifacts of Mattel's production and history—in what is or has been "out there" for consumers to see—than in insider stories. So I have focused my study primarily on texts and objects that have been available to consumers.[13] Most, like dolls, novels, television ads, and comic books, are or were previously in wide circulation, although some have far more limited circulation, such as the *Barbie Bazaar* magazine for collectors, which circulates by subscription, and Mattel Information Releases, which require some work to get hold of. Also, for convenience, I have often referred to the producers of official Barbie products and narratives as *Mattel.* I do not mean to indicate through this shorthand that Barbie and her marketing are the products of a conglomerate of individuals acting, as if of one corporate-drone mind, with a united "artistic intention." When I refer to Mattel as a producer, author, or agent of some action—"Mattel made," "Mattel says," "Mattel did"—I have in mind the people authorized to attach the official Mattel stamp of approval to artifacts, narratives, and promotional strategies. These official Mattel products are the subject of chapter 1.

Chapter 1

Making Barbie

3. *What are Barbie's measurements?* Actually, Barbie is not scaled to human measurements. Barbie doll was developed after Mattel Toys studied the popularity of paper fashion dolls (which had more adult-like figures than the dolls of the day) among children. Finding the market place receptive to the idea, a team of Mattel employees translated the paper doll concept into a three dimensional [*sic*] doll with life-like characteristics.

7. *My Barbie didn't come with panties. Are they missing?* No. Barbies do not come with panties unless the doll is wearing a short skirt.—From "Barbie Questions and Answers," distributed by Mattel

If you call Mattel with Barbie queries, you are likely to receive "Barbie Questions and Answers," a six-page compendium of information and disinformation that, with the exception of the two question-and-answers (q-and-a's) above, makes the business of Barbie consumer relations look like a relatively simple matter. Of the twelve q-and-a's, most work relatively transparently in the service of two unsurprising goals: maximizing sales and minimizing those consumer-relations chores from which Mattel does not profit. Question numbers 8–12 draw attention to the Barbie fan club and to less advertised products that you can buy, such as expensive limited-edition and collector Barbies. Number 5 explains why Mattel no longer repairs dolls. Number 6 deflects questions about old Barbies to the collectors and dealers who actually profit from selling them.

Three others are a bit more devious, but no more mysterious. The answer to question 1 "How old is Barbie?" avoids the reading of that question— What age girl does Barbie represent?—that would force Mattel to provide biographical details, thereby jeopardizing the free play of fantasy that Mattel considers a major factor in Barbie's success. It gives instead the age of the product: "Barbie made her debut at the American Toy Fair, New York, February, 1959." Q-and-a 2 functions similarly: it states that Barbie has no last name, a switch from the position taken in the early years when Barbie novels identified her as "Barbie Millicent Roberts."

The answer to question 4, about why you can't find a Barbie in the store that you saw a few years ago, uses the typical corporate strategy of disguising profit motive as benevolence (e.g., we created product x to serve your needs), with the odd twist of making the personified product, as opposed to the consumer, appear to be the beneficiary. In different textual contexts, such as the business section of the *New York Times,* Mattel executives address this matter more forthrightly. In a June 1992 article about the success of the new Totally Hair Barbie, Jill Barad, president of Mattel USA, stated, "The ultimate goal of making each Barbie special is to create the rationale for why little girls need to own more than one Barbie doll," adding that Mattel is trying to get girls to think that they need more than the reigning average of seven. (By 1994 the average was eight.) [1] According to q-and-a 4, however, each theme Barbie lasts only a few years because "Barbies [*sic*] continued success is due in large part to her ability to continually change with the times," an interesting phrasing that manages to suggest that Mattel is looking out for Barbie's "continued success" more than its own and that the ability to change with the times is somehow located within Barbie herself. Mattel is simply the supportive parent or spouse who encourages her to actualize her potential; consumers who demand old versions of Barbie are the ones out for themselves.

These q-and-a's make Barbie, Mattel, and consumers look like easy-to-know entities and make Mattel's consumer-relations task look simple as well—simple to accomplish and simple to decode. Not so with q-and-a's 3 and 7. How can Barbie be "life-like" and "adult-like" but not at all "human"-like? The relative incoherence of the text makes Mattel look shifty and discomfited. To readers who have encountered other accounts of Barbie's origin, Mattel may look outright duplicitous. The most widely circulated tale is that Ruth Handler invented Barbie so that her daughter could have a three-dimensional version of the paper fashion dolls that she loved so much. Less widely circulated is the information so deftly camouflaged by the Ruth Handler tale, including Barbie's derivation from a German doll, Lilli, that had been marketed primarily as a sexy toy for adults.

It's easy to see why Mattel used to publicize the Ruth Handler tale. From the beginning, Mattel has had to overcome the reluctance of mothers who have considered Barbie an inappropriate toy for their daughters, either because of her advanced "age" and sexual suggestiveness or because of her bimboesque qualities. Besides obscuring the fact that, while perhaps being unprecedentedly "adult-like," Barbie was not actually the first three-dimensional teenage fashion doll, the Ruth Handler tale works against this maternal reluctance by making the gift of Barbie look like a sign of maternal devotion rather than moral negligence and by shifting Barbie's function from modeling adult sexuality to modeling adult fashions (thereby also distancing Barbie further from her sex-signifying German prototype). Why, however, did Mattel trade this in for the q-and-a version of Barbie's origin? Granted, Ruth Handler's conviction for illegal financial dealings in 1978 tarnished her good-mother image. But why this particular rewrite, which substitutes anonymous employees for a devoted mom and a "receptive marketplace" for the happy Handler daughter, a shift that is especially puzzling since money-making operates throughout the rest of "Barbie Questions and Answers" as the motive to be camouflaged?

Part of the answer must surely lie in Mattel's defensive posture against feminist critiques of Barbie. Feminists have frequently translated Barbie's measurements into human terms to underline the unrealistic ideal of beauty that the doll is said to promote. So it makes sense for Mattel to disavow a human model for Barbie, to locate her origin in representations already produced by others. But if this rather suspect answer is the best that Mattel can do, why not ignore these troublesome matters of origin and measurements entirely? Probably because too many people were asking about them and because it costs much less in labor power to send off a text than to have Mattel employees explain things over the phone.

The volume of consumer queries must also account for why Mattel included q-and-a 7, which similarly directs attention to issues Mattel often chooses to evade: "My Barbie didn't come with panties. Are they missing?" For me, this question immediately brought to mind bad-girl sex. Like many women born in the late 1950s, one of my teen sex guides had been *The Sensuous Woman,* in which whispering to one's husband in public that one was not wearing panties figured among the most memorable pieces of advice (along with that thing about greeting him in Saran Wrap when he returned home from work). I suspect that many people called to ponder Barbie's pantilessness would similarly situate its significance in the realm of the kinky.

Mattel's answer, that Barbie comes with panties only if she's wearing a short skirt, does not quite provide an exit from this realm, although it does suggest Barbie's modesty. But what else was Mattel to respond? Drawing attention to Mattel's line of Barbie underthings, which features do-me outfits instead of white cotton briefs, does nothing to dekinkify the issue. The strategies used rather unsuccessfully with regard to Barbie's measurements would be even less successful here. Coming out about the profit motive, which must be the big reason—Mattel saves money by not providing panties— would make Mattel appear to put money over morality. Claiming that Barbie doesn't quite represent a real female, the primary excuse for Barbie's embarrassing measurements, would create an indelicate mess. I can conceive of an argument that Barbie doesn't need panties because she is not anatomically correct; since she (is a representation of someone who) has no apparent sources of moisture, odor, or menstrual leaks, she doesn't need panties. But that would thrust Barbie's lower orifices into the conceptual spotlight along with her already troublesome breasts, not to mention raising a series of very weird questions: Would a plastic orifice be more likely than a smooth surface to generate olfactory hallucinations? If Barbie's need for panties resides in her reference to the real, could Mattel return her to good-girl status by giving her only one pair, or would it need to provide the artifactual illusion that she intended to change them daily? On the panty issue, it seems, Mattel has no way out: the triple problems of sex, money, and Barbie's relation to the real cannot be discoursed away.

This chapter concerns Mattel's production of Barbie objects and meanings, which has always involved trying to sidestep the minefields that Mattel avoids with uneven success in "Barbie Questions and Answers." Although I have focused above on spin-control failures, these testify more to Mattel's overall success at overcoming obstacles than to anything else. Despite Mattel's inability to account coherently for Barbie's unrealistic measurements and lack of panties, despite decades of disapproval by mothers, feminists, antiracists, and others, Mattel has sold billions of dollars worth of Barbie items, and Barbie continues to sell on, to an ever-expanding market of consumers who buy more dolls than did their counterparts of the past. According to the Information Release entitled "Barbie Fun Facts" that I acquired in 1992, placed head to toe the nearly 700 million Barbie dolls and "family members" sold since 1959 would circle the earth more than three and a half times, and a Barbie doll is now sold every two minutes. How Mattel gets so many people to buy this good girl who doesn't wear panties is the subject of this chapter.

I suggested in the introduction that Mattel's Barbie production merits study as an example of successful hegemonic discourse, and some words are in order concerning the term *hegemony* and its appropriateness here. Dick Hebdige provides a useful definition of *hegemony* as "a moving equilibrium": "The term hegemony refers to a situation in which a provisional alliance of certain social groups can exert 'total social authority' over other subordinate groups, not simply by coercion or by the direct imposition of ruling ideas, but by 'winning and shaping consent so that the power of the dominant classes appears both legitimate and natural.'"[2]

One feature of Mattel's (artifactual and discursive) line that can be seen to constitute hegemonic discourse follows relatively straightforwardly from Hebdige's definition. This is the feature that primarily concerns feminists, antiracists, and other activists: how Mattel contributes to prevailing and inequitable distributions of power and resources by contributing to dominant ideologies. As Lisa Tickner explains, "Ideology is compounded of the mental categories and systems of representation through which we make sense of our conditions of existence in the world. Ideology is a practice of representation although it does not present itself as such, but as a self-evident set of propositions which are self-evidently 'true.' This 'naturalization' of a constructed social reality serves the interest of particular social groups."[3] This is one aspect of the Barbie line that interests me as hegemonic discourse—the way, for instance, that the promotion of a white, blond doll as especially beautiful backs up the power of white people.

I am equally interested, however, in another feature, for which the term *hegemonic,* as traditionally used, does not immediately seem as relevant: Mattel's ability to get people to act on its own behalf. On this matter, I deviate a bit from the orthodox use of *hegemony,* which was originally defined against more obviously coercive forms of power maintenance such as authoritarian rule. The concept is ordinarily used to understand ways in which people in power maintain power, without using direct force, by getting people to consent to their own subordination. From this standpoint, calling Barbie production *hegemonic* appears to be both overdramatic—Mattel's power over the individual being of very limited scope—and a fancy way of stating the obvious. Getting someone to buy Barbie is clearly different than getting someone to obey orders from a dictator under penalty of death. Specifying this distinction requires little theoretical elaboration and offers little insight.

More interesting, however, is the matter of why getting someone to buy a

Barbie is often different from getting someone to buy, for instance, an Etch-A-Sketch. It is in specifying this difference, I believe, that the term *hegemony* is especially useful. Selling an Etch-A-Sketch, a screen on which you create erasable lines by manipulating two knobs, is a relatively simple matter. It primarily entails publicizing the toy's existence and promoting the benefit of an activity to which few would ascribe negative effects: drawing on a blank screen. It does not entail talking away potentially troublesome features or attending to contextual value shifts, such as changing attitudes about the status of women, that might change the apparent value of the product to consumers. Ohio Art can promote the Etch-A-Sketch today much as it promoted the Etch-A-Sketch in the 1960s.

Buying, or not buying, an Etch-A-Sketch is also relatively painless. One might be moved to ponder whether a child's creativity would be better served by a watercolor set. But making this decision does not entail entering into a widely publicized debate about the toy's effects in which the child's current and future psychological and political values may seem to be at stake. Nor does the toy threaten to inscribe many contested values from outside; if a child uses an Etch-A-Sketch to draw a woman with large breasts, the interest in breasts has come from within the child, not from within the toy.

In contrast, the traffic in Barbie is far more complicated, and many features that distinguish it from the traffic in the Etch-A-Sketch are features generally understood to characterize hegemonic discourse. The first lies in the language of infinite possibility that Mattel uses to camouflage what is actually being promoted: a very limited set of products, ideas, and actions. Mattel promotes Barbie to consumers the way capitalists promote capitalism to the people who least benefit from it. The discourse maintains that the limits come only from within you—you can be rich if you set your mind to it; you can make Barbie be anything you want her to be. The goal of the discourse is to mask external limits so that you have appeared to choose freely actions—working for low wages, buying Malibu Barbie—that will benefit the discourse spinner.

And that will not so obviously benefit you. Mattel's discourse also typifies hegemonic discourse because it is designed partly to address the consumer who suspects that buying Barbie may be harmful to the recipient. Not every consumer sounds like this reluctant mother: "We struggled for three years over whether to buy Karen a Barbie doll; she finally convinced us that she would be more damaged by parental refusal than by owning this hideous little role model." But Mattel's promotions always have in mind the suspicious consumer whose consent must indeed be "secured" or "won." When critics complained about the unwholesome sexual fantasies that Barbie's breasts might engender, Mattel portrayed her as an antigreaser; when critics complained about Barbie's antifeminist message, Mattel made her the girl who "can do anything." As a result, the history of Mattel promotion reveals a relation between seller and buyer that operates like hegemony's "moving equilibrium." As Stuart Hall explains about the way in which dominant classes preserve their power over subordinates in a hegemony, "This operates, not because the dominant classes can prescribe and proscribe, in detail, the mental content of the lives of subordinate classes (they, too, 'live' in their own ideologies), but because they strive and to a degree succeed in *framing* all competing definitions *within their range,* bringing all alternatives within their horizon of thought. This is just what Mattel does: the company continually adapts its line to bring competing definitions of *good role model* and *acceptable fantasy object* within its own conception of Barbie and to present its offerings as precisely those that fulfill consumer "needs."

Besides abetting multiple hegemonic discourses, then, Mattel can be said to model hegemonic discourse in that it uses the language of infinite possibility, continually adapted to defuse counterclaims, to persuade people to act on its behalf in ways that they may not initially or ever believe will benefit themselves. As a result, although the effects of buying Barbie do not match the effects of buying into capitalism, or working for low wages, or entering heterosexual partnerships when one is otherwise inclined, a study of the Barbie line can illuminate how other hegemonic lines work. This is one purpose of this chapter; the other is to study the content of the Barbie line as it has developed since 1959, against which consumer responses will later be examined.

Inventing Inventing Barbie

As well befits the empire that the world of Barbie has become, Barbie comes with competing, semimythic tales of origin that, like tales of early Rome, mix historical and fictional characters whose relative importance varies according to the needs of the tellers. According to the most popular story, Ruth Handler invented Barbie. When she saw how much her own daughter, Barbara, loved to play with paper dolls, she came up with the idea of translating the fashion doll concept into three dimensions. (Variations have Handler helping her daughter out of play frustration—Barbara was either bored with paper dolls or sorrowful that the three-dimensional dolls she already had were unsuitable for fashion play.)[5] What this tale accomplishes by what it states is, as I suggested above, obvious. The eleven-and-a-half-inch bane of many mothers is now attributed to a mother devoted to the needs and desires of her daughter, which, incidentally, the invention of Barbie does not seem to have fulfilled. According to Barbara, she was too old to play with dolls by the time Barbie came along. (Later, Barbara's daughter, who preferred outdoor games, didn't want Barbie either.)[6]

What the tale accomplishes by what it fails to state is no less important. To begin with, the tale of Ruth Handler, mom, obscures another key player: Ruth Handler, businessperson. Until recently, most articles failed to mention that, far from having a sole focus on creative child rearing, Ruth Handler was also a co-founder of Mattel in 1945 with her husband, Elliot, and a third person, Harold Mattson. The creation of Mattel's name from the names of the male founders only—the beginnings of *Mattson* and *Elliot*—initiated this erasure of Ruth from the corporate label, although Ruth, not Elliot, was the businessperson. According to Sydney Landensohn Stern and Ted Schoenhaus, authors of the illuminating *Toyland: The High-Stakes Game of the Toy Industry,* in the Handlers' ordinary spousal division of labor, Elliot designed things, and Ruth figured out how to sell them; Barbie, in fact, was the only toy she "invented."[7]

In many cases, the absence of Ruth Handler, businessperson, must be attributed as much to the sexism of the article writers who obligingly disseminated the story as to Mattel's particular marketing strategy. After all, her corporate role was never far to seek. Sexism may also account for the total absence of Ruth, as either mom or businessperson, in articles attributing Barbie to Jack Ryan, an engineer and inventor who had been working on the Sparrow and Hawk missiles before Mattel hired him in 1955. Articles about Ryan are full of other women: his numerous wives, including Zsa Zsa Gabor, a German actress supposed to become the next Marilyn Monroe, a Polish attorney exiled for work with Solidarity, and his Mormon secretary, as well as his numerous lovers, whom Stern and Shoenhaus describe as follows:

> According to Ryan, one was a morphine addict whom he cured by sex ("the endorphins in her brain from sexual activity made it so she didn't need drugs"); she repaid him by hiring a twice-indicted murderer to crack his safe. Another was a Miss World who had been jilted by Bob Hope. One of his favorites was the estranged wife of the platinum equivalent of Goldfinger (the real-life gold magnate whom Ian Fleming immortalized in a James Bond adventure). "She was French royalty, although she was raised in Germany. I lived with her on Park Avenue

while her husband paid all the bills so he could spy on her. She had three sable coats and drove a Porsche especially built for her in Germany."[8]

In addition to lovers with Barbie's dream accessories, Ryan also had a dream house that would make even Barbie jealous. In a 1974 article, *People* noted that his house, where he reputedly threw 182 parties one year, included a "Tom Jones room," in which people ate meals without utensils, and 150 phones, rigged up to respond to certain phone numbers by activating a waterfall or enabling him to "order caviar for eight in a sumptuous tree house with a crystal chandelier."[9]

Women are everywhere in articles about Ryan, but never Ruth Handler. *People*'s comment is typical: "[Ryan's] greatest claim to fame . . . is the Barbie doll, which he invented during his 18 years with Mattel, Inc. He also fathered Chatty Cathy and the company's other talking toys, during which time he got rich."[10] One could view Handler's absence as just retribution for Ryan's own absence from Mattel-generated tales. Mattel did not promote Ryan as a Barbie "parent"—hardly surprising, given how unsuited was his sex-filled personal history to drawing attention away from Barbie's troublesome sexuality. But revenge cannot totally explain why Barbie is described as having sprung full grown from his head without female contribution; reporters' desires to look and report no further must have contributed.

The occasional absence or diminishment of Ruth Handler got another source in the mid-1970s when the tale of Ruth Handler, mom, began to hide something else: Ruth Handler, gold-collar criminal. The most concrete evidence that Ruth was the Handler in the business pots is that it was she, not Elliot, who was co-indicted with Mattel's vice president of finance and administration in 1978 for conspiracy, mail fraud, making false financial statements to the SEC, and "[falsifying] internal records to influence the market price of the stock in order to acquire assets of other companies, obtain bank financing for the business, and sell Mattel stock for their own benefit."[11] Ruth pleaded no contest, receiving a forty-one-year suspended sentence, a $57,000 fine, and twenty-five hundred hours of community service. By this point, both Handlers had been forced out of Mattel and the toy business (although they were later symbolically reinscribed by induction into the Toy Industry Hall of Fame in 1989). Elliot went back to being a painter, and, after surviving breast cancer, Ruth started a new company, Nearly Me, that made breast prostheses for mastectomy survivors—a business not inappropriate to the "mother" of the much discussed Barbie breast.

The story of Ruth Handler, mom, omits a lot of information about Ruth

Handler, businessperson—some unmotherly, some unsavory—and one more source of Barbie's origin, the German doll Lilli. One of the first people to reinject Lilli into the Barbie origin story was Cy Schneider, who worked for Mattel's advertising agency, Carson/Roberts, in the 1950s and 1960s. He had been closely involved with Mattel since 1955, when, risking everything, Mattel put up $500,000 to advertise on the new Mickey Mouse Club show, subsequently selling $1,000,000 in Burp Guns and inaugurating the practice of television advertising for toys. Schneider's account, from his book *Children's Television,* is worth quoting at length since it is based on his day-to-day involvement with Mattel at the time:

> Lili [ordinarily spelled Lilli] was a German doll modeled after a German playgirl in cartoon form [Stern and Schoenhaus refer to her as a prostitute] who regularly graced the pages of *Das Bild,* a German newspaper much like our *Inquirer.* The Lili doll was not designed to appeal to children, but was sold to adult men in tobacconists and bars. Lili came in one of two sexy outfits, and if there was an aura or fantasy at all around this doll, it was as an adult male's pet. . . .
>
> When the Handlers first saw this doll they were intrigued with the possibilities of a three-dimensional mannequin. Ruth Handler's daughter Barbara was playing with paper dolls at the time and Ruth recognized how much more fun paper dolls might be if there were a doll or a mannequin who could wear real miniature garments made of fabric with actual bottons and zippers.
>
> An emissary was sent to Germany and all the rights to Lili were bought by Mattel. Some doll construction patents were bought from Hauser, the German manufacturer, and the cartoon rights to Lili were bought and put aside.[12]

The Handlers then tested the doll on a few hundred mothers and their daughters since introducing such a product in the United States was so "radical." Virtually all the mothers hated it; they said it was too mature for their daughters. Virtually all the girls, whose mothers were not present when they were shown the doll, loved it. The Handlers renamed Lilli, selling the new doll as Barbie.

The history of this story's circulation, and of the recent circulation of the Ruth Handler tale, well illustrates Mattel's ability to exercise spin control over the story of Barbie and, simultaneously, Mattel's dependence on the needs, desires, and cooperation of others to get its story of choice promoted. As I suggested above, Mattel's early attempt to promote the promotionally ideal tale of Ruth Handler, mom, minus Ruth Handler, businessperson, could not have been successful unless writers were disinclined either to discover or to publicize Handler's business acumen. Some writers still recount this story, although Mattel has done a relatively good job of pulling Handler out of the mix. Since the mid-1970s, Mattel appears to have given Ruth (and Elliot) Handler a fate akin to the *damnatio memorae* treatment given to Roman emperors reviled by their successors: they tried to obliterate her image, past and future, from the public domain. She is no longer mentioned in the material that Mattel puts out about Barbie's origin, like the q-and-a. I suspect, too, that the will of Mattel is also behind the fact that the Handlers hardly appear in two books about Barbie that are effusive in their acknowledgments about Mattel's generous cooperation: *The Collectors Encyclopedia of Barbie Dolls, and the New Theater of Fashion,* by Sybil DeWein and Joan Ashabraner, first published in 1977, which nowhere mentions the Handlers; and the 1987 *Barbie: Her Life and Times,* by Billy Boy, which includes only a brief reference.[13]

The results of Mattel's erasure can also be seen in the articles published about Barbie's thirtieth birthday during the first half of 1989. I surveyed over a hundred of these articles. A fair number do include the Handlers. A few tell the story of Ruth Handler, mom—and, now that businesswomen are considered more standard popular fare, these usually refer to her as Mattel's co-founder.[14] Several mention the Handlers as founders only: "Barbie was named after the daughter of Ruth and Elliot Handler, two of the founders of Mattel Toys."[15] A few others attribute the invention of Barbie to one or both Handlers without telling the mother story. But many omit the Handlers altogether; Barbie is simply a doll introduced by Mattel in 1959. The long arm of Mattel is further indicated by how few of these articles mention Ruth's conviction for financial wrongdoings.

And virtually none mention Lilli, even though her tale, by this point, had been moving into broader circulation owing to the increasing visibility of the people with a financial stake in bringing her to the fore: Barbie collectors. Although Schneider did not misrepresent Barbie's media past when he described his 1987 text as the first published demystification of Barbie's origin,[16] his was not the only text to draw attention to Lilli during that year. So did Billy Boy's *Barbie: Her Life and Times,* a book with much wider circulation among Barbie fans, whose account is interesting for several reasons. First, it seems to have Mattel's stamp of approval: "It is with great joy that, with the generous support of Mattel, Barbie's 'parents,' I have had the opportunity to show my collection to the world."[17] This does not mean that Mattel wanted to see Lilli publicized. It does suggest, however, that Mattel considered her inclusion and his version of the story acceptable, or at least an acceptable trade-off for the good PR that this book from a fan gives Barbie.

Second, his account appears to be remystification more than demystification. Mattel's editorial input, and history of suing people who use Barbie in a way deemed to tarnish her image, may well be behind the disclaimer with which he begins—"Some believe that Barbie was fashioned after 'Lilli,' a German doll produced in the mid-fifties"—as well as the cleaned-up story:

> Lilli was originally conceived by the German cartoonist Reinhard Beu-thien for the daily newspaper *Bild-Zeitung,* when they needed an emergency filler for the June 24, 1952 edition. The cartoon was originally meant to make a one-time appearance, but the public adored Lilli. Beuthien's wife Erika gave him suggestions for Lilli's (or "his daughter," as he once referred to her) fashionable wardrobe. His credo was "I love to send up women but without portraying them as ugly or nasty—rather with warmth and humor." Lilli became very popular to the point of being honored in a Hamburg artist's club, *die insel,* by putting copies of the naive darling on its walls. The cartoonist also created a second character almost identical to Lilli for the "Munchen Abendzeitung" newspaper called *Schwabinchen.* She had a different hairstyle than Lilli, but it was Lilli's success that brought about the idea of a three-dimensional doll version.

Billy Boy goes on to describe in detail the development of the Lilli doll, naming corporate sponsors, creators, and fashion designers, and then briefly discusses her transformation into Barbie: "Lilli's success was short-lived, however, and she was eventually sold to Mattel. Through the coordination of Jack Ryan, then Mattel executive, and Ruth and Elliot Handler, the remake of Lilli's image thus gave birth to Barbie."[18] (Note how the concrete details of production and patent transfer undercut the "some believe" disclaimer with which he began.)

What is fascinating about this account is that it pulls the same discursive move as the one effected earlier through Ruth Handler, mom. Billy Boy shifts the terrain of Barbie's origin from sex to parenthood, although he switches the inventing parent's gender. Ruth Handler has been reduced to a coordinator of unspecified contribution, and Lilli's status as a sex toy for men is nowhere to be found. In their places stand the loving cartoonist father and the "naive" daughter on whom he lavishes great care. The father lovingly designs the daughter's wardrobe in consultation with his wife—who, by extension, would be Lilli's mother and thus, according to the ordinary division of labor among parents, the logical one to dress the children. Billy Boy does mention Lilli's sexiness: "The *'Bild* Lilli' doll was a tall, slim, fashion model type of teenage girl. She had a lot in common with the newly popular movie star Brigitte Bardot, whose honest sexuality and startling frankness were hailed during the *yé yé* years in France." But he adds, "Lilli and Bardot had blond ponytails and wore similar clothes. There may be a physical similarity between Lilli, Bardot, and Barbie, but any further similarities are debatable."[19] If the body and the clothes match, what's left? Just the sexual persona.

Overall, Billy Boy has obligingly penned a legend that erases the mother of the past, now tarnished, while preserving her function of de-oversexing Barbie. Despite her Bardot-like characteristics, Lilli is by far the best candidate from the Mattel archives for this job; drawing attention to Jack Ryan, whose own story is all about sex, not to mention real-life (and highly phallic) war toys, would hardly fit the ideological bill here. Billy Boy's Lilli tale also serves the people who have kept Lilli in view, the adult Barbie collectors among whom is Billy Boy himself, described on the book jacket as "jewelry designer, couture historian, and Barbie collector *extraordinaire.*" Certainly, besides giving to this highly selective account the illusion that all has been told, many details included about Lilli—the markings on Lilli's stand, the history of the packaging—are intended to guide the collector.

And it is among collectors especially that Lilli's name primarily circulates still, although her reputation is spreading. *Barbie Bazaar,* "the Barbie Collector's Magazine," founded in 1989, contains frequent references to and articles about Lilli. These articles differ from articles in the general press in that they are directed to a small subset of the public, Barbie collectors, who, in turn, represent only a fraction of Barbie consumers. They differ from Billy Boy's book in that they are "Mattel authorized" only in the negative sense that Mattel has not taken legal action to block them. Each issue of *Barbie Bazaar* states on the masthead, "Barbie ® is a trademark of Mattel, Inc. and is used with permission. The research and publication of this magazine is [*sic*] not sponsored in anyway [*sic*] by Mattel, Inc."

The treatment of the Lilli-Barbie connection in *Barbie Bazaar* reflects the magazine's relative independence from Mattel as well as the particular culture of knowledge of Barbie collectors. In *Barbie Bazaar,* Lilli's role as Barbie's progenitor is generally taken for granted. A photo-essay by Helmut Jahn, in which a (very rare) black-haired Lilli contemplates wardrobe possibilities, does not even mention Barbie. The reader is presumed to know why a Barbie magazine would include a Lilli piece. The article's informational purpose is to provide images of various collectible Lilli outfits from the summer of 1956, which are itemized in captions such as "11½″ 'Bild' Lilli in #1105 cocktail dress, yellow, with original poodle." Jahn also has no Mattel-type interest in making Lilli look wholesome enough to be worthy of giving birth to Barbie. One photograph depicts a group of Lillis clad only in underpants. Another shows her from the waist down, with her skirt flying up in classic Marilyn Monroe, walk-over-a-sidewalk-vent fashion. A third shows her in a V-neck top that closes well below the breasts, with a text underscoring Lilli's status as an object of male sexual delectation (and of male sexual control): "Oops . . . did the little black dog eat the front of my blouse or what? . . . My friend will like seeing this on other dolls, but I don't think he will let me wear it! You've got to know he's such a jealous guy!" [20]

Writers who do discuss Lilli's role as progenitor have moved beyond the question of whether Barbie was modeled after Lilli to consider details of interest to specialists. A typical example is "Javanese Lilli" by Sumiko Watanabe, which well reflects the importance of Lilli's role in the culture of Barbie collectors as both a marker and a source of Barbie expertise. The text begins much like an article in an academic journal, reminding the reader of previous scholarship on Lilli and Barbie with a brevity that presumes shared bibliographic expertise. The author then recounts discovering two dolls who looked a lot like Lilli, dressed in "splendid traditional Javanese outfits," at a doll museum in Yokohama, Japan, and trying to determine whether they could have influenced the makers of Lilli, which might explain why the *Bild* Lilli, a blond German girl, had black eyes. If so, Watanabe contends, we'd know more about Barbie, who owes her own black eyes (switched early on to blue) to Lilli, not, as some maintain, to having been first manufactured in Japan. After extensive research, however, including a consultation with Billy Boy and a subsequent museum discovery of more easily datable dolls with blue beehive hairdos and "mod" clothes that seemed to be part of the same series, Watanabe ultimately concludes that the dolls probably came from the 1965 World's Fair, thus postdating Lilli. [21]

Watanabe's article stands in opposition to the Mattel "story of Barbie" discourse, without ever articulating this, not only because the author presumes Lilli's place in Barbie's history, but also because of the desire to acquire and present facts. Some of this search for facts tacitly implicates Mattel as an obstacle to knowledge; Mattel, presumably, might be able to end the mystery of where Barbie's black eyes came from, thus rendering scholarly searches unnecessary. Watanabe abets Mattel, however, in the vague articulation of Lilli's genealogical role: "It is well known that the Bild Lilli doll had a major influence on the post WWII modern fashion doll world, particularly the Barbie doll."[22] Like Billy Boy's "some believe," Watanabe's phrasing avoids implying that Lilli's role is either a corporate secret revealed by hostile exposé or a provable fact of specifiable nature. Whether Watanabe's approach reflects the influence of Mattel's line on Lilli is not clear, although two forms of indirect influence seem quite possible: (1) Watanabe's version derives from Billy Boy's Mattel-friendly version; (2) *Barbie Bazaar*'s editorial decisions are made with an eye toward what Mattel might consider defamatory and, consequently, actionable.

Such a conclusion seems plausible in light of how often "some believe"–type phrases occur—and "bought the patent"–type phrases do not occur—in *Barbie Bazaar* articles on Barbie's origins. Even "The Rise and Fall and Rise of Ruth Handler," which has something of an exposé flavor, is vague on this point: "[Ruth Handler's] legend is that of a keen business woman who, after observing her daughter play with high fashion paper dolls, decided to create a three dimensional expression of the teenage ideal. With a body inspired by Germany's Bild Lilli doll and a wardrobe straight off the runways of Paris and Milan, Barbie was launched in 1959 and the rest, as they say, is history."[23] Every topic that Mattel would just as soon bury stands revealed, but obligingly labeled *legend,* and without any firm position on the thornier issues, such as whether Mattel (or Handler) saw Lilli before or after having the three-dimensional paper doll idea.

Like the survival of the Ruth Handler, mom, story long after Mattel tried to kill it, the treatment of Lilli in *Barbie Bazaar* reveals the limits of Mattel's ability to control Barbie discourse: Mattel has no great fondness for the Lilli tale, but people keep it going anyway. Yet these articles also suggest what might be called Mattel's "hegemonic smarts." Once the Lilli tale was out, and clearly out for good, Mattel authorized, by apparent endorsement or legal silence, versions of the Lilli tale to accommodate one group of Barbie fans, collectors, thus working to maintain itself as the hegemonic agent in "moving equilibrium" with Barbie consumers, the people it needs to maintain its own position as the fashion-doll powerhouse. (Although Mattel profits little from the traffic in Barbie collectibles, it does have a stake in maintaining a cordial relationship with collectors, who give Barbie much free publicity.) With the exception of Schneider's, most Lilli texts give the impression of lying within rather than outside Mattel's arena. Mattel, that is, functions in the way Stuart Hall describes successful purveyors of hegemonic discourse as functioning: "They strive and to a degree succeed in *framing* all competing definitions *within their range,* bringing all alternatives within their horizon of thought."

Two different features of Barbie writing thus testify to Mattel's success at controlling the story of Barbie's origins. The first is simply the tendency of Barbie writers to follow Mattel's prevailing line of choice. The second lies in how rarely texts that deviate from Mattel's line appear to be challenging Mattel in doing so. Embarrassing details come off looking more like further information than suppressed information. Otherwise put, one rarely reads anything like this: "Mattel doesn't want you to know this, but a business-woman later convicted of financial fraud bought the patent to a plastic German sex symbol and turned it into Barbie with the help of a guy whose other credits include designing missiles and, he says, fucking one of his numerous lovers out of drug addiction." The absence of "Mattel doesn't want you to know this, but," is as important as the rarity of the rest of the sentence.

Dream a Little Dream of Me

The rest of the chapter concerns the Barbie meanings generated by her makers. My project here is akin to the art historical project of studying "artistic intention," even though Mattel's major intention certainly ought to be deemed other than artistic; Barbie's meanings are primarily crafted in the service of product sales. As a result, many art historians will shudder to see the term *artistic intention* used anywhere near Barbie, as will anyone who suspects that artists turn away from their "artistic vision" every time they turn an eye toward the market. The common distinctions between art and craft, between fine arts and applied arts, and between art and popular culture are underpinned by a false separation between art and capital—by the idea that, the more artists "do it for the money," the less they are "expressing" the special vision that makes them artists.

To these shuddering readers I have three responses. First, relax. I do not use the term *artistic intention* to ennoble Barbie by raising her to the exalted category in which you place art and artists, nor do I intend to validate the idea that a certain category of objects deserves such exaltation. I reference this term to designate a subject for study—what cultural producers intend their work to signify—that corresponds to the material ordinarily viewed as constituting the artistic intention of people deemed artists. Second, get over it. No distinction between artists and everyone else can be founded on a distinction between people who don't do it for money and people who do; if this were the case, any object made on commission, such as the *Mona Lisa,* would be disqualified.

Third, consider this proposition: Barbie is the art historian's dream date.

Most art historical projects, ranging from traditional artist exaltations to more newfangled reception studies and social context analyses, depend on having some theory or conclusion about the role of artistic intention. They depend on a conception about how much of what an artwork signifies is "put there" by the artist intentionally, as opposed both to what is put there by the artist less than intentionally—via unconscious internal factors (e.g., an oedipal crisis) or the influence of social context (e.g., the cold war) or identity features (e.g., race, class, gender, sexual orientation)—and to what is put there, more or less consciously, by the viewer.

But, with most cultural producers, we have relatively little information about intention. Many artists now dead left little on record. Even if they did leave letters, treatises, or other written documents that later generations considered worthy of preservation or gave interviews committed to print, they cannot be called on to answer questions that were not asked of them while they were alive, questions deriving from new technologies or habits of thought. We cannot ask Giorgione why he painted over the figure revealed by X ray to lie beneath the surface of *The Tempest;* we cannot ask Leonardo da Vinci to comment on the similarity, suggested by a computer jock, between his face and that of the *Mona Lisa;* we cannot ask Picasso if he had anticolonialism on his mind when he painted *Les Desmoiselles d'Avignon.*[24] People studying living artists are not guaranteed such information either; many artists are reluctant to talk about their work, to answer particular questions, or to respond to particular questioners.

With Mattel, in contrast, we have lots of information. Mattel constantly produces and publicizes meanings, narratives, and identities for Barbie— in press releases, commercials, and articles; in Barbie magazines, comic books, and novels; on and inside Barbie boxes. This material hardly provides direct access to corporate intention or represents a desire to bare all to the consumer. Some of what passes for information, like "Barbie Questions and Answers," is more precisely disinformation. But both information and disinformation provide evidence about what Mattel intends Barbie to signify.

This vast amount of producer-generated material, combined with the vast amount of consumer interpretation available for study (the subject of chapter 2), provides a rare opportunity to study the relation between intention and reception in the production of meaning. I will not argue that the relation between them in Barbie meaning can be ascribed without modification to other cultural products; several specifics of the culture of Barbie point, as I will argue later, to the opposite conclusion. Yet I do propose that studying intention, reception, and resistance in Barbie culture can yield issues and insights to bring back to the study of other objects, including those labeled *art*. I consider the *intention* component of this intention/reception duo below.

Barbie Goes Infinite. From her first appearance in 1959, Mattel has worked to situate Barbie in carefully crafted, if vexed, relations to both fantasy and reality. On one level, Barbie's intended relation to each has remained consistent.

> Fantasy: Mattel has always promoted Barbie as a catalyst for the free play of fantasy.
>
> Reality: Barbie "changes with the times" so that the face that Barbie wears will match the concept of "beautiful and glamourous" perceived to reign among girls and so that the outfits you can buy facilitate fantasizing about up-to-date career and leisure options.

From this standpoint, reality serves fantasy, and fantasy serves girls.

But ideas about how to make reality serve fantasy and to make both serve sales have changed over time. According to Mandeville, who interviewed Ruth Handler for a 1990 series of *Barbie Bazaar* articles on Mattel's early years, her original idea about how to make Barbie serve fantasy was to avoid giving Barbie any physical or biographical details that would limit the owner's imagination. To this end, Handler told Mandeville, "the face was deliberately designed to be blank, without a personality, so that the projection of the child's dream could be on Barbie's face." To this end, also, the face and hair were changed early on from the Lilli-based first Barbie to the "blond, blue-eyed vision of the American Dream" (fig. 1). As Mandeville recounts, "The Handlers felt the [original] doll looked 'too foreign.'"[25]

blank face

This second change points to many limits of the Handlers' vision of unrestricted fantasy. The Handlers apparently had no desire, for instance, to enable children to fantasize about being "foreign." They also had no sense that, as consumer comments indicate, a child's ability to hang her fantasies on Barbie might be impeded if she knew she was unlikely ever to look like Barbie. Nor, it seems, did they consider as potentially limiting the one narrative detail given to Barbie: a specific career. Mattel's first catalog copy for Barbie describes her as a "shapely teenage fashion model," a career also announced on early boxes for the Basic Barbie Fashion Model Set, which came with "a special pedestal to keep Barbie on her feet for all her fashion shows."[26] If Mattel's artistic intention at this point was primarily to abdicate authorship of Barbie meaning, to transfer authorship to the child, the Handlers clearly did not have the vision, the artifact, or the text to make that happen for everyone

1. Nonethnic Barbie as seen on 45-rpm records, 1961.

(although, in their defense, it is hard to imagine an object in the likeness of a human that actually could serve everyone).

I will return later to why promoting the absolutely free play of fantasy cannot be construed at any point in Barbie's history as having actually been Mattel's primary goal, even when abdicating authorship was apparently the reigning concept: Mattel has always wanted to direct children to fantasy play that would be abetted by buying specific additional Barbie products. But something else must be discussed first: Mattel's early decision to give up abdicating authorship as a primary marketing strategy, in the hope that Barbie would sell better with a biography and personality. The changes that happened at this time were not permanent. Mattel later moved back toward infinite possibility and dropped some of the details it had given Barbie. Despite its relative brevity, however, this period deserves close study, both as an interesting episode in the history of Barbie meaning construction and as one against which to compare later meaning-construction (and anti-meaning-construction) strategies.

Barbie Gets a Life. Mattel's change in policy came, not from some realization that, even without a biography, Barbie's possibilities were far from infinite, but from the realization that infinite possibility was not selling and that generating details could mean generating sales. According to Mandeville, Mattel gave Barbie a bit of biography for two reasons. First, thousands of letters from children indicated that the Handlers had not correctly predicted the source of Barbie's appeal: "Children WERE in love with Barbie, but were NOT projecting their own identity on her, nor living in the future with her. They wanted to know more about her. Where did she live? How did she become a model?"[27] Second, financial advisers for Mattel wanted to begin authorizing other companies to make licensed products: "The year, 1961, the subject, Barbie teen-age fashion model doll by Mattel. The word 'licensed products' has come up in board meetings. Advisors say it is necessary for the survival of the product. The Handlers resist, the agency insists! Select firms would be allowed to develop the personality of Barbie, under the watchful eye of management of Mattel. The image must be wholesome, all-American, beautiful yet naive. The list of demands were [*sic*] endless."[28] Although the Handlers still felt that Barbie's lack of a "personality" was the key to her success over other teenage fashion dolls, they reluctantly gave in. Once the way had been cleared for generating a personality, a number of products were authorized: licensed products such as vinyl record totes and Barbie novels and also other Mattel dolls, starting with Ken.

In most texts about Ken's beginnings, as in those about Barbie's, the discourse of infinite possibility sometimes masks telling limits and sometimes stands side by side with, and in bald contradiction to, another narrative about intentionally closing fantasy options. First of all, writers often describe the creation of Ken as another step in expanding Barbie's possibilities toward the infinite, even when they also ascribe Ken's creation to the abandonment of "infinite possibility" Barbie. Mandeville, whose four-part *Barbie Bazaar* article on Ken sets the stage with another recounting of Ruth Handler's resistance to giving Barbie a personality, argues that Ken's primary importance was to do just that: "What made the introduction of Ken so important in 1961 is that he made Barbie REAL. He helped her acquire a personality."[29] Cy Schneider, who was working for Mattel's ad company at the time, has a similar take on what Ken offered Barbie: Ken enabled her, in nineties terms, to "get a life": "With the advent of Ken, a richer story in Barbie's life blossomed. It was easier to take Barbie on her 60-second (later 30-second) television adventures when an escort was involved. Her activities became virtually unlimited."[30]

Well, not quite. Today, the sexist presumption in the idea that Barbie needed a boyfriend or, as Schneider terms him, a (male) "fantasy escort" in order to have a personality and a life needs little discussion. Granted, one's personality might be more manifest in interaction with others, but obviously a woman can have a personality, a life, and activities alone or in the company of other females. Mattel would hook into some of these activities in 1963 when it introduced Barbie's friend Midge; Midge, however, was never

2. Barbie and Midge Travel Pals case, 1963. Photo: Jay York.

described as completing Barbie's personality. Also noteworthy is the hetero-sexist presumption that Barbie's activities became virtually unlimited once she had a male date; surely the "dates" that some girls fantasized about were not dates with males.

These limits, I think, are limits of presumption rather than intention. I doubt that anyone at Mattel worried much about the limits to child sexual fantasy caused by giving Barbie a potential boy date without simultaneously giving her a potential girl date. No one seems to have considered the possibility that Midge would be a potential fantasy date for Barbie either before or after her creation. Certainly, whoever authorized the vinyl Barbie and Midge Travel Pals (fig. 2) makeup case during Midge's early years wasn't think-ing about it. The case shows Barbie and Midge embracing, breast touching breast, while Midge touches Barbie's face with her hand and the two look out at us with a "don't tell Mom" slyness. We may owe this queer moment, I suspect, to a queer accessory or two working on the inside. Heterosexual presumption might have blinded its designer to the homoflirt implications of the hug and conspiratorial glance; maybe even those fingers framing Barbie's lips were intended to signal merely best-friend playfulness. But what about that semi-disembodied hand-like form that seems to be feeling up Midge? If there's a heterosexual presumption accident here, the presumption seems to belong not to the designer but to spin-control higher-ups who don't seem to have worried about catalyzing fantasies of Barbie dating Midge, or two Barbies "dating" each other, or, for that matter, Barbie engaged in autoerotic activity—a lack of concern that stands out against the huge concern about child sexual fantasies about Barbie and Ken, which is where the limits of intention come in.

Alongside the narratives of how Ken made Barbie's possibilities infinite are narratives, in the same texts, about Mattel's desire to avoid fostering, or to appear to have avoided fostering, certain kinds of fantasy. Mattel needed to cater to those who were interested in controlling children's mental and physical sexual life—most important, parents in charge of the toy money. Since preproduction days, Mattel had been contending with the suspicion, ascribed primarily to mothers, that Barbie was too much of a sexpot for children. Not surprisingly, then, Mattel wanted to promote Ken as a boyfriend or an "escort" without being blamed for giving Barbie a sex partner. So, according to Schneider, "Mattel was careful to give him boyish, clean-cut looks, and the overall, non-threatening, asexual appearance of a wimpy little jerk." Mandeville describes him more lovingly as having "the 'boy next door' wholesomeness about him that instantly inspired trust."[31]

Mattel also worried, Schneider recalls, about whether to give Ken a penis: "If his genitalia were included, some mothers would object. If his genitalia were omitted, would he look like some wounded Hemingway hero? Would mothers think we were putting out heads in the sand?" Mattel consulted Ernest Dichter, a psychologist often consulted by the toy industry, who watched girls playing with Barbie and then posed the following problem: "[Dichter] pointed out that the primary play mode for Barbie and Ken dolls was dressing and undressing them. He questioned whether children would understand that Ken was a boyfriend, or comprehend what a boyfriend really was. Would they see Ken as their fathers, brothers, or the boy next door? And if so, was it healthy to see him undressed? And when he was naked, why did he or didn't he look like Daddy?"[32]

Mattel's solution was to have Ken molded in "a permanent set of jockey shorts with a lump in the appropriate spot." This way, Ken would appear to be anatomically correct, but no one could actually see his penis. Alas, this solution was not to be: when Mattel sent the prototype to Japan for manufacture, a supervising engineer decided that eliminating the shorts would make the doll easier to produce; eliminating the lump would cut a cent and a half off the cost of production. So he eliminated both, apparently without disastrous effect: "Ken was brought into the world a neuter and it didn't matter one whit. Barbie's virginity was not threatened. Children did not think Ken had been in some horrible accident. These issues had all been concerns of adults who had over-stressed the problem. Ken was, and still is, accepted as a necessary escort to many of Barbie's activities. There was a lesson in this for all of us: do not substitute your own tastes, thoughts, or imagination for a child's."[33]

One might, I think, learn several other lessons, although this one certainly merited learning. First, it serves as a reminder of how tricky it is to try to read "artistic intention" from the created object. Without Schneider's account, one might ascribe Ken's lack of genitalia to a more premeditated Mattel intention; Mattel's decision not to return to the original prototype, however, ultimately returns the responsibility of Ken's penislessness to headquarters. It also highlights some differences between solo and corporate intention/ production—although some that first come to mind are false ones. It would be wrong to downplay the role of accident in the creation of works labeled high art, to presume that every stroke of the paintbrush signals the meaningful workings of the artistic mind. It would also be wrong to forget that cost of production often plays a role in the material or form of one-of-a-kind art objects, that many artists produce with an eye to sales, that many art objects are produced in editions greater than one, that many art objects are designed by one person and executed by others who may alter the designer's intention in the process, and that even artworks designed and executed by one individual always bear the influence of others with whom that individual came into contact, thus being far more collectively produced than the solo signature would suggest.

Nonetheless, even if few features actually render the production of Ken's crotch wholly alien to the production of art objects, the particular role of money is specific to the mass production of objects unashamedly produced for sale—well, relatively unashamedly, given the tendency of Mattel players and fans to describe money-related concerns (Will mothers be willing to buy it? Will children want to own it?) as altruistic ones (Will children be traumatized? Will children be able to project their hopes and dreams on the doll?). A cent and a half matters more when so many objects are produced. So does projected consumer response: had Mattel been aiming for a smaller number of buyers, akin, for instance, to the number needed to sell out a limited-edition print, Ken's penis could very well have been erect.

The story of Ken's penis also offers some lessons about Mattel's blind spots besides the one Schneider identifies. Some are apparent from related issues that Mattel does not seem to have pondered as extensively, at least not in the presence of anyone who considered it worthy of historical record. These include, besides Barbie dating Midge, Barbie's own lack of anatomical correctness. Why did Mattel presume that girls might be traumatized by the sight of a plastic male without a penis and fail to worry about the sight of a plastic female without a vagina?

The answers are far from elusive: sexist and heterosexist presumption.

It's no surprise that Mattel considered the penis to be a crucial feature of girls' sexual fantasy and psychological health, given the assumption widely promoted by Freud and his followers that child psychosexual development hinges on the discovery of the penis—not the vagina, which, overall, is rarely described as something to see—followed by an immediate realization of the penis's great value and an inevitable conclusion that people who don't have one are incomplete or wounded. Mattel certainly acknowledged that Barbie's breasts turned children's minds to sex and that it was Barbie's sexiness that impelled the decision to avoid making Ken too overtly a hunk. But the relative lack of concern over this issue—and over the possible fantasies generated when you put sex-signaling females together—is striking in comparison to the penis issue. Schneider merely states that the breasts were "necessary for realism and to allow Barbie's costumes to hang properly" (with no question apparently about whether looking good in clothes entailed having a miniature version of a 39-21-33 figure, another interesting presumption).[34] Yet, just as getting a boyfriend enabled Barbie to get a personality and a life, it also, apparently, gave her a sex life worthy of study, via the object that is presumed to matter most: the penis.

What Mattel studied Ken's penis instead of is telling; so, too, are the particular speculations about what its presence or absence would mean to children. Again as simplistic as Freud: presence means that everything necessary for (heterosexual) sex is in stock; absence means wound. Yet so many other interpretive options present themselves. One woman found that Ken's lack enabled her to fantasize about being him: "I preferred Ken. I cross-dressed as a child, and he had no penis anyway." And questions emerge about the extent to which fantasy about a body part or anything else depends on the sight of it. Apparently Barbie doesn't need holes in order for numerous people to decide she needs panties, which, in real life, serve little function without genitalia to cover or fluid to absorb. How much, then, does fantasy involving Ken's penis depend on seeing it? This is to suggest not that the Mattel people should have been spinning out every possible theory about the role of the visible in fantasy—a matter still insufficiently understood—but merely how much more is at issue in the plastic penis problem than the matters apparently up for debate at Mattel during Ken's development and how much more may explain girls' apparent lack of Ken-castration anxiety than that girls didn't think about it.

So Ken the artifact came into the world lumpless and intentionally unsexy, with an origin heralded alternately for expanding and foreclosing Barbie's options. As he unfolded in Barbie novels, however, Ken the character neither performed the function of making Barbie's activities unlimited nor rested secure in his status as Barbie's dream date. Ken did seem to be Barbie's possibility-expanding dream date in early commercials, which explain that, once Barbie met Ken, her weekends were full and signal the boyfriend/girlfriend relationship by the two demurely holding hands. When Midge comes along in 1963, she often spends her time as their third wheel, although, for those with an eye to the queer, brief shots that betoken another possibility pass by. In my favorite one, Ken stands behind the two female dolls, whose hands seems to be inching toward their own hand-holding position.

But, in the Barbie novels, Ken's boy-next-door lumplessness makes him always insufficient for Barbie. The short-story anthologies almost always presume that Ken is firmly situated as Barbie's boyfriend. In the novels, however, Barbie usually has another, more exciting love interest. In fact, sometimes the promise of a cute boy to date in a far-off destination is the only thing whetting her appetite for travel. While she wrestles with a bit of guilt about straying, the lure of the more exotic never dies, and Ken's rivals are always more interesting than he, for various reasons. In *Barbie Solves a Mystery,* he's an older man, just out of college. In *Barbie's Fashion Success,* he's a rich boy. Most interestingly, in *Barbie's New York Summer* and *Barbie's Hawaiian Holiday,* Barbie dates slightly older boys who are also nonwhite: a world-weary young man from Buenos Aires named Pablo and a Hawaiian native named Apaki.

This feature of Barbie novels surprised me. One might view Barbie's extra-curricular dating as a parent-approved lesson about how high school girls are too young to go steady. Barbie's flirtations are innocent enough, all talk and no action, and short-lived; she always comes home without getting pinned, in either sense. But they still leave the impression that Barbie gets to operate according to some cleaned-up version of the to-bed/to-wed double standard usually reserved for males: Barbie has a boy in every port to get hot for and a safe one to come home to; Ken himself never shops around. And why does Barbie, who, in plastic, does not even acquire a black friend until five years later, get to "date outside the race"? Here, too, Barbie appropriates white male privilege, a privilege registered in the novels by the information that both Pablo and Apaki are products of white men and women of color.

In the novels, as in the artifacts, it is Barbie's sexuality that violates social norms and defies parental standards. True, Barbie always returns virginal to the lumpless Ken, implying that girls' dangerous sexuality can be controlled through proper socialization. Yet this control is precarious at best, and the inevitability of the punch-line return to Ken is undercut by the generous

3. Covers of *Here's Barbie* (1962) and *Barbie's Hawaiian Holiday* (1963).

portrayal of his rivals, which separates Barbie novels from many other teen books of the period. While the plot in which a good girl considers hooking up with an inappropriate mate is a common one, other novels usually wind up vilifying the male object of temptation; in Barbie's case, fidelity to Ken remains rather unexplained and inexplicable.

Barbie's liberated-woman sexuality stands out all the more in these books because, aside from these hints that Barbie may sexually, as it were, go wild at any moment, everything else about Barbie suggests a character well under control, both societal and authorial/corporate control. These early Barbie novels and anthologies are particularly interesting relics of the period in which Barbie got a life (fig. 3). And, since they require more detail than a commercial, it is possible to extrapolate from them many of Mattel's rules about Barbie personality construction. In terms of information, the books alternate between two opposing stances: tell-all openness and furtive secrecy. Some biographical material and events are described in minute detail. On other matters, however, the reader must often rely on hidden clues and onetime mentions that might well pass unnoticed unless you're on an active search mission. It is clear from these moments of textual vagueness that Mattel still believed that too many details would spoil sales. What's hidden, then, shows what Mattel worried would be deuniversalizing; conversely, overt details show what Mattel didn't worry about.

Some unobscured details: <u>Barbie's last name is Ro</u>berts. <u>She and Ken</u> <u>Carson were named</u>, quite appropriately, after Mattel's accessories in money-making, their ad agency Carson/Roberts. The frequent mention of the last name is especially interesting in retrospect since Mattel now takes pains to "disappear" it on the Barbie q-and-a and elsewhere, probably because it no longer seems so unobtrusively generic. (Mattel also never bragged about the origins of Barbie's and Ken's last names, and I've yet to read mention of it—another, minor example of spin control.)[35] Less frequently mentioned is her middle name, <u>Millicent, a name old fashioned even then, as if to reinforce</u> <u>her good-girl qualitie</u>s. Barbie's parents are George, an engineer formerly in the navy, and Margaret, a housewife. Barbie goes to high school. She lives in a small town called Willows. She loves fashion: designing, wearing, and, on occasion, modeling it. She has blond hair. She dates boys. (Detail discovered by inference: Barbie dates boys only.) She has a typical teenage life of high school and dances. She does nothing outrageous; unlike her friend Jody, she doesn't weigh astrological compatability in picking a boyfriend.[36] She learns typical teen lessons, too: to be kind to the unfortunate, poor, and elderly; not to be jealous of other pretty girls. (Mostly she learns that she needn't be since her jealousy always turns out to be unfounded; Ken only has eyes for her.)

She also learns how to be a consumer of mass-produced goods. In the short story "The Size 10 Dress," she learns how to personalize mass-produced out-fits by using accessories creatively and how to work within a budget to make the same outfit serve for different occasions, also via accessories. The plot concerns Barbie's altruistic attempt to help "Big Bertha" make herself over into a popular size 10 girl. Barbie envisions Bertha being her own individual person, only thinner and, therefore, prettier. But Bertha, already in the habit of "inspecting Barbie like an art lover admiring a favorite sculpture" (one of many allusions in this story to the Barbie character's plastic prototype), tries instead to make herself over into Barbie, copying trademark features like her ponytail. Barbie is none too pleased, but the shock comes in sewing class when the girls model their creations. Barbie has adapted a purchased pat-tern for a more unique look. Bertha comes out in the same dress—material, adaptations, and all. After the teacher forbids Bertha to wear the dress, Bar-bie explains to Bertha that she needs to "be herself" for both their sakes: " 'When you try to become me, you're just half a person, and you make *me* less than myself." Barbie then gets the teacher to approve a plan so that Bertha does not have to wear the green plaid, size 14 dress she had made earlier, with the happy result seen through the eyes of Midge:

Midge stared in surprise. This was a *new* Bertha, hair cut short and fluffy, curving gently at her face. Bertha removed her coat, and Midge's eyes widened. It looked like Barbie's dress, yet it was different. The accessories, Midge decided, were what made the difference. A tiny nosegay of flowers was fastened at the waistline, where the streamers [a Barbie adaptation] met, making it a perfect dress for dancing on a summer evening. Bertha's pumps were pale yellow, matching her dress. Midge looked again at Barbie. Her yellow dress seemed more casual: a long strand of bright white beads matched the fresh whiteness of her gloves; her pumps were a cheerful orange, a color that would dance in sunlight.

The teacher then remarks on the two girls "as different as night and day—in the same dress!" adding, "Which only goes to show that any smart girl can take a style and make it her own."[37]

This story addresses the reader as mass consumer on many levels. Underneath, it addresses the reader as a consumer of Barbie clothes, suggesting how girls can make their own Barbie unique while still buying the same Mattel outfits that their friends buy: make adaptations or, better yet, buy Mattel accessories. More obviously, it addresses the consumer/reader as a consumer of clothes for herself. It explains to girls the two age-old contradictory fashion requirements: you need to imitate trends enough to be recognizably fashionable while appearing also to have a unique personal look. And it shows girls how to manage these requirements both in the general situation of mass culture and in the specific situation of being middle class in the 1960s. It presumes that readers will be able to afford only a limited number of dresses, all bought off the rack, and will be defining ready-to-wear against the option of homemade, which makes sense during a period when mothers were expected to sew and girls took sewing class in school. These particular options and budget constraints determine the suggested strategies: buy accessories, choose your own special material, alter the pattern.

The historical and class specificity of the Barbie solution, the urgency for many people of the issues raised, and the important role in teen socialization of rules concerning what might be called the etiquette of originality were underscored for me on an airplane recently when Cecile, a stranger seated next to me, told me about a fashion tragedy from her own teen years in the 1940s. Apparently, the branch store for fashionable party clothes near her home in Waterville, Maine, catered to girls' desire to be one-of-a-kind by selling one each of various mass-produced dresses. The store thus offered an originality safeguard since no two shoppers could buy the same dress there, a safeguard that, Cecile emphasized, was available only to girls who could shop at the finer stores. For one party, however, Cecile bought her dress at the store's Portland branch, assuming it carried a different, more elegant, big-city selection. It actually had an identical collection of one-of-a-kinds. The result: another girl at the party was wearing the same dress. Cecile blamed herself for this disaster: she had violated the rules by shopping out of town; therefore she had wronged her friend. Like readers of "The Size 10 Dress," she learned a lesson, but not the same one: after that, she went to a dressmaker. Cecile's options differed from Barbie's, but her understanding of what girls had to learn was the same: to work around mass production with the resources available and to avoid diminishing yourself and other people by breaking the rules of originality etiquette.

"The Size 10 Dress," then, conveys guidelines and etiquette rules for fashion under mass production. It is also one of many texts that teaches girls how to acquire knowledge about fashion and other girl matters to which they lack ready access. In "The Size 10 Dress," Bertha needs Barbie's help because her mother is dead and her father "doesn't pay attention to things like that."[38] Other books explain how Barbie gets fashion knowledge far above what a small town can provide. The 1962 novels *Barbie's Fashion Success,* in which Barbie interns for a famous beachwear designer in San Francisco, and *Barbie's New York Summer,* in which Barbie interns as a model for a teen magazine (and learns to lose ten pounds for the camera), explain the contradiction between Barbie's middle-class "cultural capital," to borrow Pierre Bordieu's term for class-based training for cultural consumption, and her high-class fashion knowledge. Unschooled in these matters at home, Barbie learns about them in big urban centers, acquiring through her internships an insider's knowledge that few girls of her background can obtain. The novels also suggest, rather unrealistically, that acquiring cultural capital is an add-on process rather than a transformative experience. Barbie always returns to Willows with the same fundamental small-town-girl identity. *Barbie Solves a Mystery,* in which Barbie's New York training lands her a part-time job on the Willows town paper (the fashion beat, of course), has Barbie bridling defensively at the big-city pretensions of Johnny November, a farm boy turned self-made urbanite who is biding his time at the *Guardian* until he can get a city job.[39]

Parents, town name, teen activities, knowledge about consumer culture: these are the details overt in Barbie books. Some fine points may entail some pulling out, but there is no sense that they are being pulled out against the will of the authors or against the rules and spirit of the Mattel author guidelines. One detail rarely specified yet easy to discern is Barbie's age. In *Barbie Solves a Mystery,* which takes place just after the experiences chronicled in *Barbie's New York Summer,* she worries about whether her ponytail is too childish for her new reporter job and bemoans being "sixteen going on seventeen" when "one was not quite grown up, but certainly not a child."[40]

For some details one must seek farther. Primary among these is the location of Willows. One passage of *Barbie's Fashion Success* locates the town in the nowhereville of the Midwest. (Barbie's friend Jody: "Someday you'll be a big designer. Just like someday I'm going to marry a rich man and live richly ever after." Barbie: "Fat chance either one of us has, living here in the middle of nowhere." Jody: "Just because we're in the Midwest doesn't mean we're *nowhere.*")[41] Usually, however, the reader can only infer the location of Willows in relation and contradistinction to other locations and people discussed in the texts. Barbie takes a plane to get to New York, San Francisco, and Hawaii, each trip described as a journey into the unknown and a chance to get to know the "natives," a term used often. "Barbie's Big Prom," in which Barbie's cousin Lulu Belle Rawlins visits from New Orleans, reveals that Barbie and her Willows friends are "Yankees." This seems primarily to designate "not Southern" as opposed to a particular region, for, as "Captain Hooten's Return" suggests in the same anthology, New England is equally foreign to Barbie, who learns a truism about the region when she asks her Maine host if she's lived there long: "Oh, no! The native New Englanders around here consider me a foreigner—even though the house has been in my family for generations."[42] (These authors deserve credit for identifying popular truisms; I've heard this one about always remaining a foreigner countless times since moving to Maine a few years ago.)

Two other details ordinarily or only discovered by inference: most important, Barbie's geographic roots and ethnicity. Although Barbie lives in Willows, the town is not her birthplace. "Barbie, Be My Valentine," in which Barbie meets Ken, recounts that Barbie's family moved to Willows just before Barbie started high school because her father got a job transfer.[43] But from where? *Barbie's Fashion Success* explains that Barbie's parents got married in San Francisco while George was a naval pilot stationed at Alameda Air Base and that Margaret "came out here to marry him before the war ended."[44] But from where she came we'll never know, just as we'll never know where Barbie's been.

Why are these texts so vague on this topic? Geographic vagueness must be a rule because it's actually quite hard to achieve, leading to some awkward and contradictory moments. For example, "Barbie's Big Prom" indicates that Barbie and her cousin Lulu Belle Rawlins have an intersecting past: they attended Miss Potter's dancing classes as children. Where could this have happened? Lulu Belle is ensconced in the South—name, drawl, everything; Barbie bears no trace of a Southern sojourn. Stories like this would be much smoother if a place were named. So why the convolutions for geographic vagueness?

Two simple reasons present themselves. The first is plot related. Many of Barbie's adventures entail journeys to new places; if Barbie lived somewhere, she couldn't discover it. Giving Barbie a home base, however, would hardly make her world weary. The second reason, more likely, is that Mattel did not want to cut off the fantasy by giving obtructive details. What if Barbie were from Evanston, Illinois? What would this mean to children who could not conjure up "Illinois" or identify with the Midwest? There seems to be a common assumption among many producers of mass culture that geographic vagueness helps consumers see fictional characters as people just like them and that identification breeds popularity. We don't know the location of Archie and Veronica's Riverdale High. New viewers learn only that the Oakdale of "As the World Turns" is in Illinois or that the Pine Valley of "All My Children" is in Pennsylvania when characters travel to the nearest big city, either to model, like Barbie, or to get lured into seamy underworld activities, apparently unlike Barbie. Oakdalites do not discuss being typical Midwesterners; the primary point under discussion, as with Barbie books, is home town versus big city.

This second reason also explains the silence about Barbie's ethnicity, but only partly. The vagueness about Barbie's geographic history operates quite differently than that about her ethnicity. The former clearly stems from a deliberate refusal to answer a question that Mattel assumes curious consumers will pose. It's hard textual work to make Barbie come from nowhere, and the text cracks often under the pressure in scenes where the lack of information is glaringly obvious. The latter seems to leave no marks, no clues that the author is hiding something because, in one sense, the author has nothing to hide. Barbie is a blond, white girl; from the texts' perspective, this does not need to be hidden since it does not signal fantasy-busting deviation from a norm or represent a marker that belongs to the few rather than the many, as geographic location does.

In other words, being blond and white does not make Barbie "ethnic." Barbie books are in accordance with still current usage of the term *ethnic* to designate only people who have a family history, name, religion, skin tone, or other physical features suggesting that they come from some distinct else-where—as if only people of color or Irish, Polish, or Jewish Americans have an ethnicity. Soul food and Chinese food are ethnic; diner food is regular. Similarly, blond, white people do not bear the marks of ethnicity—unless they come from some geographically marking region. Being blond and being white are marks that signal being unmarked—like nothing else, apparently, does. Midge, for instance, who is not blond in the texts, at least inhabits a body in which ethnicity might be signaled. In "Barbie, Be My Valentine," Midge, "a round berry of a girl," goes to the costume dance as Pocahontas, looking like "the very model of an Indian Princess," while Barbie, "blond and fair," goes as the ethnically unmarked and unspecified Cinderella. (Several decades later, it was Midge, not Barbie, whose ancestor's house was revealed in *The Phantom of Shrieking Pond* to have been a stop on the Underground Railroad.)[45]

The place in the text where Barbie's own ethnic specificity would go if anyone noticed it was missing is filled once: in a scene in *Barbie's Hawaiian Holiday,* which elsewhere follows the convention that, while she is always constructed as a foreigner to the places she visits, Barbie is never con-structed as "the other" instead of the norm, as the person with ethnicity. The novel predominantly follows the tradition of colonizer travelogues in which white people recognize their superiority over colonized people of color as they encounter curious customs and primitive people whose lives, while simple, have been enriched by colonizers. Barbie's knowledge about Hawaii begins on the airplane, when her father explains that the muumuu, which Barbie presumes to represent Hawaiian fashion ingenuity, is actually of con-tinental U.S. origin, brought to the island by "New England missionaries." Barbie later learns more from Hawaiians demonstrating "native" customs: that U.S. missionaries brought written language, helping natives translate their twelve-sound language into an alphabet; that the Portuguese brought the guitar, which Hawaiians transformed into the easier-to-play ukelele; that native music and sound making are alternately "haunting" and "savage"; and that "going native" would mean carefree fun on the beach with thoughts of school far away.[46]

For a moment, however, Barbie's sense of being the norm against which others are measured is shaken. This occurs when Barbie meets Apaki, a Hawaiian "native" whose darker color she originally mistakes for a white person's "tan," although her observation about his gleaming white teeth, stereotypical feature in white people's description of black people, clues the reader in to his person-of-color "identity":

"What was that word you called me? Haa . . ." Barbie sputtered to a stop, trying to pronounce haole as he had.

"Oh, that's just a Hawaiian word for white person."

Barbie wasn't entirely sure she liked being dubbed with the term; it made her seem like an outsider, somehow. Of course, she was. Still. . . . But the boy had used it so casually she assumed it must be a quite commonplace expression in these parts. "I'm hapahaole," Apaki went on to explain. "That means half-Hawaiian, half-white."[47]

Here Barbie learns some of her better lessons. She learns that she has a specific, not generic, skin tone that cannot be taken for granted but needs to be uttered: there are white girls and black girls, not girls and black girls. She learns that being marginalized because of one's skin color doesn't feel good. But, textually, Barbie is still not the other. It is Apaki who is then asked to explain his origins, which are "ethnic" through and through—mother's name Mele, father's name Jim O'Hara. Barbie never responds in kind even with the authorized "I live in Willows"; it is he who has the difference to explain, the skin color to account for.

When the novel does take up white people's origins, these narratives, like that of the U.S. Navy man O'Hara marrying the island girl, reinforce and retell the story of colonial conquest that makes the nonotherness of foreign white people seem natural. The Roberts' island hosts are the British Commander Baldwin George James Hawes, who met Mr. Roberts while stationed in Pearl Harbor, and his wife Clara, née Croft, a British refugee from Hong Kong, thus a sort of colonized colonizer. The Haweses have an elderly Chinese servant, who speaks in stereotypical broken English: "Pardon, please. . . . Is Mistah Roberts, maybe?"

The conquest narrative, too, cracks once. Barbie questions Clara's love of monarchy after Clara praises the violent unification of Hawaii by King Kamehameha, who, she explains, forced resistors over a cliff. Perhaps Clara's British origins, Barbie muses, make her think so highly of powerful kings, no matter how many deaths they caused.[48] But this is primarily a way to declare the superiority of the forty-eight contiguous states over both Britain, former colonizers of the United States, and the Hawaiian others, who are marked, not surprisingly, with a capacity for violence that Barbie considers uncivilized. No wonder Barbie has no explaining to do here. In addition to being the nonother, even on the other's turf, she has U.S. authority backing up her right to be the questioner and not the questioned: explicitly, the moral authority of U.S. democracy; implicitly, the military power of U.S. imperialism. One would no more expect Barbie to explain herself than one would expect a job seeker to demand a résumé from a potential boss. People in power get to ask the questions.

But they don't get to be absolutely sure of the answers. Although Barbie notices her whiteness only once, whiteness is perpetually being constructed. It is clear from Barbie's frequent musing about her own values and identity, and typical of portrayals of racial others, that the colonizer biography and travelogue patter also function to help Barbie understand herself as white, even if "native," not "white," appears to be the obvious object of inquiry.[49] "Native" and "white," to paraphrase David Roediger, are "created together,"[50] along with, importantly, Barbie's understanding and affirmation of her class identity. As writers on the social construction of whiteness have noted, white people often define their race and class status in tandem against people who are simultaneously of different color, economic position, and work situation and who are also often perceived as having access to pleasures that the white race constructor has had to foreswear.[51] This happens in *Barbie's Hawaiian Holiday,* in which Barbie, we learn, takes school more seriously than Apaki (the first college student in his family of fishermen), who seems to Barbie nonchalant about his mediocre grades and content to be more at home on his surfboard than in the classroom. Similarly, in *Barbie's New York Summer,* Pablo, the jet-setter who plays around while Barbie fulfills her strenuous intern responsibilities, is also a character of different color and class whom Barbie associates with freedom from work and responsibility. Barbie thus stands as the righteous representative of hard work embraced from neither above nor below but only in her middle class, which, by the omission of nonwhite examples, is implied to be occupied by whites only.

And, not surprisingly, Barbie's way turns out to be the superior one. By the end of Barbie's encounter with them, both young men have been "enlightened." Apaki has resolved to stick it out at college. Pablo has entered the working world—and, in a subplot confirming the association of whiteness and hard work, Barbie's (white) cousin, mistakenly considered shamefully unproductive by his father, turns out to have been working hard all along. Barbie, meanwhile, has tasted the pleasures that Apaki and Pablo embody and offer. (In one scene, Barbie eats the pizza that Pablo induces her to share in violation of her stringent diet when he entices her away from her disciplined schedule for a night on the town; as Kelly McCullough pointed out to me, eating this pizza was wildly out of character.) Barbie has even delighted in them. But she has restricted them to their proper, circumscribed place as vacation or occasional treat.[52]

4. Barbie fondles Apaki's surfboard in *Barbie's Hawaiian Holiday* (1963), p. 88. Illustration by Clyde Smith.

It is important that Barbie finds such pleasures in appealing individuals (fig. 4), whom readers are also encouraged to like, that she embraces both the people and the pleasures (in just measure), and that she redefines herself repeatedly in relation to them. All these features of the novels bear witness at once to the mixture of attraction and disdain, appropriation and rejection, characteristically present in white approaches to nonwhite others and to the nonfixity of dominant ideologies, which need to be actively maintained, re-inscribed, and re-created. Yet it is also typical that defining white identity and justifying white privilege rarely show up as active projects of either Barbie or the authors. These matters, the texts suggest, can be taken for granted.

The Barbie books' position on Barbie's (non)ethnicity reveals one point of continuity between when Barbie went infinite and when Barbie got a life and a personality, two periods that are not as different as many narratives imply. In both, Barbie is constructed to be <u>nonforeign and nonethnic</u>, on the basis of the assumption that there exist physical features that signal a desirable non-foreignness, an assumption made so confidently that Barbie's nonethnicity is one of the few characteristics that does not seem to be constructed at all in the texts (although, as I have suggested, they are). Once the Handlers had made the Barbie artifact blond, ethnicity became a nonissue. The issues to be addressed, the questions to be answered (or not), the details to be constructed, concerned Barbie's name, social life, home and origins, and moral character.

Several other significant areas of continuity also stand out. One concerns Barbie's sexuality, which remains under tenuous control at best. In the novels, as with the artifact, Barbie is a good girl whose possibilities for being a bad girl protrude like her pointy breasts. A critic of a more deconstructionist bent than I would linger much more lovingly over these points at which the public relations and fictional texts undo themselves, disrupting their own narrative continuity. A more Marcusean critic would revel in this testimony from such an unexpected place as Barbie literature that perhaps it really is sexual freedom that will undermine repressive social order. What pleases me more is the image of the Barbie books' two authors, named (pseudonymously?) Cynthia Lawrence and Betty Lou Maybee, rebelliously stretching the boundaries of what went out under the corporate label in a deliberate move to present other possibilities to girls—by reversing teen gender roles so that it's Barbie who gets to play around and by refusing to confine Barbie's choices to white boys, a refusal that, although occurring in texts marred by racial exoticism, does represent a challenge to the taboo against interracial dating that still makes dating outside the race a bold plot move for soap operas.

Presumably, Mattel higher-ups exercised veto power over licensed products then as they do now; in 1993 Mattel forced an author of *Barbie Fashion,* one of two Barbie comics published by Marvel, to degrit a story about homeless shelters.[53] Were these authors pulling a sexual fast one on Mattel? How about Clyde Smith, who did the illustrations? Did he want me to see what I do in the vignette illustrating "Barbie's Big Prom?" (fig. 5), which, instead of showing Barbie and Ken in formal wear, shows one girl seated on the floor looking up adoringly at another girl in a chair? Is this vignette a by-product of the standard "you two affectionate women must be sisters" heterosexual presumption, so that a sexual reading of the scene never crossed his mind, or a subversive little gift to readers for whom girl-gets-boy is not the happy ending that story after story, including this one, makes it out to be? Presumption or subversion? I'd like to think the latter.

For me, however, partly because the authors' resolutely heterosexual articulation of Barbie's bad-girl possibilities dampens my rebel pleasure in them, how Barbie's roving eye might serve the freedom of girls stands out less than something else: how the articulation of Barbie's sexuality as almost out of control yet always heterosexual—aside from the occasional subtly dyke-friendly visual or subtext—serves Mattel. It does so in two ways. It caters subtextually to child sexual fantasy, known to be a key feature of Barbie's appeal to girls. It also helps keep alive Mattel's infinite possibility

BARBIE'S BIG PROM

By Bette Lou Maybee

5. Who is Barbie's dream date really? Clyde Smith, illustration for the short story "Barbie's Big Prom" in *Here's Barbie* (1962).

discourse, which remains, if subdued and semi-disavowed, in this period when Mattel supposedly abandons infinite possibility to give Barbie a life. This discourse operates in the novels and anthologies in the deliberate refusal to answer certain questions that might restrict girls' abilities to hang their fantasies on Barbie. It is also visible, inversely, through the questions that do get answered, which stand as evidence about what Mattel considered either demographically unobstructive to fantasy (small-town middle-class life) or fantasy generating by virtue of being an ideal to which others would aspire (blond hair, blue eyes), the latter being more easily construed as unobstructive because it is presented simultaneously as something of a blank slate. To have blond hair, blue eyes, and white skin is, it appears, to have no ethnic specificity at all.

And it operates, within and outside the novels, in the presentation of the Barbie/Ken relationship, which reveals, more clearly than other meaning-producing textwork of the period, why Mattel's particular brand of infinite possibility discourse, with all its limits and contradictions, serves Mattel. By presenting Ken as someone who expands Barbie's possibilities without preventing her from exploring other options, Mattel promotes Ken as a desirable purchase while preserving Barbie as a workable fantasy catalyst for girls who do not like the lumpless Ken. By declining to author or even to articulate certain possibilities (Barbie never even thinks about having sex in the Barbie books), and by failing to author others (Barbie never dates girls), Mattel also works to avoid the wallet-closing wrath of parents.

The marketing advantages of gesturing toward the infinite explain why Mattel would understandably hedge its bets by trying to leave Barbie's options somewhat open during this period in which the dominating marketing decision was to abandon infinite possibility. It also explains why Mattel would inch back toward infinite possibility in subsequent marketing and product design moves. From the mid-1960s through the present, Mattel has been working to return infinite possibility to the foreground of meaning. This shift in strategy can be seen through a comparison of three commercials: a 1961 commercial introducing Ken, a 1965 commercial for the game Barbie's Keys to Fame, and a 1967 commercial introducing Twist 'N Turn Barbie.

The first commercial explains how Barbie met Ken and describes their activities:

> It all started at the dance. Barbie, the famous teenage fashion model doll from Mattel, felt that this was to be a special night. And then it happened. She met Ken. And somehow she knew that she and Ken would be going together. So now Mattel brings you Ken, Barbie's boyfriend, with a complete wardrobe of perfectly tailored clothes of unmatched quality. Now, Ken and Barbie meet for lunch at school, go to fraternity parties, and just relax together. Think of the fun you'll have taking Barbie and Ken on dates, dressing each one just right. Get both Barbie and Ken, and see where the romance will lead. It could lead to this [Barbie and Ken in wedding outfits].

This commercial conforms exactly to the strategy that Schneider, of Mattel's ad agency, describes. It tells who Barbie and Ken are and what they do, with each activity keyed to a costume you can buy. There remains, as in the novels, some intentional biographical vagueness, suggesting again that, given the opportunity to avoid specification, Mattel often took it. Mattel never states, for instance, here or in other commercials of the period, whether Barbie attends high school or college. Nor do ads ever mention Barbie's surname, home town, or parents; they mention only characters with plastic incarnations. There also remains a small gesture toward the unscripted in the directive to "see where the romance will lead." But the punch line implies that you will see where it leads, not in your mind's eye, but in a scenario presented by Mattel. How can you find out where the romance will lead? Tune in tomorrow to the next Mattel commercial, or scan the shelves "wherever toys are sold." As with the novels, the discourse of infinite possibility lingers, although subordinated to the Barbie-gets-a-life strategy, which presumes that children will buy Barbie products in order to act out the scripts provided by Mattel.

This presumption guides other commercials of the period. One begins, "It was the start of the fall semester, and Barbie, the famous teenage fashion model doll from Mattel, made plans for every weekend." It then shows a series of Barbie-and-Ken activities and concludes with another suggestion that Barbie fun lies in acting out Mattel-generated scenarios: "You'll love dressing Barbie and Ken for school and fun times. It's almost like going along with them to share their adventures." Others specify personality traits, events, and relationships to act out, with the same small gesture toward consumer-crafted plotlines subordinated to Mattel-generated ones: Midge, Barbie, and Ken hang out together, and one of the really great things they do is go to a costume ball. They also show ingenious strategies for giving Barbie a specified life without foreclosing costume options. One ad, circa 1963, explains why Barbie, a famous teenage fashion model who goes to school, would own a nurse's outfit, which one would hardly expect a glamourous model to wear, and a cap and gown, which signal the end of a school sojourn. The voice-over tells us that Barbie is dreaming about the represented activities and careers and that you can help her dream about them. Barbie's identity as a fashion model stays intact while the wardrobe necessary for it expands. Mattel is further ensconced as the author of Barbie, now bringing us not only Barbie's "real" life but her fantasy life—and ours too.

The complicated narrative twist of this ad, however, suggests that Barbie's fashion line was outgrowing the fashion-model career story, and Mattel soon took one of its first steps to undo the narrative it had authored. It turned fashion modeling into one Barbie career among many, a narrative unclosure announced in the commercial for the 1965 board game called Barbie's Keys to Fame. It begins with a male voice-over intoning, "Someday, maybe you'll be an airline stewardess like Barbie," followed by a picture of a smiling little girl in a fantasy-indicator bubble dressed as a stewardess, saying, "Coffee, tea, or milk?" as she extends a tray with three glasses. Seven other possibilities follow, each with fantasy bubble—schoolteacher, movie star, fashion designer, nurse, ballerina, mother, and astronaut. He then states, "Now you can be all of them with Mattel's wonderful new game called Barbie's Keys to Fame. It's all about the marvelous careers you might have someday," and describes how the game works, adding that it will be even more fun if you play along with Barbie and Midge dolls, shown in costumes you can buy that match the career choices in the game.

This commercial makes Barbie a doll with multiple possibilities, which, from one angle, seem far more vast than previously since they add a new field of activity in which choices might be made: the working world. It also gives Mattel a somewhat different authorial role in relation to the child, who now has a variety of different Barbie narratives from which to choose instead of one master narrative. There is still, nonetheless, a master author, Mattel.

But in 1967 the discourse of marvelous possibilities becomes the discourse of infinite possibility, which, submerged but not expunged in the earlier commercials, moves from subtext to text in the ad for Twist 'N Turn Barbie:

> She looks prettier and more real than ever before. But what kind of girl *is* the new Twist 'N Turn Barbie? Is she a famous fashion model? Does Barbie like sports, and music, and dancing? Would she rather go to the beach or go for a walk in the country? Does Barbie know all there is to know about what's new and exciting? What kind of girl *is* the new Twist 'N Turn Barbie? Whatever kind of girl you want her to be. She's got a beautiful new face, a new hairstyle, all kinds of new outfits to add to her wardrobe, and a twist 'n turn waist that you can pose any way you want. Mattel's new Twist 'N Turn Barbie can be whatever you want her to be, when you pretend together.

This commercial preserves the key moneymaking advance of the Barbie-gets-a-life strategy and of its successor, the Barbie-gets-several-lives strategy. It names specific activities and personality traits with which Barbie products can be correlated; for each Barbie characteristic mentioned in the commercial, Barbie is shown in a different and appropriate outfit. Also unchanged, interestingly for a commercial about unlimited options, is the spectrum of characteristics from which consumers are invited to craft Barbie's personality. Indeed, the paucity of choices stands out all the more against the question they purport potentially to answer: "What kind of a girl *is* Barbie?" In other contexts, one might expect the poser of such a question to lay out different alternatives: good girl or bad girl, virgin or slut? This is the usual query behind "what kind of a girl" questions and the hot topic of many contemporary teen novels. Here, however, as in Barbie novels, the range of possibilities does not extend beyond the good-girl side of the spectrum.

Despite these similarities, the commercial also marks a return to the vision of Barbie pushed by Ruth Handler before Barbie got a life, a return to the idea that artistic intention resides in the consumer. The ad underscores this idea by showing a child playing with Barbie and by presenting each named characteristic against a crayon-drawing background. Although a bit more sophisticated than the average child's drawing, they suggest that it is the child who will create Barbie's scenarios. But it is a doubling back with two significant adjustments. The understanding of what limits fantasy has changed. Barbie's modeling career, first a nonissue in the construction of Barbie as a blank slate and later relegated to one career among many, has now been disavowed as a core feature of Barbie. Is Barbie a fashion model? You decide. Also, the language of infinite possibility, which existed behind the scenes in the beginning and between the lines when Barbie got a life, has moved to the foreground of public sales promotion.

The history of Barbie meaning production from this point on can be described as a continuing refinement of the strategy used in the Twist 'N Turn ad. On the one hand, Mattel presents Barbie as a character who can be whatever you want her to be. On the other hand, Mattel works to promote a few options as particularly attractive, options that can be enhanced by the purchase of Mattel items and that avoid associating Mattel with the bad-girl side of the available-option spectrum.

In the next sections, I discuss both prongs of this strategy, which reveals, like Mattel's changing story of where Barbie comes from, Mattel's hegemonic smarts—already visible in the Twist 'N Turn commercial, which exemplifies the use of infinite possibility language without any corresponding attempt to increase possibilities. Nothing in the commercial actually heralds an expansion in Barbie's options. Although Barbie has a new face and a new waist, these changes, as the commercial states, are designed not to expand Barbie's options but to make her look more "real." Barbie has new costumes, but these only enable her to remain fashionable. They do not expand her options.

Actually, Mattel has narrowed her options, retreating, in the year of the Twist 'N Turn ad, from the expansion into the workplace trumpeted in Barbie's Keys to Fame. In 1967, Mattel introduced nothing new in the career department, except that Barbie as stewardess moved from Pan Am to Braniff. Appropriately, the costumes of the commercial are all keyed to leisure activities, which differ little from those discussed in the ad where Barbie meets Ken. In fact, they could all be accounted for under the old story of Barbie being a wholesome fashion model with a boyfriend. Otherwise put, the shift in artistic intention resides only in the producer's description. Mattel is like an artist who describes a work's meaning one way and then offers a different reading later. The artifact remains unchanged, and only what it is meant to signify shifts: Barbie still has clothes to model and clothes to wear on dates; now, however, this array gestures toward infinity.

Another feature of hegemonic discourse, which is visible, I argued, in the changing story of where Barbie comes from, cannot be seen in one product but only over time: Mattel's adaptation of Barbie's artifactual and ideological line to bring competing definitions within its range so that its presentation of infinite possibility expands and changes to account for and incorporate the changing views of consumers. This feature has less place in Barbie's first five years and little place over the next fifteen years. Although many early twists and turns in the Barbie story presage Mattel's ability to embrace the definitional elasticity that hegemonic discourse requires, Mattel did little through the 1970s to adapt Barbie to changing concepts of female possibility. It hardly nodded to feminism in the ERA years. Indeed, the list "Barbie Doll's Careers" provided in "Barbie Fun Facts," a 1992 Information Release, lists only three new careers between 1966 and 1984: surgeon (1973); Olympic athlete (downhill skier, figure skater, or gymnast; 1975); and aerobics instructor (called Great Shape Barbie; 1984). Keeping Barbie up with the times entailed basically working from a relatively unchanging concept of the audience: children want to emulate teens, teens spend money, so the best way to keep Barbie current is to tap into teen consumer culture or, more precisely, a fragment of it (I couldn't have bought Barbie a McGovern T-shirt like mine). This consistent emphasis is well reflected in Mattel's 1992 Information Release "The Barbie Doll Story":

> Over the years, Barbie has remained one of the most popular dolls ever created by changing with the times. Fashion and teenage customs were evolving at a startling rate. . . .
>
> The "British Invasion" of 1964 brought hemlines way up and hair way down as teenagers adopted the "Carnaby Street" look.
>
> Mattel's design and development staff has been adept at identifying trends for Barbie doll that related to the lives of teenage America. Barbie went "Mod" with new face sculpting in 1967 that brought her current with the next generation who adored her.
>
> In the 1970s Barbie doll wore up-to-the-minute designs reflecting the "prairie" look, the "granny" dress, the "California Girl" suntan craze, and the frantic "disco" glittery styles.

Mattel's elasticity turns hegemonic, however, in subsequent years and particularly during the 1980s, when Mattel refined Barbie's infinite possibility to incorporate, among other things, two growing ideological trends that threatened to position many consumers as Barbie opponents: feminism and "diversity." In the following sections I discuss the place of these two forces in Mattel's recent construction of Barbie meaning.

We Girls Can Do Anything, Right Barbie?

Barbie has always seemed to have more freedom than the average teenage girl. Even when novels characterized her as a middle-class small-town good girl, her plastic, cloth, and cardboard world—the world that most consumers knew best—betokened an allowance for clothing, accessories, travel, and activities far beyond what the Roberts' apparent income in the novels would support. William K. Zinsser, writing as a bemused father, recorded in 1964 that Barbie and her friends had travel costumes that enabled them to dress "like natives" in Japan, Switzerland, Mexico, and Holland: "Pity the father who comes home to learn that Barbie and Ken have decided to take the Grand Tour." He also alludes to one of the weirder implications of turning Barbie fantasy environments into artifacts for purchase, which, he points out, give new meaning to the concept of providing for one's child's future: "Should [Barbie] want to go to college, she can buy a 'campus,' which consists of a dormitory room, soda shop (with phone booth), football stadium and drive-in movie. Should she flunk out, which seems likely, she has her own fashion shop with modeling stage, display corner and model's dressing room."[54] Artifactually, Barbie seems to inhabit the "Dallas" and "Dynasty" "Daddy, I'm bored, buy me a boutique to run" world of seemingly endless cashflow more than the off-the-rack world of "The Size 10 Dress."

Zinsser put himself in Barbie's father's shoes, but Barbie's freedom must surely depend partly on the fact that Barbie ordinarily comes with neither history nor authority figures to restrict her actions. Even during the period when Barbie got a life, Barbie didn't seem to have parents unless you read Barbie literature. When Barbie acquired a plastic family, she got only a sister, Skipper. Mattel never turned Barbie's parents into dolls, and eventually made them disappear altogether, along with Barbie's age and last name. In the early 1960s, inquiring minds could go to the bookstore with Mattel's blessing; today, they must do archival research, with no help from Mattel. Mattel now has enough of a stake in revaguing Barbie to devote one of twelve q-and-a questions to denying that Barbie has a last name and a policy, apparently, of denying this in other contexts. A research assistant called Mattel and asked if Barbie had a last name. A public relations person told her no. "I thought her last name was Roberts." "Oh, I guess it is." One might borrow, here, from Eve Kosofsky Sedgwick's characterization of the Romantic rediscovery of ancient Greece and say that Mattel's primary goal throughout was to "[clear] out—as much as [create]—a prestigious, historically under-furnished imaginative space in which relations to and among human bodies might be newly a subject of utopian speculation."[55] Mattel sometimes aided those who preferred their imaginative spaces to come furnished but never showed the furnished spaces first.

Barbie's world has always been about "relations to and among human bodies." Her plastic body signals a sexiness that belied the chaste dates of early commercials and novels, and Mattel catered to child sexual fantasies, even while claiming attempts to forestall them, by making a boyfriend Barbie's first anthropomorphic accessory. Altogether, as Don Richard Cox noted in 1977, Barbie's sexiness, combined with her apparent lack of adult supervision and huge collection of habitats, clothing, and recreational gear, might well lead one to conclude that Barbie was a liberated female, sexually and otherwise. In his eyes, this made her a dubious role model: "Will [young girls], like Barbie, resist the responsibility of having children, or, following Barbie's lead more completely, resist the responsibility of marriage and family altogether? There is also the question of the sexual mores of today's Barbie owners. Barbie is a physically attractive woman with no visible permanent attachments. Will she produce a generation of sexually liberated playmates intent on jetting from resort to resort?"[56]

Massive amounts of disposable cash, no parents, and sexpot breasts made Barbie a liberated woman of sorts from day one, although not because of any corporate-stated artistic intention. "Girls, Barbie's boyfriend is coming over, and her parents aren't home" was never on the ad copy. In the 1980s, however, Mattel went official about Barbie's liberated woman status, apart from sex. It turned Barbie into a role model for girls with career aspirations and came up with a slogan to match: "We girls can do anything, Right Barbie!" This wasn't Barbie's first exploration of careers outside modeling. In the early 1960s, remember, Mattel outfitted Barbie for a number of other ones. Granted, these careers were traditionally female (nurse, stewardess) or largely unattainable (astronaut) or both (ballerina), but they were careers nonetheless. Mattel also anticipated Barbie's feminist future in the Keys to Fame game by plugging Barbie as a catalyst for career fantasy—"It's all about the marvelous careers you might have some day." But the Keys to Fame did not initiate a sustained linkage between Barbie's possibilities and career options. For the next twenty years, Barbie got few career costumes; Barbie kept up with how teens might spend money, not with how they might later make money.

All this changed in the mid-1980s, largely through the work of Jill Barad. Barad, previously a cosmetics executive, got her start at Mattel in 1981 by pitching to her prospective employers the idea of marketing cosmetics for children. Although Mattel didn't buy the idea at the time—it did, however, market a Barbie who comes with makeup for girls in 1992—they acquired her anyway. In 1985, Barad conceived and introduced She-Ra, Princess of Power, the first action doll for girls, as a female counterpart for the Masters of the Universe line. She-Ra was short-lived, partly, according to Barad, because "she wasn't very popular with moms" (something that never stopped Mattel from marketing Barbie).[57] In 1985, too, apparently in tandem thinking with her idea for She-Ra, and also as a result of focus-group research that revealed that little girls were playing at going to work, she introduced the Day-to-Night Barbie line.[58] The first entry was an executive whose pink suit could be transformed into evening wear by reversing the skirt and removing the jacket. Career updates in 1989 and 1990 include Doctor Barbie and Flight Time Barbie, "who doubles as a pilot and a flight attendant—with a sparkly after-hours outfit."[59]

Day-to-Night Barbie came with the slogan "We Girls Can Do Anything," which became Barbie's all-purpose slogan and set the stage for many careers Barbie has undertaken since. In 1985 Barbie was also a dress designer (again), a television news reporter, a veterinarian, and a teacher. In 1986 she was an astronaut and a rock star (this was the famed Barbie and the Rockers series); in 1988 a doctor; in 1989 a UNICEF ambassador, a doctor, an army officer, and a dancer on a television dance club show; in 1990 a U.S. Air Force pilot, a rock star, a summit diplomat, and an Ice Capades star; in 1991 a music video star and a navy petty officer; in 1992 a Marine Corps sergeant, a rap musician, an in-line skater, a teacher, a chef, a businesswoman, and a doctor again.[60] Besides these careers undertaken in 3D, Barbie took up others in Barbie comics and *Barbie* magazine. In the issue of *Barbie* magazine with Day-to-Night Barbie on the cover, Barbie became the star of her own cooking show, the "Glamourous Gourmet," in the Barbie Drama—a regular comic-strip-like feature using photographs of staged doll action tableaux.[61]

With the help of Barad, then, Mattel expanded its language of infinite possibility to pick up on a somewhat feminist revision of the American Dream, according to which anyone, girls included, can be and earn whatever they want, if only they try hard enough. Barbie, actually, never has to try very hard. Getting a cooking show entailed merely throwing one party for friends, which led to a write-up in the paper, a subsequent invitation to appear on someone else's cooking show, and, because the ratings "went through the roof," an immediate invitation to host her own. But this magical erasure of obstacles is really quite appropriate to the feminism invoked here. It merely exaggerates, in typical Barbie exaggeration mode, silences all too common in career-focused feminism: about the obstacles most women face in making their talents pay off so lucratively; about the inequity of any distribution of resources that enables the few to amass an inordinate proportion of the goods. Day-to-Night Barbie is feminism according to *Cosmo:* women can be happily sexy (minus *Cosmo*'s permission to have sex) and get glamourous jobs.

Besides feminism, Mattel has been following the discourse, and marketing potential, of "diversity." The company, which gave Barbie a black friend in 1968, introduced "black and Hispanic" Barbies in 1980. In 1988, Mattel introduced dolls of color with other names, reversing a decision made in the early 1970s to call all the dolls "Barbie." It also changed these dolls' expressions from a pout to a smile, apparently in response to complaints from consumers of like ethnicity, and decided, for the first time, to create ethnically targeted ads.[62] In 1991, after "black" Barbie sales rose 20 percent as a result,[63] Mattel introduced a new line of African American Fashion Dolls: Shani, Asha, and Nichelle. Each has a different skin tone and is "realistically sculpted from head to toe to reflect the natural beauty of African American Women," although all have long hair, which Mattel considers regrettably inauthentic but necessary for a totally fulfilling play experience.[64] A Mattel Information Release epitomizes Mattel's ability to pull the glitz out of liberation discourse and liberation discourse out of the conditions that require it:

> SHANI is tomorrow's African-American woman. She's young, strong, beautiful, and fresh. She exemplifies every attribute insinuated by her Swahili name, which translates as "MARVELOUS".
>
> . . . SHANI knows what she wants and has the self-confidence to go after it by being the best she can be.
>
> SHANI is fun, but she is also serious. Not "just a pretty face," she has high aspirations for her future. She's also very conscious of her culture, which she views as a rich tapestry of history, custom, and family values.
>
> With a look that moves easily across the terrains of West Africa to the sunny horizons of the Caribbean and on to the cosmopolitan metropolis' [*sic*] of America, SHANI is equally at home in kente cloth or glittering glamour. . . .
>
> SHANI is many things. She is light and darkness. Sweetness and courage. Committed, sincere, and inquisitive.
>
> SHANI is what we want our little girls to be—the best of all worlds— a hope for the future which will make us proud.[65]

As with Barbie feminism, Barbie diversity knows no obstacles. Mattel seems to have mastered the discourse of infinite possibility: according to Mattel, now all "we girls" can do anything.

Or has it? And can we? Well, almost, and no. Although Mattel's Information Release on Shani carefully avoids perpetuating racist stereotypes so blithely reinforced in *Barbie's Hawaiian Holiday,* the language of exotic otherness creeps into Mattel's toy catalog for 1992, once through the actual use of the word *exotic,* once through *ethnic,* more often in the coded term *outrageous.* Virtually every description of Shani products incorporates *outrageous,* which, like the words *ethnic* and *exotic,* appears nowhere in the catalog's Barbie descriptions. The dolls are "glamourous fashion dolls with an outrageous sense of style and contemporary fun" and have "an outrageous flair for exotic elegance." The boyfriend "wears an elegant golden tuxedo designed with outrageous Shani style." The clothes are "outrageously fashionable high style looks designed for Shani and her friends," which are accented "with a shimmering ethnic print."[66]

This hint of breathless thrill with the exotic occurs elsewhere, too, in texts with much wider circulation than toy catalogs such as *Barbie* and *Barbie Fashion* comics. An August 1993 story gives the overdramatic appreciation treatment to Jews (of whom I've seen no mention elsewhere) when Barbie accidentally walks in on a bar mitzvah reception. After informatively thinking, "Bar Mitzvah? That's when a Jewish boy turns 13 and becomes a man," she puts her hand to her head in a gesture of great emotion as she thinks, "That was a lovely prayer." Appropriately, the invited guests seem relatively unmoved; for them it is not the drama of the foreign (or a standard tearjerker moment like the singing of "Sunrise, Sunset").[67] One month later, in the "Letters to Barbie" column, "Barbie" told Czamira, who wrote "I think I have a weird name," that it gave her "an interesting, almost mysterious air."[68] And in December, responding to a child's query about what "it's like" in New York, Barbie added multiculturalism and multiethnicity to a list of tourist attractions: "Like any big city, [it] has good things and bad things. Homeless people, crime, dirt, overcrowding—these are some of the bad things cities try to overcome. But the good things in New York far outweigh the bad! Wonderful theater, dance, music, museums, galleries, beautiful architecture, a multi-cultural and multi-ethnic environment, many varied opportunities for employment—the list goes on!"[69] Apparently, Barbie does not make New York multiethnic; she visits multiethnicity as she visits museums. (Note also the unfortunate implication that homeless people, not homelessness, are to be "overcome.")

These are subtle goofs. Mattel sometimes goofs less subtly. "All That Jazz," in the September 1993 issue of *Barbie Fashion,* retells the popular story of parents learning to accept their child's disinclination to follow in the parents' footsteps. Here, the African American jazz greats "Dizzy" and "Sassy"—in typical gender coding he does instrumentals and she sings scat—want their son Duke to take up jazz also, but he's really into a different kind of music. Hip hop? No, rock and roll. If this were a story about challenging dominant race-coded expectations, this might not be a goof. But "All That Jazz," which race codes the parents' tastes and nowhere addresses race issues in the music biz, is not such a story. The writers come off looking clueless about contemporary music and African Americans in general.[70]

This goof reached more people and lies closer to the surface of the well-meaning text than the ad copy for Shani in toy catalogs. Even more obvious and widely circulated was Mattel's goof over Barbie's math woes. In 1992, Mattel was criticized for making "math class is tough" one of the phrases that might be uttered by Teen Talk Barbie, each of which comes programmed to utter four phrases randomly selected from a pool of 270. After much protest about Barbie reinforcing sexist stereotypes, which it couldn't quell by pointing out that Barbie also said things like "I'm studying to be a doctor,"[71] Mattel took the phrase out of the mix.

Mattel might be accused of even bigger goofs if the infinite possibility line with its feminism/diversity components were intended for all Mattel's audiences, which it isn't. Before discussing the products, narratives, and promotional material that expose the limits in this line, it is worth specifying its intended audience. Until 1993, it did not include shareholders. The cover of the annual report for 1991 (fig. 6) offers a far different spectacle of racial diversity than the one proferred in the promotion of Shani, for whom skin color was no barrier—and who, significantly, does not appear in this annual report even though Mattel had introduced her in that year. The cover features eight photographs arranged around a photograph of the Earth. Five include people. One shows a middle-class white woman in a store who might be taken for an affluent consumer reaching for a Mattel toy but whom a nametag and a description inside reveal to be one of Mattel's "retail service representatives" or "point-of-purchase experts." Another features a Japanese man at a computer apparently designing a video game. In the other three photographs are also people of color: a man crafting a mermaid-doll prototype; a woman bent over a sewing machine diligently at work on blond Barbie hair; and people working on an assembly line, people whose expressions range from diffident to weary to angry, constructing "white" Barbie heads (no multicultural Barbie here). These photographs represent the production of Mattel products in the "geographically diverse locations" that Mattel claims to have chosen for "optimum flexibility in sourcing, production and distribution options" but that, with the possible exception of Italy, scream out cheap labor

6. Cover of Mattel's
Annual Report for
1991.

more than anything else: Malaysia, China, Mexico, Indonesia (fig. 7).[72] (Mattel pulled out of the Philippines in 1988, partly owing to labor unrest and several months after negotiating a new agreement with the employees' union to raise minimum pay to about $5.00 a day, an increase forced on Mattel by a new minimum-wage law.)[73]

We don't need mentally to add the photograph on page 6 of John W. Amerman, chairman of the board and chief executive officer, the distinguished white-skinned, white-haired gentleman sitting behind his desk (in white shirt and largely white tie), to get the full picture here. Mattel's unabashed presentation of classic exploitation scenes and race/gender stereotypes—Japanese at the computer, Malaysian at the factory, or, alternately, woman bent over the sewing machine, man at the computer—hides nothing. Different diversity for different people. This world of Mattel is as diverse as Barbie's plastic world; people come in two genders and many colors. Yet the woman at the sewing machine does not have "a look that moves easily" across continents, from "sunny horizons" to "cosmopolitan metropolises"; her look announces geographic, racial, and social fixity, not mobility. Nothing in the pictures or the text suggests any attempt by Mattel to enable her to be one of the girls

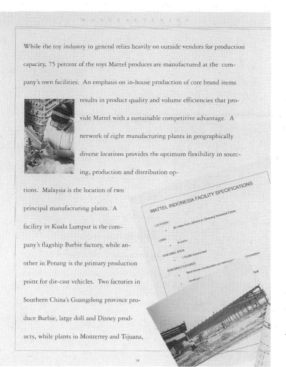

While the toy industry in general relies heavily on outside vendors for production capacity, 75 percent of the toys Mattel produces are manufactured at the company's own facilities. An emphasis on in-house production of core brand items results in product quality and volume efficiencies that provide Mattel with a sustainable competitive advantage. A network of eight manufacturing plants in geographically diverse locations provides the optimum flexibility in sourcing, production and distribution options. Malaysia is the location of two principal manufacturing plants. A facility in Kuala Lumpur is the company's flagship Barbie factory, while another in Penang is the primary production point for die-cast vehicles. Two factories in Southern China's Guangdong province produce Barbie, large doll and Disney products, while plants in Monterrey and Tijuana,

7. Mattel's geographic "diversity." *Annual Report* for 1991, p. 28.

who can "do anything" or to camouflage a corporate lack of concern about the conditions that make her spectrum of possibility so different than Barbie's. Mattel didn't even bother to ask the assembly-line workers to smile for the camera. Happy workers and corporate do-gooding are not the point.

Unless they sell products. While Mattel might genteelly refrain from committing to print the indelicate phrase "cheap labor," annual reports before 1993 mince no words about why Mattel performs good deeds. In the 1990 report, which includes a less cropped version of the assembly-line photograph, Mattel appropriately announces its socially conscious activities under the heading "Marketing": "The job isn't done when toys reach store shelves. Innovative marketing is needed to drive retail sales, and Mattel is the industry's marketing leader." After reminding readers that Mattel led the way with toy-company television advertising and discussing new promotional tie-ins with MasterCard and Coca Cola, the text turns to "cause-related activities which enhance the company's image":

> A Mattel France radio promotion of the past two years, also timed for
> the prime toy-selling season, is just one example of promotional efforts

developed in international markets around the world. Radio listeners were encouraged to call the station, and each call activated the delivery of a Mattel toy to a hospitalized child.

Mattel has established itself as a cause-related marketing leader. The Barbie Children's Summit, held in 1990, brought together 40 children from 28 countries to determine the most important issues facing children today, and Mattel committed $500,000 to support that cause. [The children obligingly chose the uncontroversial causes of world peace, homelessness, and drug abuse, rather than, e.g., exploitation of labor in developing nations, to be the target of Mattel's largesse.] In addition, an ongoing program of the Mattel Foundation installs Computer Learning Labs in elementary schools to help children with special needs learn to read, write and speak.[74]

As if this text were too subtle, two photo captions reiterate the point that image enhancement is the primary goal here.

Again, however, this is not image enhancement directed at shareholders. The photo illustrating the summit, like the factory shot, was not composed with a Shani-public-relations eye. There is no diversity in the foreground of the diplomatic corps (shades of Bella Abzug in the girl with the wide-brimmed hat notwithstanding): the five girls at the front delegate table are white. Behind them are two more white girls and a black boy. At the back of the room, another young male of color seems to be training for a position, not in the diplomatic corps, but in the diplomatic corps service staff; in white shirt, red vest, and black tie, he learns how to operate a videocamera from a similarly dressed adult.

Mattel, then, does not ordinarily strut its diversity stuff for shareholders, although it has tried a bit harder recently. The report for 1992 showed Jill Barad along with John Amerman—underneath him, actually, since she sits while he stands leaning over her shoulder. It also put Mattel's do-gooding (placed even before "Totally Hair Barbie: A $100 Million Success") in its own category, subheaded "One week after civil unrest devastated Los Angeles . . . , the Mattel Foundation committed $1 million to better the lives of the city's children." Nor does Mattel hide the profit motive for advertising-magazine or business-page readers in general. Articles in these forums rarely downplay sales as the primary reason behind changes in the image and color of Barbie and her friends.

I do not offer this evidence of Mattel's fundamental disinterest in the causes for which today's Barbie stands as an exposé of Mattel's profit motive. It's no news that Mattel is into Barbie for the money, which, besides being the nature of toy companies, is obvious even if you never pick up the business section. Just cruise the toy shelves, and shameless bucksucking gimmicks jump out. To take just one example from 1992, Rappin' Rockin' Barbie came with one of four little boom boxes, each imitating a different instrument. You couldn't buy the boom boxes separately; to get the full "rap" experience, you had to buy four dolls. This is just a minor extension of the recent career-doll strategy in general. In the early years, you could experience Barbie's many options by buying costumes alone. Now, although some costumes are still "sold separately," advertising is directed to induce you to buy additional Barbies. It's not Barbie with available Rappin' Rockin' outfit and Lights and Lace outfits; it's Rappin' Rockin' Barbie or Lights and Lace Barbie.

Nonetheless, while the profit motive of companies that sell products goes without saying, the shallowness of the corporate good-intentions rap does not. At least, the degree of shallowness needs to be specified. Mattel might have backed up the apparent politics of Day-to-Night Barbie, whether primarily for public relations or not, in the way that Ben and Jerry's backs up the apparent politics of Rainforest Crunch Ice Cream. Feminist-diversity Barbie would be proud of the Ben and Jerry's Foundation funding criteria: it funds projects that "will lead to broad social change or help ameliorate an unjust or destructive situation through empowering constituents or addressing the root cause of problems." [75] The company is also well known for fairer-than-usual workplace policies, out of which, by the way, it has gotten major public-relations mileage—I have rarely stood on a supermarket line with a pint of Ben and Jerry's ice cream without having someone I've never met before tell me about how the company provides masseurs for its packers or restricts the disparity between owner and worker salaries.

With Mattel, in contrast, the apparent politics of the Barbie line are little more than skin deep. Mattel puts some money behind them, and some projects do more than donating toys to sick children in the direction of "empowering constituents" or "addressing the root cause of problems," albeit uncontroversially; proceeds from the special Summit Barbie doll created to mark the Children's Summit went to a fund promoting education and literacy for children. [76] Mattel also set up an eight-member environmental task force after they got a petition from a group of San Antonio twelve-year-olds that asked Mattel to "make Barbie recyclable, set up a scholarship fund in environmental science, and establish rebates for returned dolls." Although Mattel probably won't change the five-plastics makeup of its big moneymaker, it did make a small environmental gesture: it announced a plan to collect old Barbies, fix them up a bit, and give them out free to poor children around the world. According to Donna Gibbs, Mattel's media director, "We think re-use, instead of recycling, is an acceptable [read 'convenient'] alternative for now."[77] But Barbie's "we girls can do anything" politics operate primarily in the realm of Barbie meaning construction: in the dolls like Animal Lovin' Barbie or Friendship Barbie, which was produced for the German market to celebrate the tearing down of the Berlin Wall;[78] and in the narratives addressed to Barbie buyers, including both promotional material for wholesale (Information Releases) and retail (commercials, packaging) and texts like Barbie novels and comics.

So neither the fact nor the spectacle of unhappy Malaysians bent over pink Barbie heads and blond Barbie hair constitutes a goof in terms of Mattel's position on, or discourse about, the infinite possibility of all humans, as long as the spectacle appears in annual reports only. They bear little on the issue of whether Mattel has mastered the discourse of infinite possibility. They merely make it possible to define the boundaries within which it is meant to operate, the audience to whom it is addressed, and the artifacts among which the content and coherence of the infinite possibility line need to be studied. With these specified, I now return to the conclusion suggested by dolls like Day-to-Night Barbie and her multicolored friends about Mattel's message and the query I posed about it. A few goofs aside, Mattel has clearly mastered the discourse of infinite possibility; according to Mattel, now all "we girls" can do anything. Or can we?

No, not even within the limited arena of doll meaning and doll "play." Barbie can't do anything, we girls and boys can't do anything with Barbie, and, if we take Infinite Possibility Barbie, as Mattel has crafted her, to be a model for what we girls can do, we girls can't do everything either, and only a few of we girls can do what Barbie can do anyway. The most blatant signs of Mattel's desire to circumscribe Barbie's options are its lawsuits against those who would besmirch Barbie's reputation. In the past few years, for instance, Mattel forced a stripper duo to stop using the stage names Barbie and Ken; apparently Barbie, who is constantly taking off her clothes, cannot do so for money, even if, as "Ken" a.k.a. Michael Cherwenka said, she does it in "a tasteful way."[79]

Nor, it seems, can Barbie be implied to have acquired her unnaturally thin figure through excessive dieting. To Mattel's credit, Barbie comics have taken up this topic several times. When readers write in for dieting advice, Barbie reminds them that Barbie is a doll, that people should not try to achieve a figure that is unrealistic for their body type, and that nutrition and exercise are the best routes to fitness.[80] (These letters suggest that some readers expect Barbie to function as a sort of Dear Abby, although no one I talked to described wanting advice from Barbie; they wanted, if anything, information about Barbie, which readers also sometimes ask for. If readers are also asking for advice about, e.g., dating, the columns provide no evidence of this; Barbie answers only questions asking for personal advice that pertain to being thin.) And, in one story, Barbie teaches Skipper's friend Jennifer, who is dieting to be a model just like Barbie, that being too thin isn't in. Although the story is ill designed to validate other body types—Barbie herself is presented as exemplifying the healthy figure, and she admonishes Jennifer not to risk stunting her growth since models need to be tall—it does offer concrete nutritional advice.[81] But explicit or graphic reference to eating disorders is out, as is any implication that Barbie herself might have splurged and purged. Mattel tried to prevent the showing of Todd Haynes's 1989 film *Superstar,* which uses Barbie dolls to portray the life and death from bulimia of Karen Carpenter (a censorship successfully pursued by Karen's brother Richard).[82]

Mattel also sent a cease and desist letter to Barbara Bell, the woman who channels Barbie. The letter, reproduced by *Barbie Bazaar* in an article wonderfully titled "Tapping the Collectible Unconscious," warns her of Mattel's intention to sue anyone who "may significantly adversely affect the wholesome, positive, family-oriented image of BARBIE and Mattel . . . [that] Mattel has spent considerable funds and resources to develop."[83] Actually, much of what Bell utters as Barbie in the *Barbie Channeling Newsletter* seems rather Mattelesque in content, if new agey in vocabulary: "We all have disabilities in life. Some may have physical disabilities. Some do not know how to love or be loved. Barbie tells us that even when appearances are cosmetically flawless, as is her plastic physique, subtle cosmic limits exist to show us that we all have areas to grow into, to improve, to strive toward." But then again, Mattel would probably not let Barbie use her "deformed" feet to exemplify her own imperfect state or answer a transsexual's question about why her estrogen pills—the transsexual's, that is—are pink. The answer: "Pink is the color not only of the Divine Feminine, but also that of Universal Love, so the color choice is appropriate."[84]

Stripping, dieting, channeling—these are some things Mattel won't let Barbie do. Many others Mattel won't help Barbie do. As both critics and fans have long noted, Barbie's accessories have always worked to predetermine her choices in the world of infinite possibility she purportedly inhabits. Barbie never could do anything or wear anything. Her career must be glamourous: "Barbie would never be a waitress," commented Kitty Black-Perkins, one of her fashion designers, in 1989.[85] Her look must be antisubversive. In the same 1964 interview in which Ruth Handler stated, "These dolls become an extension of the girls. Through the dolls, each child dreams of what she would like to be," she also noted proudly that Barbie got girls out of jeans and into a dress.[86] Barbie scorned the leather-jacket look, although she, like James Dean, was, and remains, a teenager without much of a cause. Barbie is clearly meant to have no politics beyond the mild fondness for the environment and "world peace" enshrined at the Barbie Summit. In Barbie comics and novels now, Barbie occasionally engages in a bit of environmental activism and animal rescue; in *Wildlife Rescue,* a 1991 novel from the new series, she saves a baby elephant from evil poachers in Africa.[87] And one Barbie comic gives "step by step instructions on writing to public officials": "The mayor explains that public officials work for you, so even if you're a child, there's no one more important than you. It explains that you have a right to write to your public officials and tell them how you feel about anything."[88]

For some people, even this level of political consciousness makes Barbie a tool of the Left. In 1990, for instance, the Oregon Loggers Group, which lobbies against much pro-environment legislation, protested ads for Mattel's Barbie Children's Summit in which children sing, "The world would be a better place if we could save the trees and the eagles," and, "We can save our world together . . . we can stop the trees from falling," claiming that the Barbie Summit might promote the "radical agenda" of preservationists.[89] But a survey of Barbie's plastic and textual artifacts suggests that this group was unduly alarmist. As presented by Mattel, Barbie's love of nature and peace seems unlikely to move her beyond letter writing to radical action. For one thing, it only goes so far. Mattel did not rush to pick up Laura Philips's 1984 idea for "Michigan Barbie," accessorized with menstrual sponge, Barbie's new name, and Barbie's healing herbs 'n' stuff.[90] Nor does Barbie's commitment to world peace make her antimilitaristic or anti-imperialistic; Barbie even did a tour of duty in the Persian Gulf. And her political activism does not extend beyond these hardly controversial areas. Mattel accessories include no pro-choice buttons, no ANC T-shirts, no Silence = Death stickers. Barbie is just not that kind of girl.

Not any kind of girl can be Barbie either, at least not in all her glory. In many stores, it's true, Barbie comes in different colors. African American Barbie has a doctor outfit and can wear all Barbie's glamourous clothes. She also comes with her own consultant. Dr. Darlene Powell-Hopson, a "licensed clinical psychologist and certified school psychologist," was hired by Mattel in conjunction with the creation of the Shani line, to "advise the company on issues related to positive play products for African American children." Her credentials, publicized in a Mattel Information Release, include co-authoring *Different and Wonderful: Raising Black Children in a Race Conscious Society* with her husband, Dr. Derek S. Hopson, and being "the proud parents of a four year old daughter, Dotteana Karyn Hopson, 'the beautiful Black African-American princess that God blessed us with.'"[91]

But Mattel's commitment to diversity does not transport Barbies of color, or even white Barbies who aren't blond, to the heights or across the breadth of the Barbie world. Many Mattel and Mattel-licensed Barbie products come in one edition only. In these, she has the same skin and hair color designated not "foreign" in 1960: "white" and blond. While children of many ethnicities people the video "Dance! Workout with Barbie," a white, blond Barbie and a young, white, blond woman lead them. In 1991, a blond, white Barbie graced the cover of the new Barbie Queen of the Prom game and also of Barbie's CD "The Look"—produced four years after Mattel hired a blond, white woman, Cana Cockrell, to impersonate Barbie in eight lip-sync concerts a day.[92] The list of products that come in blond Caucasian only goes on and on: lunch boxes, sleeping bags, paper plates, umbrellas, children's clothing.

Barbie also appears only white and blond in the textual products that expand Barbie's options beyond those committed to three dimensions: Barbie novels and books for small children and *Barbie* and *Barbie Fashion* comics. If the diversity displayed on the toy shelves suggests that any kind of girl can be Barbie, the diversity displayed in textual products suggests something quite different: any kind of girl can be Barbie's friend. Some of Barbie's best friends are people of color, who populate the comics in appealing professions and in fair number, along with an occasional person in a wheelchair.

Yet the talents and possibilities given to people of color pale in comparison, so to speak, to Barbie's. This is partly an unfortunate side effect of characterizing Barbie as a girl who appears to be a "natural" at everything she tries, which happens every month in Barbie comic-book stories like "The Heart of Art." The story begins when Barbie's Asian American friend Chris takes Barbie along for moral support to her appointment at an art gallery where Chris hopes to exhibit her work. Alas, the gallery owner ignores Chris, going nuts instead over the painting that Barbie, on her way to the frame shop, happens to be carrying, a painting of hearts made by Barbie herself. Barbie tries to redirect the woman's attention: "But, Ms. Svenson, this painting I did for fun. Chris is the real painter." To no avail—Ms. Svenson invites Barbie to be in her next show, and Barbie rushes home to dash off a batch of heart paintings. (Notice that Barbie's concern over the injustice of it all does not extend to questioning whether *she* belongs at the top.) Barbie is a hit, and one painting water damaged by a ceiling leak is immediately bought by a collector who screams, "Look! Live art! So bold! So daring! I *must* have that right away." Chris does eventually get her chance, but only now that the walls have a blank spot. Barbie pulls out one of Chris's paintings, to which Ms. Svenson, in desperation, will now pay attention.

"The Heart of Art" typifies Barbie comics, in which Barbie always manages to outshine her friends of any color despite some authorial intent to minimize the effect. It's the painting altered by weather that gets plucked, and by a collector parodied as an art snob. The comic makes the gallery owner, too, an object of some ridicule. She has wild hair, a funny foreign accent, and is "overweight"—too thin may not be in, but praiseworthy characters some- how always have Barbie's fat ratio. It also provides some visual and textual material to back up Barbie's contention that Chris is the "real" artist. A frame showing Chris's studio reveals her paintings to be more arty that Barbie's heart designs: abstract pieces and blue nudes, demurely cropped, allude in style and color to the work of Matisse. A subtext also contrasts Barbie, who paints for fun, for her friends, and, now, on commission, with Chris, who paints "because I *have* to paint, and not for everybody else," thus making Chris a truer artist in the Van Gogh tradition, driven to create from within with a vision that can't be bought. Yet Barbie, a natural, unschooled talent whose fame depends only on being "discovered," has the artist aura, too. And these correctives, many details of which seem too subtle for most young readers to pick up, do not outweigh the central message that in an area that Chris can conquer only with Barbie's help, Barbie has succeeded effortlessly, as she had succeeded effortlessly the month before at solving the mystery her female African American detective friend was hired to solve.[93] Barbie miraculously emerges at the top even of professions in which she dabbles.

Stories like "The Heart of Art" make the best of a bad set of guidelines. It's impossible to describe a world of equal opportunity while simultaneously telling the story of a white, blond girl who has the talent, destiny, and luck to triumph at anything she sets her sights on. Or merely stumbles across: Barbie merely enters the art world, suddenly she has a gallery to repre- sent her. Similarly, in "The Memory Book, Part Two," Barbie gets flown to a Hollywood audition after an African American friend sees an ad about a movie role and sends in Barbie's picture—again, a person of color whose pri- mary function is to be an agent, here somewhat literally, of Barbie's success. Barbie, of course, beats out the other auditioning actresses including two black women, one with dreadlocks; winning is Barbie's destiny.[94] In a just world, white people would not always occupy center stage and stand at the top whenever they choose to do so; in Barbie's world, by definition, this must always happen. From this angle, Barbie comics present the most insidious justification for preserving white supremacy; a white person just happens to have the most qualifications for any exalted position.

Most comics counteract this negative message by also portraying people of color as positive role models. Sometimes, however, comics perpetuate negative stereotypes more actively, particularly when it comes to foreigners. The most horrifying example is the story "Barbie or Princess Barbirita?" (fig. 8), which concerns ethnic and national otherness more explicitly than racial otherness, although the story manages to cast aspersions on several continents in which many U.S. residents of color locate their ancestry. The story concerns King Mondo of Exoticzonia and his "chief aide" Fasuli. The king mistakes Barbie for his long-lost daughter Barbirita after he sees a print ad showing Barbie wearing a necklace that matches one he had given her. He anonymously sends Barbie extravagant gifts care of her modeling agency, including a harem-type outfit complete with elaborate veil and matching pointed high-heeled green boots. As Barbie models this outfit for Skipper, King Mondo and Fasuli show up, King Mondo in a white suit with gold buttons, with a bellmanesque overcoat suggesting a service role for the foreign king that is not wholly inappropriate to U.S. perception of sovereignty over other nations, Fasuli in a bizarre outfit designed to designate who knows where—harem pants alluding to the Near East, a fur cap suggesting Russia, and a coat recalling the aristocratic milieu of Louis XV more than anything else. The two command her to return with them to her homeland, giving her first, as "a token of [her] family's love," a huge emerald, which Barbie recognizes immediately as "the *Eye of Mogombo*—the prize of the royal family jewels." After the men refuse to entertain Barbie's protest that she is not the princess, Barbie resorts to dramatic measures to get their attention. She threatens to throw the emerald off her balcony. This ploy works: fear of having their priceless gem destroyed distracts them from their mission. Once they are at Barbie's mercy, she proves her true identity by forcing them to sit through six hours of home movies. Barbie then takes the men to the necklace's designer, who, lo and behold, turns out to be the real Princess Barbirita (she had fallen off the royal boat wearing such a necklace and was rescued and adopted by a childless couple).

Now, on the one hand, the overt prejudice and implicit U.S. chauvinism displayed in this story are highly unusual for Barbie comics and constitute a goof. It's a huge one. Mondo comes off as the worst caricature of a for-

8. Barbie versus the foreigners in "Barbie or Princess Barbirita?" *Barbie* comic, vol. 1, no. 26, February 1993, p. 14.

eign head of state: a dictator who operates by fiat rather than dialogue, who neither uses his head enough nor listens to reason, who revels in ostentatious display, and whose love of wealth transcends his feeling for family. Yet the characterization of Mondo and Fasuli is as much a logical consequence of Barbie meaning-construction guidelines as is Barbie's frequent habit of accidentally displacing or stepping over people of color. Mondo needs Barbie's help to find his daughter, and she accomplishes in minutes what he failed to do in twenty years of searching. So what? Barbie's always called on to rescue people.

And how, other than by exaggerating the alienness of King Mondo, could Barbie's true identity be proved? Under other narrative circumstances, one would expect Barbie to invoke the name of her own parents or place of origin. But, since Mattel won't let her have those, she can only keep protesting, "I'm Barbie," and show highly unconvincing evidence—an image of a six-month-old smiling baby alone on a red cloth, with no hint of a familial or geographic context. The only way to make King Mondo's claim look preposterous is to overload his character with signals that he is wholly alien, foreign, other to Barbie.

Thus, nothing much has changed since only the Hawaiians had curious customs in *Barbie's Hawaiian Holiday,* except that the range of characteristics that Mattel can presume to be unmarked or generic has shrunk. We can attribute Barbie's loss of a last name, I suspect, to Mattel's growing consciousness of ethnic diversity. *Roberts* probably no longer seemed so benignly generic once Mattel started paying more attention to consumers like Jennifer Maria Perez, who wrote in from California to the "Letters to Barbie" section, "I have a lot of Barbies and my sister has some, too. My sister's name is Maricela Gabriela Perez and we are Hispanic." ("Barbie" ignored Jennifer's discussion of ethnicity in her response: "Hmmm, all the winter and snow stories we've been doing in BARBIE and BARBIE FASHION must seem sort of strange to you, Jennifer, out in sunny California.")[95] But the effect of refusing to specify Barbie's ethnicity is the same as the effect of presuming that Barbie has none. Barbie's identity can only be specified now as it was in the 1960s: by making other people different than Barbie. The contrast between Barbie and someone else is never presented as between two people of specific ethnicities, dialects, etc.; rather, it is a contrast between a person who represents a norm that needs no explanation and a person who deviates from that norm.

That the primary purpose of King Mondo's characterization is to signify difference from Barbie is evidenced by the names of his country, "Exoticzonia," and his princess, which sounds too much like "little barbarian" for my comfort, and by the huge mishmash of cultures to which names and objects allude: the Arab world (Fasuli); generic Africa (Mogumbo); the Near East in the Western-constructed guise of the exotic Orient (harem clothes); Siberian-esque Russia (fur hat). It is not, as King Mondo's name would suggest, that *he* is the world; he is the world of the other. The same logic of otherness from Barbie guides the construction of another foreigner, Ms. Svenson, the gallery owner. Under another logic of ethnic signification, one would expect Ms. Svenson, given her Swedish name, to be blond since blond hair is a common shorthand designation for Swedish origin. But Ms. Svenson cannot be blond because Barbie is blond, and Barbie is nonethnic; hence, blond signifies *nonethnic*. Ms. Svenson's hair needs to signal ethnic, so it's red and kinky. She also has an accent that, like King Mondo's costume, oversignifies ethnic by allusive mishmash. Sometimes her native language seems to be French—"Entré! Entré! And vat have ve got to show moi?"[96] At other times, she seems to be a weird hybrid of someone who would fail to pronounce *r* (stereotype of a Chinese speaker) but pronounces it as *v* (stereotype of how French, Yiddish, and Polish speakers pronounce not *r* but *w*), thus generating the word *alvight*.

The logic of otherness that guides the portrayal of foreigners also often appears to guide the portrayal of U.S. people of color, who often seem to designate "person of a color other than Barbie's" as opposed to any specific race or ethnicity. The model with dreadlocks aside, most people of color have shiny blue-black hair and brownish versus pinkish skin that might designate Asian American, Chicana, or African American. In one sense, this is as it should be; we often can't read ethnicity from appearance. What makes this silence vagueness rather than realism is the lack of other ethnic markers; characters never say, "I'm Hispanic." And it's not that people of color have acquired Barbie's privilege of silence, so they needn't explain themselves either. In the context of the comics, where the ultimate privilege of utter self-determination belongs to a white, blond person, and in the context of the "real" United States, where people of color are always considered "ethnic" while white people often are not, the silence about Barbie's ethnicity works to far different effect than the silence about the ethnicity of people of color. Barbie looks like someone with no ethnicity; others look like ethnics that white people do not bother to look at very closely.

In the 1960s, there were nonethnic Barbie and her sometimes ethnic friends. Today, nothing has changed in the textual world, and little has changed elsewhere. Although some "ethnic" dolls now get the name *Barbie*, a "nonethnic" Barbie still occupies center stage, and only she can do anything. When there can be only one, she's white and blond, suggesting—especially given the appearance of most ethnic Barbies, which are ordinarily manufactured by merely changing the skin color of white Barbie without changing the mold to suggest other body or facial types—that the "real" Barbie is white.[97] Other skin colors are merely temporary costumes that Barbie puts on in certain situations and, importantly, that you can buy: Ann duCille well suggests that "would-be multicultural Barbies make racial and ethnic difference a kind of collectible."[98] The cover of the March/April 1993 issue of *Barbie* magazine well illustrates the place of ethnic Barbies in Barbie's world. A photograph of white, blond Secret Hearts Barbie takes up most of the page. On the left are a vertical row of small photo inserts: from bottom to top, white Madison Avenue Barbie (an FAO Schwartz exclusive); white, blond Skipper with a white, blond boy doll and a white, brunette girl doll; a young Asian girl; and a head shot of an African American version of Secret Hearts Barbie. Ethnic figures remain on the periphery in Barbie's world.

I distinguished earlier between areas in which Mattel represents itself as an agent of feminism and diversity and those in which it doesn't. I suggested that the representational skin displayed to consumers camouflages the corporate body, both as it operates and as Mattel represents it more honestly to shareholders: Mattel would never display Shani working in a factory, and it will never promote the Malaysian woman bent over a sewing machine to chairman of the board. But the representational skin also suits the corporate body quite well. In the world of Barbie—which operates without camouflage, like the corporate world of Mattel, on the fundamental capitalist principle that some people deserve to amass a disproportionate amount of power, prestige, and accessories—diversity comes into play only when it does not entail significantly displacing white, blond Barbie. Barbie's counterparts and friends of color never displace or even discomfort her. Barbie never troubles herself about racism. She doesn't stop to wonder whether Ms. Svenson will not look twice at her friend because Chris is Asian American, and Chris never brings up the issue, because she can't. If she did, Barbie might have to turn down the offer of exhibition space, which it is Barbie's destiny to be offered, as it is Chris's destiny to help Barbie get offered it.

Similarly, Barbie never has to confront sexism. Nor does she displace men, at least not in any way made visible. Consequently, there is no suggestion that men must give up power in order for women to gain power, no suggestion that the social structure needs to be changed. In fact, the social structure doesn't need to change for Barbie to be Barbie. Barbie does not stand for women's right to control our own bodies or for dismantling a social order in which few women have access to resources or self-determination. She stands for the ability of a few extraordinary women to be wildly successful. Patriarchy has always had room for a few exemplary women, who can easily be described as exceptions to the rule.

In other words, Barbie's infinite possibility is the infinite possibility of hegemonic discourse. It reinforces hegemonic discourses predominant in the United States at large, which describe freedom in ways that benefit rather than challenge people in power. It suggests that all "we girls" can be anything today with little more than self-confidence, determination, and some luck and without necessitating economic and social change; white people, men, and capitalists can stay where they are.

Mattel's infinite possibility thus has hegemonic-discourse *content;* it also serves a hegemonic-discourse *strategy,* which uses and adapts the concepts of infinite possibility and freedom. Again, my point here is not to expose the obvious truths that Mattel sells a finite number of products and does so to make money or to describe Mattel's exaggerated claims for its product as an unusual marketing technique; promising miraculous consumer enrichment is standard fare. What interests me is not that Mattel uses marketing strategies but that it uses this particular one, which is absolutely brilliant. By promoting Barbie as a girl who can be anything you want her to be from a princess to a veterinarian, Mattel creates an appealing interpretive context in which the range of choices looks bigger and in which the act of buying a particular Barbie looks more like an exercise and affirmation of individual freedom than a choice among a few options dictated by others. Simply put, "Barbie can be anything from a to z, including x and y," sounds better than "Barbie can be either x or y."

Mattel also wins over some people it would not win over otherwise, such as Lin Poyer, who exalted Barbie as a "blank slate" in a 1989 article for the *Christian Science Monitor.* Poyer, "an unapologetic feminist," offers her Barbie tribute as a response to a friend who refused to buy Barbie for her daughter, claiming that Barbie would teach the daughter to be an "airhead." In counterargument, Poyer contends that little girls' Barbie fantasies really come from themselves and their parents' influence: "Whether your child dreams about high adventure or high fashion, saving the world or getting a date for the prom—that's up to her. And up to you." To back this up, Poyer marshals virtually every "Barbie can be anything or anyone" feature that Mattel has conveniently provided: Barbie is "available in different hair and skin colors (though not yet, alas, in alternative figure styles)"; Barbie comes from the store "nearly naked, bare of history, personality, family constraints, or economic and educational limits."[99]

Mattel's infinite possibility posture suits consumers like Poyer perfectly, as does the corollary message that Mattel's ultimate artistic intention is to abdicate authorship to the consumer. But, although Poyer obligingly repeats every infinite possibility/you-author-the-fantasy line that Mattel has thrown out, she is hardly Mattel's ideal customer. Mattel wants to sell lots of products to each consumer. A consumer who really takes Mattel up on the offer to assume authorship might very well not find her fantasy abetted by supplementary Barbie products, as Poyer's own memories of Barbie play make clear:

> My own Barbie was no pampered ingénue. The only manufactured cloth-
> ing she ever owned was the swimsuit she arrived in. After that, I clothed
> her, resulting in swift development of my fabric skills. My Barbie was
> little concerned with clothes, and even less with upholding a popular
> image. She was far too busy exploring the Amazon, discovering new
> planets, engaging in horseback Western adventures and espionage plots.
> She coincided with "Star Trek" and "The Man from U.N.C.L.E."—and
> she was the three-dimensional embodiment of the female hero that TV
> refused to provide.[100]

Mattel obviously benefits the most if it can get the consumer to think, "Barbie can do anything, but wouldn't it be especially fun to have Barbie be a rock star, with the official Rappin, Rockin' Barbie outfit and Rappin' Rockin' friends that I can buy." It benefits less if the consumer thinks "Barbie can do anything, so I think I'll turn my bathtub into the Amazon."

Or worse yet, "Barbie can be anything, so I think I'll build her a Michigan Women's Music Festival and all sorts of differently shaped lesbo pals," which would not only cost Mattel potential accessory dollars spent by that particular consumer but, uttered in front of disapproving, doll-buying witnesses, would forestall who knows what future purchases for who knows how many consumers. When it works best, the promotion of infinite possibility casts a positive light on the particular items that Mattel has to offer. It is also working when it induces potential consumers not to walk away. It is not working when it appears to promote fantasies that are anathema to the consumer. Herein lies the real benefit to Mattel of reproducing hegemonic-discourse content. For its hegemonic-discourse strategy to work to maximum effect, Mattel's definitions of *freedom* and *infinite possibility* must be plausible, acceptable, desirable, and unoffensive to as many people as possible. If most people believed that Barbie's disproportionate wealth signaled social injustice rather than the promise of each person's infinite possibility in a free society, Mattel's line simply would not work.

So Mattel gave Barbie careers only when these become necessary signals of a girl who can do everything. It gave Barbie racial diversity when the number of consumers who might consider this feature necessary was seen to be sufficiently large, although in such a way as to enable people who don't look fondly on racial diversity to ignore or bypass diversity Barbies. It gives Barbie popular but largely uncontroversial forms of political consciousness—environmental awareness and love of world peace. Hegemonic-discourse content serves hegemonic-discourse strategy.

We can see these hegemonic strategies and contents at work in Mattel's incorporation of feminism and diversity. We can also see them at work in Mattel's position on Barbie's sexuality and sexual affiliations. Unsurprisingly, Mattel's presentation of Barbie's sexuality has changed little since the 1960s. Barbie still doesn't go all the way, date girls, or question her sexual orientation. Mattel doesn't invite us to do so either. Mattel remains silent on the issue of sexual orientation unless it is dragged into this arena of discussion against its will, which happened in 1993 after Mattel, in response to little girls' requests for a cooler Ken, came up with the infamous Earring Magic Ken—tamely described in the *New York Times* as a "gender bending" new Ken who had "gone MTV" with streaked hair and an earring. At first, Mattel didn't address Ken's sexuality except through the veiled reference of Mattel's "manager of marketing communications" Lisa McKendall: "'We never would have done this a few years ago. But now you see more earrings on men. They are more accepted in day-to-day life.'"[101] The not-too-hidden message? It's not just gay men who wear earrings now. Mattel didn't speak the name until it became big news, spreading from the queer and otherwise alternative press to *People* (and from there to, among other places, the German edition of *Elle*), that Mattel had not only dressed Ken in not-quite-the-latest gay fashion. It had also given Ken a cock ring, or, as *People* more delicately phrased it through an obligingly discreet informer in "Has Ken Come Out?": "Mattel insists it was thinking straight, but gay men are flocking to buy the earringed update of Barbie's beau," a "plastic ring [that] looks an awful lot like what gay men were buying at sex shops."[102]

This is clearly another embarrassing goof for Mattel's spin police, although some people, like Dan Savage, spread the attribution of cluelessness around: "Lisa [McKendall] seemed genuinely unaware of the origins of Ken's necklace—and it's highly doubtful Mattel's design teams were lurking at queer

9. "And now for you men. . . ." Earring Magic Ken in the photo-drama "Making Earring Magic." *Barbie: The Magazine For Girls,* May/June 1993, p. 19.

raves. Queer imagery has so permeated our culture that from rock stars (Axl Rose and his leather chaps) to toy designers, mainstream America isn't even aware when it's adopting queer fashions and mores." [103] I'm not so sure about Mattel's design teams. I imagine a scenario closer to what got all those penises drawn onto *The Little Mermaid*'s magic castle: subversion from within by at least some people who knew exactly what they were doing. Queer intention seems also to have figured in the production of publicity for Ken. In the *Barbie Magazine* photodrama that shows Barbie and Ken modeling the Earring Magic line in a fashion show (fig. 9), Ken is actually introduced by an announcer saying, "And just for you men, check out this great look." [104] Could this screaming gay subtext here be mere accident? What about the slightly more subtle dyke pleasure offered by the beach towel in the Barbie for Girls line of licensed products sized for human girls? The towel (fig. 10), which shows Barbie in a bikini under the phrase "Barbie for Girls," seems to beg for the dyke reading always latent in the tag line, especially given the towel's most obvious forerunners: the Budweiser beach-party genre of products in which bikini-clad women are obviously supposed to represent the object of (male) desire. But Savage is probably right about many of the parents who bought Earring Magic Ken for their kids and also about McKendall and many other Mattel higher-ups. Everything else indicates that Mattel doesn't want to raise the queer issue.

The decision to remain silent is hardly remarkable: encouraging children to fantasize about queer sex is far from a widely acceptable goal; many cultural producers operate as if queer sexuality does not exist. More remarkable is Mattel's position on Barbie's marriageability, which reveals the extent of Mattel's attempt at Barbie image control and, above all, Mattel's hegemonic smarts. Since 1965, Mattel has refused to marry off Barbie because, spokespeople say, they don't want to cut off girls' ability to fantasize that Barbie is doing something else: "Little girls find marriage too confining"; "Little girls are marrying and unmarrying Barbie all the time. If we were to officially set

10. Barbie for Girls beach towel. Manufactured by R. A. Briggs, 1994. Photo: Jay York.

11. In 1959 Barbie could really get married in her "Wedding Day" outfit, illustrated on a 1990 Barbie trading card.

it, it would cut off the fantasy."[105] But, of course, they don't want to be seen as promoting Barbie dating Midge, and they do want to sell wedding dresses, one of the most expensive and popular Barbie outfits. Mattel sells more wedding dresses than any other costume—5 million by 1991.[106] So how does Mattel manage to keep Barbie's "options open," to dissociate the company from truly open options, and to get people to pick one option—buying wedding dresses—all at the same time? It makes dolls called Wedding Fantasy Barbie or Dream Wedding Barbie and then explains on the box that Barbie is not really getting married but merely fantasizing about it (figs. 11 and 12).[107] Here, Mattel, tapping again into prevailing hegemonic discourse, offers one of Barbie's most true-to-life social-context accessories: compulsory heterosexuality. Mattel doesn't force Barbie to get married or even to date Ken, but it clothes her in garments and ideology that make marriage seem like her natural, her most desirable, and her freely chosen destiny—the destiny that Barbie fantasizes about.

As important, to girls who have read the box, marrying Barbie to white-bread Ken may even appear to be transgressive play since the law of the

THE MAGAZINE FOR GIRLS

Barbie®

ENTER THE BARBIE
PHOTO CONTEST!
WIN A TRIP TO
OUR MAGAZINE!

FRESH, FUNKY
FASHION!

US ON
PARTY"
L

12. Now Barbie is
only allowed to
fantasize about
getting married.
Dream Bride Barbie
on the cover of
*Barbie: The Magazine
for Girls,* Fall 1991.

corporate father dictates that Barbie's marriage is not supposed to occur now. In a classic hegemonic move, Mattel has managed to carve out a permitted space for subversive play in which the subvertors actually abet dominant discourse. Mattel also carefully allots such a space to adults. Although Mattel sues people who besmirch Barbie's image in public, it also permits some mild Barbie bashing. In 1990, for instance, Mattel authorized the use of Barbie in the American Postcard Company's 1990 series Nostalgic Barbie, which gently pokes fun at her plastic world through captions like, "Every morning I wake up and thank God for my unique ability to accessorize," and, "I recommend no-fuss, machine washable plastic children. . . ."[108] Again, the rules expand enough to make the regime appear liberatory.

Conclusion

Despite Mattel's repeated claim, presented throughout most of Barbie's history, that Barbie is meant to serve as a catalyst for children to fantasize about whatever they want to be, the company has always had an "artistic intention" that is not confined to abdicating authorship. Whether by giving Barbie bio-graphical specifics or behind and by means of biographical vagueness and the language of infinite freedom—and usually by playing both angles at once—Mattel has been working, since 1958, to situate Barbie in carefully crafted, if purportedly unfixed, relations to both fantasy and reality. Mattel has continu-ally adapted its account of Barbie's "invention" and identity as its sales goals have changed, as its presumptions about what constitutes a blank slate have changed, and as its consumer profiles and perceptions of dominant consumer ideology have changed.

What remains consistent is that, no matter how many consumers Mattel expands its infinite possibility line to bring in, Mattel, and Barbie, always re-mains faithful to those who buy into the prevailing idea that the best thing to be is white, skinny, blonde, glamourous, rich, largely apolitical, and hetero-sexual, although it caters to some of these values more subtly than before. Racist consumers now have to see Barbie living in a racially mixed world sometimes. But dolls of color still remain Barbie's "others": defined against the white, blond norm as different, lesser, and, occasionally, "outrageous."

I have argued that Mattel's success, particularly in the past ten years, de-pends on its mastery of hegemonic-discourse content and strategies, which court the mainstream, accommodate the margin, and even provide a per-mitted space for (not too) subversive play. Whether these parameters, mean-ings, and nonmeanings stick, or can be unstuck, in circulation can be de-termined only by looking at the consumer response. This is the subject of chapter 2.

Chapter 2

Older Heads on

Younger Bodies

Of course, Bug understood that after so many tellings, the truth was only half the truth and the other half was reverie. Later she would realize that a truth's foundation could be eaten away by time and the little changes, the little slips in memory, the unconscious bits of self-preservation, while the rest of it might droop to the ground, so full of a mother's minor embellishments, like a neglected fruit tree or an unpruned bush. So years later when she finally asked about Georgia and the mother said too quickly "no, you weren't there," Bug wasn't one-hundred-percent convinced. —Gary Fisher, "Storm"[1]

This chapter studies adult testimony about childhood Barbie consumption to address several issues. The first concerns the relation between intention and reception in the production of meaning. What meanings do consumers give to Barbie, and to what extent do Mattel-generated meanings accord with consumer-generated meanings? The second concerns resistance. What constitutes resistance to given cultural objects and norms? When does cultural resistance signal social or political resistance? Where, if anywhere, in the relation between intention and reception can resistance be located? Although I have used the concept of hegemonic discourse to describe Mattel's strategy, I argue here that, while the opposition between hegemonic and counterhegemonic is valuable, it does not by itself present a model for locating resistance and that resistance cannot always be determined by assessing the degree of fit between intention and reception.

A third issue, which underlies the first two, concerns the reliability and usefulness of personal testimony as evidence about the relations between intention, reception, and resistance. As Gary Fisher eloquently states through the projected consciousness of Bug, his twelve-year-old narrator who is about to experience a Barbie disturbance, memories never represent a transcription of what happened. People who vividly remember some details have forgotten many others. What I get from adult consumers is what they remember minus what they have forgotten, supplemented occasionally by evidence they have found—testimony from others, dolls they discovered but don't remember having had, photographic documentation.   *accuracy*

Memories, even the most vivid, are notoriously unreliable, their veracity hard, if not impossible, to test. Most of my own childhood Barbie struggle occurred in my head. I could try to verify only some elements. When I did, I got conflicting accounts. In my memory, both my Barbie items and my brother's G.I. Joe entered our home via family friends. My mother was quite relieved to hear my version of things; she'd felt guilty for years because she thought that her fears about my brother growing up without a male role model had induced her to betray her political values and buy him war toys. Spencer doesn't remember how he got G.I. Joe. He just remembers setting him up on the windowsill as a protector during one scary night.

On one level, their stories validate mine. We all remember a plastic male hero that stood, for my brother, in the place of our recently dead father. Yet each of us recrafted the tale according to our own emotional stakes at the time and later: my stake in making my brother rather than myself the needy one and in aligning myself with my mother through matching political values and consumer tastes (she and I would never like Barbie or G.I. Joe); my mother's stake in remembering herself as sacrificing her politics to my brother's needs; my brother's stake in having, being, or providing for the family the missing male protector. Each story has some objective truth. My brother, in fact, did have a G.I. Joe doll in the mid-1960s, a recently dead father, an antiwar mother, and an older sister—and a younger sister who complicated all these family alignments among the living and the dead but did not make it into this story because she has no memory of Spencer's G.I. Joe. (She does, however, remember, as I did, that her Barbie didn't have too many clothes, although, unlike me, she does not remember attributing this to our economic status and nonsewing mother.) Each also has some emotional truth that makes certain contested details seem like factual truth to the teller, although they might not be.

I presume that most of the stories I examine here have some combination of emotional and factual truth, although a few, I imagine, are more deliberate fictions. Andrew Parker recounts that he asked students in a women's and gender studies seminar for majors at Amherst College about their childhood relationships to Barbie. The students, all women, reported that they didn't have Barbies, citing the disapproval of feminist mothers. But as the class progressed other truths emerged. Most had made use of ready access to Barbies belonging to cousins, neighbors, etc. One woman recanted totally. In truth, she desperately wanted to have been a child with a feminist mother who refused her a Barbie; in fact, her mother had bought her one. How many people have served up invented or semi-invented Barbie tales as flattering images of themselves?

I also presume that many people remember what they do precisely because they have some impetus to remember it. It might be a huge emotional stake, as in my story. Or it might not. My research assistant Kelly McCullough was surprised to discover recently a photograph of herself, age six, that showed a Barbie Town House. She hadn't remembered owning one. Instead, she remembered being frustrated by Barbie's feet. As a child who studied gymnastics, she thought that Barbie's feet should be either pointed or flat, rather than arched with flexed toes. In some cases, there might be less an emotional stake than something else, such as repeated use or remembered pleasure in a particular object or game. What follows, then, is not just a study of what people did with or said about Barbie; it is also a study of the transformations by which childhood events or thoughts become adult memories of them and by which adult memories of them become discursive or textual artifacts.

(A note on naming consumers: I've listed consumers by their correct first names except in several circumstances. I use full names when I am quoting from an article or if the consumer appears also in another context. I use pseudonyms or no name when consumers requested anonymity, when I decided that naming them would be inappropriate or cause them undue embarrassment, or when, on very rare occasions, they spoke to me in passing and I didn't catch their names.)

Adult memories of Barbie suggest several general conclusions. First, Mattel has had stunning success at making a doll who is memorable, particularly to women and girls. It's not just that many, many women have approached me with Barbie stories, although the numbers themselves speak to Barbie's memorableness. A more striking indication, however, is that almost everyone I ask has an answer to the question, "Did you have a Barbie doll when you were a child?" that is not, "I don't know." Most adult women remember whether they had a Barbie. Some remember specific dolls or products: "I had the Barbie camper"; "I had the Barbie perfume factory"; "I had Francie, Barbie's mod friend." Those who did not have Barbie often remember why, the reason often being Mattel's early-identified problem, a reluctant mother. A few had no memory of Barbie specifically, usually attributing this to a general distaste for female dolls: "I only wanted to play with trucks"; "I never got the whole doll thing." But typically people remember the issue of having a Barbie as at least slightly distinct from the issue of having dolls in general; having a Barbie required a separate or additional decision. Most people also remember an attitude toward Barbie in particular: they loved her, hated her, or something in between.

Second, most people remember Barbie as having been of great value and desirability, either to themselves or to others. Barbie's status often depended on the brand name as well as the product. Early Barbie commercials direct viewers to look for the Mattel tag to make sure of getting authentic Barbie products; apparently, however, children did not need a tag to tell the difference. Many people differentiated between official Mattel products and less desirable pretenders. "I only had a fake Barbie," Joleen recounted.[2] Although the similarity between her doll's fate and that of many a real Barbie—"my perverted brothers took needles and poked holes in her breasts"—suggests that knockoff status did not always render a doll ineligible for the Barbie treatment, the distinction between fake and real nonetheless mattered in the assessment of the doll's worth.

In the child's world, too, custom-made originals frequently had less value than clothes off the Mattel rack. As Lise states, "I had a friend whose grandmother sewed her hundreds of matching Barbie outfits. My mother disapproved of this; she thought it was a colossal waste of labor and time. Martha and I secretly knew they were worthless for a different reason: they didn't come in those plastic packages."[3] Nor did they come from official Barbie patterns. It was possible to buy patterns from which to better imitate Barbie's look—which meant that Mattel, via its licensee McCall's, still wound up making money off people trying to avoid the cost of Barbie ready-to-wears in this way. Mattel also devised various nonbargain ways for children to make official Barbie clothes themselves: the Sew-Free Fashion-Fun kits of the mid-1960s with precut fabric and adhesive strips; the Sew Magic machine, with "add-on" kits, of a decade later.[4] But the girls who disdained their homemade clothes remember clothes that came from spending labor instead of money, from thriftily putting to use fabric scraps left over from money-saving home production of grown-up clothes.

This was the case with Georgia, whose mother made Barbie clothes that

13. Georgia's Barbie clothes, made by her mother, circa 1963. Photo: Jay York.

matched the clothes she made for herself (fig. 13) and who remembers being "always enraged" about not having store-bought Barbie clothes. This was partly because her mother could not make appropriate accessories, matching shoes and purses, and also because, as copies of her mother's dresses, the clothes seemed inappropriately middle-aged: "These clothes were alternately sources of excitement and disdain. I didn't want Barbie to look like my mother, but they were actually great clothes." As important, however, was the class status that they signaled, the constant reminder of not being able to afford real Barbie clothes: "I didn't want to take Barbie in her homemade clothes around kids who had the store-bought stuff. I tried to compensate for quality with quantity, . . . but it didn't really work."[5] As with Lise, labors of love conferred less value than the official Mattel tag, no matter how elegant the clothes. (An interesting feature of these clothes is that Georgia's mother seems to have had an eye for the upscale fashion markers that seem to have guided Mattel's designers. For instance, while—if I and the people I casually surveyed remember correctly—many economically unprivileged home sewers applied rickrack liberally in the 1960s to both casual and fancy-dress clothes as a designator of care, craft, and good taste, Georgia's mother, like Barbie's designers, put rickrack only on casual daywear.)[6]

The Mattel tag, then, conferred value. Barbie was also perceived as valuable for what she represented. From the evidence of many accounts, Mattel was highly successful at creating a doll who was <u>recognized as a model</u> of <u>ideal teenhood</u>: "When I started to feel like I did not measure up to standards of ideal womanhood I compared my image to my sister's Barbie rather than to my Tammy doll because I knew somehow that Barbie had more status." Like many people who remember Barbie as a valued object, the woman who told me this, now an artist in her thirties who makes art about gender issues, was not quite sure how she knew Barbie had great value; she just knew. Others remember sources of value more clearly, citing Mattel and/or the opinions of others. They knew that their friends or people they admired liked Barbie or that their parents wanted them to have Barbie, often despite their apparent disinterest or professed distaste. Or they knew, conversely, that their parents did not want them to have Barbie, adding the appeal of the forbidden to Barbie's charms. Carole Nicksin writes, for instance, that her sense of Barbie's supreme value was constructed through attention to conflicting value-mongers, her mother and "the big girls":

> When I was three years old in 1963 I informed my mother that I was ready for my first Barbie. She obligingly took me to the Shopper's Fair and by that afternoon I was the proud owner of a . . . Tammy. "I couldn't buy that Barbie doll for my three year old," I heard Mom tell Grandma on the phone. "—why, that girl has a . . . a . . . a . . . full bust!" I didn't know what a bust was then but I found out that and many other differences between my Tammy and the Barbie I could not yet have. The older girls spelled it out for me in a way Mom never could—Barbie's Cool!; Tammy? a Nerd![7]

Nicksin's assessment of Barbie's value contains a number of common features. Many people knew that <u>Barbie's value was contested</u>. Virtually everyone knew that in some eyes Barbie was great. Value options might go from good to great or from great to terrible; they never went from bad to worse. Like Nicksin, too, most people remember having taken a position on Barbie, which is remarkable considering how many items are passed over or appropriated routinely, without fanfare, anguish, or conscious decision making. Barbie, in contrast, seemed to demand a stance, which often had to be fought for, or fought over, because more than Barbie was at stake. <u>Taking a position on Barbie meant taking a position about other issues, or defining oneself, or defying authority.</u>

Nicksin's account is also typical in that she remembers locating meanings in the doll itself: she "found out" who Barbie was and what Barbie meant. From adult accounts, Mattel was right to conclude early on that Barbie was not being perceived as a blank slate awaiting the consumer's inscription of meaning. Although no one I encountered remembered having been one of those children Mandeville described who clamored for biographical information about how Barbie became a model etc., his account well registers what seems to have been a prevalent childhood sense that Barbie had an identity and meanings. If you didn't know them, someone else did. Meanings, and consequently the cause of Barbie's value, were to be discerned rather than invented; when unavailable, they were concealed rather than absent. These meanings might be seen to reflect, represent, or inform about meanings external to Barbie; at the same time, however, they inhered in the doll itself.

One of the best textual encapsulations of the complex interplay between artifactual and external sources of Barbie's meaning and value comes, not from a consumer account about Barbie, but from a fictional account about a baby doll. In Toni Morrison's 1970 novel *The Bluest Eye,* nine-year-old Claudia describes initially being "bemused" by the "blue-eyed Baby Doll" that was always "the big, the special, the loving gift" on Christmas, then learning what she was supposed to do with it, "rock it, fabricate storied situations around it, even sleep with it," and finally wanting to do something quite different:

> I had only one desire: to dismember it. To see of what it was made, to discover the dearness, to find the beauty, the desirability that had escaped me, but apparently only me. Adults, older girls, shops, magazines, newspapers, window signs—all the world had agreed that a blue-eyed, yellow-haired, pink-skinned doll was what every girl child treasured. "Here," they said, "this is beautiful, and if you are on this day 'worthy' you may have it." I fingered the face, wondering at the single-stroke eyebrows, picked at the pearly teeth stuck like two piano keys between red bowline lips. Traced the turned-up nose, poked the glassy blue eyeballs, twisted the yellow hair. I could not love it. But I could examine it to see what it was that all the world said was lovable. Break off the tiny fingers, bend the flat feet, loosen the hair, twist the head around. . . .
>
> But the dismembering of dolls was not the true horror. The truly horrifying thing was the transference of the same impulse to little white girls. The indifference with which I could have axed them was shaken only by my desire to do so. To discover what eluded me: the secret of the magic they weaved on others. What made people look at them and say "Awwwww," but not for me?[8]

I return later to why this fictional text, like so many others, bears a striking resemblance to adult Barbie stories labeled nonfiction by the tellers. What concerns me here are the elements of this resemblance, which are many. To begin with, Morrison's text captures in Claudia the imaginative process by which every Barbie consumer identifies human referents for the anthropomorphic artifact. Equations between anthropomorphic artifacts and human beings always, of course, entail imaginative leaps: plastic denotes skin, yarn denotes hair, etc. But Claudia makes other leaps such as age; the baby doll stands for little girls. Her correspondence is also partial and depends on her own sense of identity. Conscious of her own color, Claudia focuses especially on the pink skin, yellow hair, and blue eyes, which she views as being about race. In Claudia's correspondence between white female dolls and white female girls, race matters the most, whereas, in Nicksin's correspondence between Barbie and teenagers, race (being "white") never gets mentioned, and sexuality matters the most. "It is no wonder," Nicksin writes, after lauding Barbie's stiletto-molded feet and firm bust, "that myself and countless other prepubescent girls (if my independent survey is any indication) used this doll in particular to act out budding sexuality."[9]

I do not mean to suggest here that thinking about race is the same as thinking about gender or sexuality or to set up a distinction between Barbie consumers of color who think only about race and white Barbie consumers who think only about gender or sexuality. Although the second characterization has much truth to it, the first has little or none. White Barbie owners from Barbie's prediversity period generally seem to have noticed Barbie's race even less than did the early novelized Barbie, who recognized herself as white for one brief moment. Even if they remember Barbie's blond hair and blue eyes as significant physical features, they do not, as Claudia did, recognize them as ethnic or racial markers. In contrast, Barbie's race seems to have been noticed by most people who lacked the privilege of ignoring their own, whether or not race was not the primary focus. Cheryl, an African American dyke who told me that she "hated that stupid white doll," then proceeded to outline a series of despicable characteristics that were not race oriented: Barbie's hard body; the model-young-lady gender behavior for which she stood and that, Cheryl believes, induced her mother to foist one on her over her protest. (The mother's attempt did not work; Cheryl refused even to open the box.)[10] My point, then, is not that consumers pick one category to think about—race or gender, gender or class, etc.—but that every interpretation, like Claudia's, is based on partial vision in which certain artifactual attributes are transformed and transported into human referents.

This passage also well describes diverse paths of meaning into and out of the artifact. In Claudia's narrative occur, in characteristic interrelations, all the different places, sources, and paths of meaning that come up in Barbie tales. While Claudia knew that she was supposed to generate some meanings, to "fabricate storied situations," she also believed that meaning and value resided in the object independent of what she or anyone else fabricated. It is not that "adults, older girls," or people in charge of "shops, magazines, newspapers, window signs," implant content; they interpret and value content that is already there. Meanings come from both inside and outside the artifact and traverse the boundaries between them. Decoding the doll will help decode social values because valuing the doll means valuing the human characteristics to which the doll refers. Similarly, interpretive or physical acts performed on the doll reverberate beyond it. They are viewed as acts of allegiance to or rebellion against those to whom the doll refers or those who ascribe to it opposing value, especially when the referents or interpreters have authority, power, or status over the child.

Not all these places and paths of meaning occur in every Barbie story. Nor do all Barbie stories contain such a logical correlation between thought and action as does this one—in which hatred lead to destruction and resistance to the doll matches resistance to human referents—although, just as important, some do. What follows are some adult memories about Barbie. I am interested precisely in the mixture of messiness and tidiness within these stories and in the frequent use and unfixed place of resistance in them. In deliberate Barbie subversions by adults such as the photographs from *On Our Backs,* although resistance is sometimes complex and multiple, it is usually relatively easy to locate, as are the people, dominant ideologies, and institutions against whom or which resistance is directed. One can assume that the makers of "Gals and Dolls" intend to be subversive and conclude with some assurance that they aim to subvert Mattel and heterosexual presumption. The big uncertainties here, which I take up later, concern whether their subversive meanings can adhere in circulation.

I decided to study childhood Barbie use after I began to take seriously the implicit connection between child consumers and adult interventionists suggested by many adults who dumped unsolicited Barbie memories in my lap: if you think *On Our Backs* is subversive, wait till you hear what *I* did with Barbie when I was only six years old. These first informants often defined resistance as a rejection or subversion of Mattel's product: if thinking and doing weren't fit for a Barbie commercial, the consumer was resistant; if they were, the consumer wasn't. I discovered, however, that resistance did not always lie on the rejection/subversion side of things and that, while Barbie storytellers often make use of tidy oppositions between acceptance and rejection or conformity and subversion, the relation between intention, reception, and resistance is much messier.

One result of this messiness is that this material resists organization.

Anecdotes can't be placed on a continuum from acceptance to rejection, mainstream to marginal, or straight to queer. Nor can they be organized according to the consumer's take on one particular issue (like "identity," with subheadings on ethnicity, class, gender, and sexuality) or one particular artifactual feature (with subheadings on breasts, hair, skin, clothes, and cars). These organizing principles leave too many anecdotes without assignment to any category or with multiple or debatable assignments. And, regardless of their particular insufficiencies, they impose a false sense of orderliness that is too high a price to pay for narrative flow and easy topic sentences. So, as an attempt simultaneously to respect the mess, to tame it for readability (and writability), and to suggest patterns and categories that do emerge, I organized the material by dividing it into categories that are not apparent kin or subsets of a conceptual whole. The first section deals with acts considered alien to the teller or the doer, another deals with predyke Barbie games, and so on. Each section focuses on one feature of Barbie consumption narratives that occurs often enough to be classified as a trend; from the whole, I hope, the unwieldiness of consumption will remain visible.

Sister from Another Planet

By some accounts, Barbie has strange and unnatural powers. Like an alien from another planet, she enters the home of unsuspecting victims and turns them into aliens too. Sometimes it happens right away: "When I was about four, I was given a Barbie. I grabbed Barbie and hurled her into the fire. I don't know why I did it. It was the only violent act of my childhood."[11] Sometimes it takes years. Teresa Ortega, who reported getting a fake Barbie at age three and a real Barbie soon after, did "heavy Barbie bonding" with her friends from the second through the fifth grades. Nothing seemed out of the ordinary, except, perhaps, for the intensity of her desire to get Barbie into an elevator—"I just wanted to see her ascension." (The desire itself was quite ordinary; several others told me about its fascination.) Then, in one unexplainable moment, Barbie sucked her out of the world of the law abiding: "The only thing I ever stole was a brown fringed suede vest for Barbie. My friend had it, and I wanted it desperately, and I took it. I never admitted it or returned it; I think I still have it."[12]

These possessions were only momentary. In other cases, possession recurs repeatedly: "I had this friend Ann. She was the quietest little girl, always very well behaved, except for one thing. When her parents weren't around, she used to paint nipples on Barbie with a red magic marker and then rub them off with her finger. Over and over. She'd just sit there painting them on, rubbing them off, painting them on, rubbing them off."[13] Or possession lasts a lifetime, as one woman suggested to me after a lecture I gave at Wayne State University: "Do you have any ideas about how to keep girls away from the terrible influence of Barbie? I didn't buy into Barbie, but my sister loved Barbie, and now she's just like her. She's materialistic. She cares too much about her appearance. She has a superficial life with superficial values and a gross husband, and I think she's really unhappy. She's never satisfied with what she has. And now her daughters are into Barbie, and I don't know how to counteract Barbie's influence."[14] The narrator is one of many people who seemed to view Barbie as a character in a drama of cultural affect whose human players were divided into the possessed and the unpossessed—and who usually located themselves among the latter. "I hope you're going to write about how fascist Mattel is," a woman told me, summing up her point that Mattel forced little girls to want to be Barbie. Her own memory of a much more discriminating and imaginative relation to the world of Barbie— which involved transgender and cross-dressing—did nothing to modify her perception that Barbie took over the masses.

What accounts for all these tales in which Barbie turns people into aliens: alien to their friends, to their sisters, to themselves? Or to me. I often find myself thinking that people are not who I thought they were before I heard their Barbie stories or that I'm some unpossessed observer of a Barbie-possessed mind, even though I view such claims as arrogant and delusional and recognize how questionable such a self-assessment would be in this case—no matter what the seemingly possessed person is telling me, I'm the one writing a book about Barbie. Nonetheless, the more my Wayne State conversation progressed, the more it seemed like I was talking to someone whom Barbie had robbed of the ability to think or hear. I realized after her initial comments, reproduced above, that she had misunderstood my talk. She presumed that I shared her view of Barbie completely, although I'd spoken about how frequently children subvert or bypass Mattel-generated meanings. This itself didn't seem weird. I might have been unclear; her attention might have wandered. But subsequent attempts to clarify my stance or to introduce counterevidence simply "did not compute": no reaction, no response, no reevaluation of me. She just kept telling me about how Barbie was stealing little girls as if I had never spoken.

In part, besides lending them an aura of shock value, the science-fictional tone of these accounts registers something mysterious that is not in Barbie or caused by Barbie. Each concerns something else frequently understood to be unknowable or unexplainable. The first—besides dealing with childhood sexuality, which often seems like evidence of a secret life revealed—is also the stuff of television interviews with the surprised neighbors and coworkers of someone who seemed to be normal until he shot up McDonald's. It rehearses the common wisdom that you never really know what's going on in the minds of other people, especially the quiet ones. The second reveals the teller as a stranger to herself: she experienced earlier the often-recounted feeling of watching yourself doing something as if it were someone else doing it and later the frustration of looking for causes lost to memory. The third has elements of the first two and adds the mysteries of compulsion: the urgency that propels you beyond the dictates of reason, socialization, training; the compelling force that cultural products exert (I had to have it; I had to destroy it). The fourth engages the mystery of many a family, which, as Sedgwick points out, theoretical systems that give primary explanatory authority to categories of identity such as class, race, gender, and nationality will always fail to explain: How did my sibling and I turn out so differently? [15] I recast this one as the mystery of noncommunication: We seem to be speaking the same language, so why can't she hear me?

Yet, if these mysteries occur often without Barbie in the cast of characters, it is not surprising that Barbie often appears in them. Barbie herself is premade for a number of roles: the sister from another planet (eerily human looking but not like anyone you know, or, as Mattel states in the q-and-a, "life like" but "not scaled to human measurements"); or, conversely, the sister from another planet's victim (fixed stare, brain susceptible to being taken over by whomever gives her one). And she has a long history of alien casting. The last story, which sounds the most science fictional, merely exaggerates the terms of the debate that has surrounded Barbie since she emerged in 1959. If you let Barbie into the house, will she steal your daughter? Will she turn your daughter into a clone, a plastic personality? Will she take over her mind, possess her soul, erase everything you've taught her? Will she fill your daughter with sexual thoughts, thereby forcing her maturation process to proceed at an unnatural rate? Will your daughter be strong enough to resist Barbie's spell? Will you be strong enough to bring her back?

I do not describe this debate in science-fictional terms to discredit the claim that culture affects people; I believe that it does and that we need to be concerned about the cultural products circulated. I draw this comparison instead to denaturalize the conventions of cultural debate. As William Pope.L points out, the statement "Barbie turned my sister into a materialistic bimbo" has the same truth value as "Barbie loves Ken." Barbie cannot actually do either of those things.[16] Yet the first, unlike the second, often stands as a credible description of reality because phrases like "turned my sister into" are understood as figures of speech. But recognizing them as such does not thereby render them meaningless or neutralize their effect. As James Clifford points out in his introduction to *Writing Culture,* the "tropes, figures, and allegories" that people always use in descriptions "select and impose meaning as they translate it."[17] Embedded through the science-fiction convention in my first three examples is an acknowledgment that certain phenomena escape explanation. Available theoretical systems cannot account for them; the incompleteness of memory and the opaqueness of personality prevent us from accessing the data that we need to figure them out. Embedded in those that divide the cast of human characters into the possessed and the unpossessed is the assumption that certain people escape culture. Barbie captured my sister, but she didn't get me, and no cultural products have captured me enough to prevent me from seeing what Barbie really is.

Dykes to Watch Out For

In contrast to stories about alien behavior are stories told by people who see in their Barbie past a sign that the seeds of adult identity had been sown early in life. I focus below on one subset of the prefiguration tales I heard: dyke destiny stories.

The most obvious signs of dyke destiny occur in stories about female sexual desire for females. Not every junior dyke could get off on Barbie: "I hated Barbie; you couldn't spread her legs." But some could. Penny Pollard remembers using Barbie to act out fantasies about her baby-sitter Janet, with help from Janet's mother: "I had a crush on my baby-sitter, Janet (who was also the only person who could get me into a dress). Her mother had turned two Barbies into 'Janet' and 'Carol' dolls, named after her and her sister, dressing girls and dolls in matching clothes. I got the dolls when they were too old for them and used my 'Janet' doll to act out what I wanted to do with the real Janet."

Here Barbie gets transformed into the object of dyke desire. Penny Lorio turned Barbie into the agent of dyke desire. Her "Uncloseting Barbie: Get Over It, Ken, It's a New Age" concerns Lorio's attempt to make her unasked-for Barbie a usable toy—"the last thing I needed when we were hiking through quicksand was to have her gimping along in high heels"—and her mother's distress that Barbie was not a socializing tool as she'd hoped:

"So Barbie should start acting like a young lady," Mom explained, reading the dumb expression on my face. "Because someday she's going to meet someone and fall in love. And then she's not going to want to be a tomboy anymore."

Oh, right, like falling in love was more fun than climbing trees.

"Do you understand what I'm trying to say?" mom asked.

Of course I did. I wasn't born yesterday. I was 7. I knew about life.

"Barbie's already been in love," I said, vouching for the heart of a tomboy.

Mom smiled eagerly. "Oh, she has? Does she like Freddy's G.I. Joe?"

I made a face like a person who's just been served ketchup on pancakes.

"Of course not. Barbie loves Midge."

And that was a whole different subject.[18]

Not necessarily. In all the stories above, the perception of sexual desire for women arose in the context of being a gender-role outlaw. The woman who couldn't spread Barbie's legs (to which she did not attribute dyke content until I raised my eyebrows) was as much disgusted by getting a girl's toy foisted on her. Disgust for girl's clothing was a subtext of Pollard's tale of lust, and the two issues met in her interaction with the same person. Many other dykes told me stories that indicated, if not a childhood intermesh of sexuality/gender issues, then a sequential progression from gender outlaw at the Barbie age to sexual outlaw sometime later.

To many women who later self-identified as dykes, it seems, Barbie did not provide a role model or suitable imaginary friend. A number just could not see any potential: they preferred boy's toys, often mentioning trucks. Some found a different doll in the Barbie line to identify or pal around with. Teresa Ortega, who spent lots of childhood time playing with Barbies, nonetheless shunned her as a role model: "I wanted to be Skipper; she had a teenager look, flat feet, and could do sports." Later, when she got into the Los Angeles punk scene at age fifteen, she retrieved Skipper from the discard pile, punking her out with tattoos and other unauthorized accessories. Ortega also related conducting a small survey of the four women in her office that suggested that predyke evidence might be found in the assessment of Barbie's potential suitors. The two dykes remember thinking G.I. Joe was too big to date Barbie, while the two straight women made him Barbie's dream date. What does this mean? Perhaps the woman who identified with Ken has the key. In her eyes, remember, Ken was not really a male but a cross-dressing female.

Sue also preferred Ken, although she kept asking for Barbie:

> Actually, I wanted a Ken more, but I was too scared to ask for it. Barbie was a girl, and girls were too girly. I kept asking for one because it seemed like the normal girl thing to have. All my friends [in Limerick, Maine] had one. And asking for Barbie was easy because you were supposed to ask for it; it didn't make you feel ashamed. I asked for Barbie over and over, but I only asked for each of the boy toys I wanted once, and I totally planned it out. I'd wait until a Matchbox car came on a TV commercial and then ask for it like it was a casual idea that had just occurred to me—something generated by the commercial—when really I'd wanted it for a long time. So I kept asking for Barbie, and once I got it I hated it. I never played with it. I think I threw it under the bed. My older sister loved it, though. She crocheted all these little dresses for it; she'd never gotten to have one.[19]

Sue's story underscores how misleading secondhand testimony can be. Did anyone who heard her repeated request for a Barbie know that it camouflaged a desire for Ken and Matchbox cars?

It also underscores how hard it is to draw any broad conclusions about how Barbie rejection relates to future sexual orientation or gender identity. A third dyke present during my conversation with Sue, "T.D.," had also rejected Barbie. When Sue commented, "Now I'm living my second boyhood," T.D. responded, "That's the whole thing about being a young butch dyke—living out your second boyhood." (Sue and T.D. were then, respectively, nineteen and twenty-four.) This comment suggested that Sue had hit on a typical feature of a butch dyke's childhood: rejecting femaleness. But, as the conversation progressed, it turned out that the two women had different ideas about why they had rejected female-coded toys. For T.D. it meant rejecting her own biological gender. After hearing Sue describe a mutual friend's story of burning off Barbie's breasts with matches and then giving her Ken's head, T.D. said, "That sounds like what I would have done with my Barbie if I had ever let anyone give me one. She burned off Barbie's secondary sex characteristics—actually she got rid of all of them, including her female head." Sue, however, had not wanted to be a boy and thought her toy preferences were about something else:

> It wasn't about gender as much as it was about going outside. I wanted to play outside and get dirty. Girl toys you used inside; boy toys were for outside. I resented being supposed to do the girl thing all the time. I wanted to do the boy stuff. I think the Barbie thing was also about

being treated as too young. I was the youngest of four girls, and my family kept treating me as younger than I was. Throwing out Barbie was related to this. Most girls got Barbie when they were really little, but I didn't get one until fourth grade. I think that, by then, I felt too old for Barbie. It was another example of how my family did not want to let me grow up.

Sue was protesting the gender coding assigned to activities, not the gender assigned to her, and Barbie was just as much about infantilization as about gender. *denying maturity in age*

The designation *adult butch dyke* turned out not to serve as a unifying *or experience* concept either. In subsequent one-on-one conversations, T.D. told me that she did not actually ascribe to Sue some easily fixed place on the "butch-fem scale." Sue, who identified herself as "more fem than butch but with some of both," thought that the woman who burned off Barbie's breasts would describe herself as bisexual. Among these women, there seemed to be no standard correlation between Barbie rejection and later sexual or gender identity. From this angle, Barbie loving Midge is, as Lorio commented, a "whole different subject" than turning Barbie into "the speed bump in the Driveway 500."[20]

So the connection between butchly approaching Barbie and becoming a butch and/or dyke later falls apart under the scrutinizing of a mere sample of three. But it cannot simply be dismissed. It is still the case that a large number of dykes tell Barbie stories about gender protest and that, regardless of whether the women who tell them believe that their Barbie stances predicted, caused, or were caused by a dyke identity they would claim in adulthood, they often tell them with a wink or a knowing glance that invokes such a connection, at least in fun. In other words, although the frequency of the dyke-who-did-Barbie-gender-protest story does not signal a truth about how a child becomes a dyke, two questions still remain: Why do so many dykes remember Barbie gender protest, and why do so many narrativize their tales of gender protest in a way that implies that their childhood Barbie activity makes sense given their adult sexual identities?

And where are the fem stories? My relatively dispassionate tone thus far—"some dykes said this," "it turned out that"—grossly misrepresents my interaction with this material, which has been punctuated by episodes of fem outrage, although not from the beginning. At first, I happily returned every knowing glance and in-joke verbal nudge as dyke after dyke told me about being into girl-jock Skipper or Tonka trucks. Perhaps I liked these stories also because they fed some dyke chauvinism—all these dykes who rejected given and oppressive models for appropriate female behavior. But I grew to hate my array of stories for their dearth of explicit fem content. I have stories by dykes who identify as fem, or at least as more fem than butch, but almost none that say "I enjoy(ed) being a girl." I hate the way my evidence perpetuates the invisibility of fem dykes as dykes, supporting the oppressive notion frequently articulated by both antidykes and pro-dykes that having a masculine side is some crucial element of real dyke identity. I kept finding myself mentally screaming at a variety of smug, self-satisfied culprits, dead and living, whom I imagined to be rerouting my evidence for heinous purposes. Among these culprits numbered those named by Joan Nestle in her eloquent defense of fems, "The Femme Question": sexologists from the late nineteenth century onward who defined the true, most lesbian lesbian as the one who feels like a man; those lesbian feminists who see the fem as "a lesbian acting like a straight woman who is not a feminist"; those butch women whom she remembers making "femme put-down jokes" that were going around the bars in the 1950s.[21] They go around still.

The screaming fem defender in my head pushes me to try to explain away fem invisibility in the Barbie dyke destiny tales as I interpret the stories I do have. Fem invisibility needs to be thrown into the mix of the needing-to-be-explained for another, less emotion-generated reason: it shows up certain explanations as insufficient. One might otherwise attribute the adult dyke verbal nudge to adult dyke habits of associating gender styles with sexual styles. Dressing butch or dressing fem is often seen as a possible indication of whom or what one wants in bed.[22] Gender drag may not necessarily tell a truth about sexual practice—thus the truism, "Butch in the streets, fem in the sheets." It at least, however, raises the subject of erotics. If dyke destiny stories were more mixed, one might simply conclude that adults were transferring gender-sexuality associations from adulthood to childhood. This may well be happening. But this doesn't explain why this transfer seems to be gender specific, depending not just on gender coding but on butch gender coding. Thus, fem invisibility needs either to be explained or to be explained away.

Here are several possibilities.

1. More fem Barbie stories are out there, but I did not find them. This must be true, but it doesn't explain why butch destiny stories predominate.

2. Some butch stories are fem stories in drag. Picking Skipper's suitable-for-sports feet over Barbie's pointy feet can be described as butch insofar as doing sports is typically labeled a boy thing. But it could also be described as

a fem thing: choosing from the array of available female models some things to accept and others to reject. Something similar could be said about Sue, who wanted to relabel boy-designated activities rather than shift her gender.

Why does the *butch* label come to mind first? Partly, I think, owing to the very habits of labeling that Sue protested against. If it's not a typical girl thing, the label *male* is readily available now and was certainly available in childhood. Getting dirty outside was for boys then; thus it seems, in dyke terms, butch now. But it also comes from prevalent habits of vision according to which butchness seems to represent a more complicated, troublesome, constructed, and critical stance toward gender than femness. As Nestle points out, there is a tendency to interpret a fem's use of and pleasure in certain styles and attributes traditionally labeled feminine as a sign that she has uncritically bought the whole package instead of as a sign that she has picked those particular elements and not others. I'm guilty of this myself. When my truck-preferring informants asked me about my childhood, I often disparaged it, replying, with obvious embarassment, "I had a very femmy childhood. You know, I took ballet, figure skated, hoola-hooped, hated gym class, etc." To me this story seemed lesser—less interesting, less complicated, less indicative of a critical stance. I took comfort in having hated ruffles and having let myself be "good at math"; these antifeminine choices did feel like choices about gender. But I usually didn't discuss them. The mere fact of having taken ballet made me feel like I could be no more than a pretender to the title of childhood gender critic. In contrast to me, butch storytellers did not seem to demean their own memories as boring, uncreative, and uncritical, except for one. Commenting on the *On Our Backs* photographs, she wrote, "I have to say, I never thought of Barbie as having those kinds of possibilities before. At the age of seven, as a baby butch, doll-hater and antifashion maven, I rejected Barbie without a second thought in favor of high tops and baseball bats. Now I begin to wish I'd been more creative."[23]

As Nestle argues, however, pro-feminine style is not by definition uncritical, a matter of buying the whole package. The fem also "constructs gender": "She puts together her own special ingredients for what it is to be a 'woman,' an identity with which she can live and love."[24] While Nestle's description underplays the cultural influences that affect or overdetermine choices and the less-than-conscious way that some of these choices get made (partly because I quote it a bit out of context), her point that fem identity is a construction and entails choices is crucial. Ballet yes, math anxiety no. Barbie's clothes yes, Barbie's feet no (or Skipper's feet yes).

3. Fem stories get told less often, and without the dyke destiny nudge, because dykes scan our childhoods with an eye toward the coming-out story.

Butch stories have more obvious potential to serve as episodes in coming-out stories because they concern being "different from the other girls." Tomboy-hood and dykehood can be seen to involve parallel mental activities: first you figure out that you don't want the toys girls are supposed to have; later you figure out that you don't want the object of desire girls are supposed to have. While the sequential occurrence of parallel identity constructions does not mean that the first caused or prefigured the second, the suspicion that this particular first causes or prefigures this particular second is certainly a part of popular lore. Asking for ballet classes probably won't make your parents fear that you will turn into a dyke; asking for boy's toys might well do so. This might also explain why butch Barbie stories circulate more than fem ones. As Sue's account suggests, the shame and censure that often attended crossing gender lines might make such events more memorable.[25]

Few people, I imagine, come to adulthood without having encountered the connection between gender-role rejection and adult queerness. Perhaps they saw it on television. To take just one example, an early episode of "The Facts of Life" from 1980 concerned the kindly prep-school dorm mother Mrs. Garrett reassuring a girl who did sports that she wasn't a lesbian, even though she did not yet want to date boys. (Apparently, this verbal reassurance wasn't considered enough to bring a happy, i.e., heterosexual, closure to the episode; by the end, the girl was in a party dress happily anticipating her first date with a boy.) Or they picked up on why their parents were so bugged by their activities. Or they got taunted or heard others being taunted as queers for gender-inappropriate behavior or mannerisms. My students certainly have this hypothesis in their conceptual framework. It comes up frequently as a stereotype to validate, rail against, or worry about: "My roommate said I must be a lesbian because I told her I didn't like dolls as a kid."

Given the prevalence of this connection, it is not surprising that, when dykes look through their pasts for coming-out episodes, butch incidents look like particularly likely candidates. Nor is it surprising, given the prevalent assumption that queer identity is the one to be explained, that, when dykes look through their past for whatever reason, they are looking simultaneously for sexual identity markers—and that people who identify as straight generally aren't. Consider, for instance, the Barbie narrative of my heterosexual sister the doctor:

> I had Barbie. Her joints moved in creaky motions, and once in a while a little piece of plastic or metal would stick out of her skin. She had what was considered to be a perfect figure, and her breasts were huge. . . .

Yes [in response to my query], I liked Barbie. Definitely. I think mostly I played with her limbs. Sounds like a doctor, no? I don't remember having many clothes for Barbie. I think I remember having her naked more than dressed. I think I had a Ken, too. I think Barbie and Ken were together a lot. No, nothing [in response to my question about whether she remembered anything about how she got Barbie]. I don't remember a box or anything; I think she was always just there. [Conversation in which we conclude that she must have inherited my doll.] You must have mutilated the limbs before it got to me; you must have played with it a lot.[26]

This story contains all the material needed for a <u>heterosexual destiny</u> narrative: Barbie was naked a lot; she hung out with Ken; and playing with a naked doll's limbs might well have sexual content (just as being a butch kid might not). But Cynthia didn't say, "I must have been heterosexual at an early age." Her destiny narrative was about her career choice. If people had been asking her, "When did you first come to suspect that you were heterosexual?" her spin would probably have been different.

Cynthia's story also suggests, in tandem with my own, both the compellingness and the constructedness of the destiny narrative. Had I presented our two narratives, minus her doctor spin, and said, "Guess who became the dyke cultural critic and who became the heterosexual doctor," few people, I suspect, would guess wrong. Even though my story does not really signal *dyke* or hers *doctor,* my troubled relation to mainstream culture and her untroubled relation to Barbie dating Ken foreshadow our future lives. The <u>match between our childhoods and our adulthoods is striking</u>. Yet a central contradiction between our stories—her memory of inheriting Barbie well used versus mine of rejecting the same doll—makes the directness of the passage from child into adult seem to be an adult construct. The question should not really or only be, "Who did *x* as a child and turned into *y* as an adult?" but, "Which adult remembers/narrates her childhood in each of the following ways?"

Although the constant presence of the coming-out narrative in dyke lives may account partly for the aura of destiny in many dyke tales, so too does the presence of so many other child-to-adult continuity narratives: therapy and the bildungsroman, to name a few. Lots of Barbie narratives read the present from the past. Consider one other example from my own head. While I don't remember playing with Barbie, I do remember playing the <u>Barbie Queen of the Prom</u> game. I remember preferring the magenta or chartreuse game pieces and that these were plastic silhouettes of ponytailed Barbie. I remember the rules and that one goal was to buy a dress with money you had won; the idea was to win a lot of money and get there first so that you could buy the most expensive dress. But I remember most vividly that even back then I preferred the simple "little black dress" to the frilly gown that was designated most desirable by its cost. Do I remember the black dress because an autobiographical thread runs through it? In this case, I know the answer. Yes. According to a photograph I saw of the game board, there was no black dress, little or otherwise; this vivid memory was <u>utter fabrication</u>.

There's a passage in Freud's (largely horrible) psychobiography of Leonardo da Vinci in which Freud compares adult memories of childhood to the history writing of ancient nations:

> As long as the nation was small and weak it gave no thought to the writing of its history; it tilled the soil of its land, defended its existence against its neighbors by seeking to wrest land from them and endeavored to become rich. It was a heroic but unhistoric time. Then came another age, a period of self-realization in which one felt rich and powerful, and it was then that one experienced the need to discover whence one originated and how one developed. The history-writing which began by noting successively the experiences of the present, threw also its backward glance to the past; it gathered traditions and legends, interpreted what survived from olden times in ethics and customs, and thus created a history of past ages. It was inevitable that this pre-history was more the expressions of opinions and wishes of the present than a copy of the past. For much had escaped from the memory of its people; other things became distorted; some trace of the past was misunderstood and interpreted in the sense of the present; and, besides, one did not write history from motives of objective curiosity, but rather because one desired to impress his contemporaries, to stimulate and extol them, or to hold the mirror before them. The conscious memory of a person about the experiences of his maturity can now be in every way compared to that of history-writing, and his infantile memories, their origins and reliability, actually correspond to the tendentially corrected history of the primal period of a people which was compiled later.[27]

My encounters with children like Hannah suggest that Freud was wrong to hypothesize a long preinterpretive period when children merely do things and do not interpret them. This seems as little true of children as of the ancient peoples to whom Freud compares them; the lack of textual artifacts from either front is poor evidence that histories were not being formed and told.

But the testimony provided by many former children suggests that Freud's understanding of the project of autobiographical history telling may be largely on target. Although not all adults tell Barbie stories with an eye toward explaining the present, many presume that one's present can be explained by identifying incidents in one's past from which the present appears to be a logical outgrowth. I rarely had to ask people if they thought their Barbie story prefigured their adult identity; they virtually always brought up this issue themselves, either by explicitly announcing or denying the connection, or by indicating less directly that they presumed this to be an issue, as with the dyke destiny verbal nudge. The huge number of such statements and nudges suggests that they came from just the impulse that Freud describes; the frequency with which they unravel under scrutiny suggests that they were made of the same mixture of history and myth that he describes as well.

If the coming-out narrative in particular and habits of narrating the past into the present in general account in part for the dyke destiny verbal nudge, some credit for its prevalence must also belong to Barbie. As has often been noted, Barbie's body signals sexuality to adults. It is a commonplace that Barbie might induce precocious sexual thinking, and adult narratives indicate that Barbie often signaled sexuality to children. From this angle, the dyke destiny verbal nudge can be viewed as an acknowledgment, hypothesis, and/or trace memory that, no matter what is remembered about Barbie, some sexual assessment was or might have been going on, too. That is, if the coming-out narrative overlays my questions with, "Was I a dyke at age seven?" Barbie's body overlays it with, "Was I sexual at age seven?" This lurking question about sexuality is another one that seemed to be present in the minds of many people I talked to. When I asked one of my aerobics instructors whether her daughter had ever "done anything weird" with Barbie, the defensive and panicked haste with which she responded, "Oh, no, she's a very good girl," made me realize that she interpreted my albeit untactful query as necessarily a query about whether her daughter had done anything sexually weird. Dykes don't need Barbie to associate gender with sexuality, but Barbie's sexpot rep certainly helps the cause.

Some credit, too, must belong to Mattel. Barbie would not be so well suited for gender-outlaw rejection if Mattel had not successfully sold her as a model of ideal womanhood and as a proper toy for girls. For some consumers, Mattel's success in this area led to its failure to achieve its other promotional goal of making Barbie a catalyst to fantasize about their own futures: girls who did not like the model threw her out instead. Others, however, found Barbie more adaptable. For Lorio and Pollard, Barbie could be turned into such a fantasy catalyst, although in each case some changes had to be made: Barbie had to be rolled in the dirt or dressed like the hot baby-sitter next door. Thus transformed, she fulfilled *her* dyke destiny.

Matching Outfits

In the previous two sections, I focused primarily on mix and match in the consumer's mental wardrobe, surveyed during childhood and over time. Did the child and the adult have matching mental outfits: did the mental style of the past predict the mental style of the present? Did Barbie appear to instigate a temporary or a permanent mental wardrobe change? Did she cause the consumer to appear in mental garb that ordinarily remained "in the closet" or reveal the closet to have items that the consumer or her witnesses had not known to be there?

This section concerns the relay between the consumer's wardrobe, both mental and artifactual, and that of Barbie: people who outfitted Barbie's body or mind to match their own (present or future), or that of others in their lives, and those who, conversely, wanted to refashion themselves after Barbie. Many stories discussed above show that, as Mattel promotions argue, Barbie could indeed sometimes be outfitted to suit the style of consumers, although neither Mattel nor Barbie gets all the credit. Consumers did a lot of the work required to relate artifact to reality, sometimes abetted by people like Pollard's neighbors' mother, who dressed Barbie like her hot daughter. This section recounts some other successes and failures.

Mattel's early dilemma about whether to give Barbie a personality is described in terms of two basic imaginative models: children view Barbie as either a blank slate or a distinct character. Consumer narratives suggest, however, that these were hardly the only two models. In some cases, Barbie became a specific adult character in the child's life. One more reason that Sue lost her desire for a Barbie was that she hated the Barbie games her friend Karen had forced her to play: "My friend Karen used to make us play with Barbies. [Karen] was physically abused and would put us in these weird situations. She would be the poor dejected child, and I had to play an abusive mom. I didn't have to hit her, but I had to be mean and exile her to the basement and stuff." Another woman made her sexual abuse the subject of Barbie scenarios, although the characters did not have a one-to-one correspondence with people in her life: "My Barbies were always having sex. Sex with Ken, sex with each other, sex all the time. I know why I did this: I was sexually abused as a child."

Barbie seems often to have been a composite of known characters in a child's life, both living and fictional, extrapolated into a general sense of what adults do. Joleen, whose brothers poked needles into her fake Barbie's breasts, remembers observing her daughter Melanie playing Barbie with (only) one special friend, Alicia. Ordinarily, the scenarios revolved around disasters—shipwrecks, car crashes—with Barbie perpetually crying out, "Help me, Ken." But one day Joleen witnessed Ken and Barbie having a fight in a kind of marriage-counseling discourse: "Maybe we should try such-and-such." Suddenly Melanie spat out, "Oh, just leave him!" At this point, Joleen speculates, Disaster Barbie turned into Mom, reflecting the "laissez-faire attitude toward bad relationships" of Joleen herself, divorced and unmarried at the time. "Help me, Ken" did not come from Mom; "Oh, just leave him!" did.

Lise, who considered homemade Barbie clothes worthless, also remembers mother/antimother components. On the one hand, Lise remembers a succession of Barbie-line dolls coming into her family whose personae were alien to her own household adults. There were the dolls of her older sister's time, including Midge, whom she remembered as Barbie's "beer-drinking and bowling" friend—that is, stereotypically white, working class and different from her own class status, although her family, living on the modest salaries of her minister father and librarian mother, was middle class more in outlook than income. Later, "by the time I came around, they [Mattel] had ditched the downbeat, small-town friend for the Twiggy look. It was Francie, her mod friend, representing the 'British Invasion' with chain belts, mini-skirts, day-glo tights. She wore clothes like my sister did against my parents' wishes. I remember my father trying to get my sister to wear some gross, cheap, [unmod] thing and saying, 'It's mod,' to try to convince her."

On the other hand, when Barbie got down to sex, Lise's family reappeared, mixed with June Cleaver:

> I remember vividly being ten years old and not quite knowing how men and women did it. So Alan and Barbie would go on a date, and then they'd go back to her apartment. And Alan would hypnotize her ["by waving his stiff little arm back and forth in front of her eyes"] and take her clothes off to the waist. But then I couldn't figure out what would happen next. So I'd have Alan have Barbie serve him drinks on a tray. Sex got played out through those middle-class bourgeois private-sphere roles I saw around me. It was a mix of "Leave It to Beaver" and other things . . . we had trays at home. Barbie was acting really cheerful and serving people things.

(This is another destiny story. Twenty years after doing sex through June Cleaver, Lise was writing on fictional representations of a gendered private sphere under different historical manifestations of capitalism. Did she carry a childhood inquiry into adulthood, merely trading in Barbie for George Eliot, or does the present inquiry determine the content of the memory or what is available to it? Probably both.)

Bee Bell also remembers having Barbie perform a forbidden act that she had insufficient knowledge to script. In this case it was a speech act. Bell is another white dyke with a tale of gender-role rejection and hating Barbie, who "knew at age three that these female dolls were a plot to oppress women":

> I'm pretty sure I hated Barbie. I think I got it partly from my mom, who hated Barbie, and also from my aversion to everybody female. I col-lected superheroes: Hulk, Kirk, Spock, Shazaam, Batman. I had about twelve. I had to save up for them; they cost more than three dollars. I didn't have any woman superheroes. Even some boys had those, but I disdained Wonderwoman. I did, though, when I was about six, play Barbie once with my friend Tanya. She was German; her family was Lutheran. My mother set me up on a date with her—the kind of date mothers set up for their geeky bookworm children—"Tanya's a nice girl; wouldn't you like to play with her?" Anyway, we took off her clothes and had her say, "Goodbye fuckers, I'm going to hell." We had this idea that if you swore you went to hell; actually, neither of us was sure about what hell was and how you got sent there. I think it was really that Tanya and I wanted to swear but we didn't want to go to hell, so Barbie swore instead. Oh, I think that even though she was naked she still had her shoes on—Barbie, that is, not Tanya.[28]

The disparity that Bell saw between Barbie's options and her own figures in many other tales, like Bill's. As Lise's Barbie was and was not her mother, his was and was not his cousin Treesi, who owned the Barbie he played with. "Treesi, like Barbie, was very heterosexually precocious then, as she is to this day. Playing with Barbie might have been a safe way to have a relation-ship with her." But he was more fascinated by something beyond his world— her clothes: "It might have been as much about clothes. . . . Her clothes were much more exciting than the ones I saw in real life. I liked her clothes. I didn't like to see her naked. I undressed her and dressed her, but not to see her naked. I took off the top layer and put other things on."

Eve also got turned on to Barbie because of her special clothes. I was passing on an apology from her mother's ex-lover, who had co-parented Eve several decades earlier, about having made Eve wear hated yellow rubber rain boots to school. Eve, who didn't know of my work, told me that she'd really wanted boots like Barbie had: "Those clear plastic boots with one of those clear, mushroom-shaped umbrellas with the thin colored border." She then added, after I told her that I was writing about Barbie, that she hadn't paid much attention to Barbie—whom, twenty-four years later, she considered a terrible role model—until age six, when Barbie became her fashion ideal, an ideal that she couldn't imitate because her hippie rural Maine mothers (with little disposable cash) made her go to school in tie-dye.[29]

Georgia, whose Barbie wore mom clothes, suspects that she, too, involved Barbie in her own consumer drama. Three years after getting Barbie in 1961, she chopped off Barbie's hair in a fury, right around the time a bit of snooping revealed that she was indeed getting the go-go boots she'd requested for Christmas, but the wrong ones. The ones she wanted zipped up the front; she was getting a cheap pretender that zipped up the back. This discovery, she thinks, may have turned her against Barbie. At least the two incidents were spatially as well as thematically related: the hair-cutting incident occurred in or near the little room where the gifts were stored, and either the hair or the doll got thrown into it. She added, however, that, while shearing Barbie seemed a logical displacement, she would never have cut the hair of her Tressie doll, the doll whose hair "grew" when you pushed a button in her back: "Barbie competed with Tressie [for my affection]. Hair was a big issue for me. I was embarrassed about having curly Italian hair that was too thin. Tressie made a big impression on me" (fig. 14).

Georgia's identification of her (brown-haired) Tressie, not Barbie, as the doll with "nonethnic" hair surprised me. To me, blond Barbie seems like a paragon of nonethnicity. But Phyllis, another white, ethnically marked woman, told a similar story of having had fantasies of ethnic erasure that Barbie did not serve. Phyllis had Barbie, loved her, and used her as a character in many fantasy scenarios. While she doesn't remember these, she does remember one fantasy game she concocted often, but never for Barbie, although it would seem to suit Barbie well: she used to pretend to be living in a "nonethnic" family on the West Coast, like the television families she saw in the early 1960s, instead of being what she was, a Jewish girl growing up in New York City. While Phyllis had no theories about this, I wonder whether Barbie's failure to fit the part of Ms. Nonethnicity had something to do with Barbie's wardrobe, which consisted primarily of clothes handmade by Phyllis's aunt to match the aunt's clothes. Unlike anyone else I talked to,

14. Georgia's Barbie with hair chopped off in 1963 and her nonethnic Tressie, with hair intact. Photo: Jay York.

Phyllis loved her handmade Barbie clothes and did view them as a token of familial love, like the birthday cake she got one year that was in the shape of a dress with a Barbie doll standing up inside (fig. 15). Perhaps these clothing artifacts and family participation turned Barbie into a member of the family.

Georgia and Phyllis played with Barbie even though she couldn't function as a nonethnic other. Rebecca, who describes herself as half Native American and half white, was put off by the opposite problem. Rebecca played with Barbie through age fifteen in 1986, thus well into the diversity years. But, like Hannah, she thought that Barbie came only in blond, with a bit of diversity residing elsewhere in the Barbie line—a perception, which I heard elsewhere, that supports my suggestion that Mattel undercuts its diversity rap by circulating so many products in the white, blond version only. As Rebecca told Kelly McCullough, "What pissed me off is that Barbies usually look the same, but sometimes Ken has brown hair or blonde hair. . . . Barbie never had any black friends; there's no black Ken, and that's wrong."

For Rebecca, Barbie's apparent monoethnicity created some play problems. "I grew up in the city [in New Jersey], and I used to say, 'Come over

15. Good enough to
eat. Phyllis holding
her birthday cake built
around Barbie in
August, 1962.

and play Barbie,' and some of my friends [many black and Latino] would say,
'I don't want to be that blonde Barbie,' but I didn't want to be blond Barbie
either." Nonetheless, she liked Barbie better than her Cher doll, even though
Cher was Native American like herself, and even though Barbie's dubious
ethnicity was only one problem. Rebecca hated the excess of pink clothes,
Barbie's name, the illogics and offenses of repetition: "I didn't know how one
could be Barbie and then the other one could be Barbie." "It always bothered
me . . . that Barbie was a scientist and yet she also worked in McDonald's?"
"You don't have any butch Barbie. I used to cut off all my Barbies' hair to make
them bald because they looked pretty much the same." Note that this solution
doesn't solve the problem of multiples but instead repeats it: each longhaired
Barbie got replaced by a hairless one. The same thing often happened when
Rebecca solved the problem of one being Barbie and the other being Barbie;
during the period when she watched "Days of Our Lives," "Barbie's name
had to be Kayla."

Here, it seems, is an example, to recall Iain Chambers's phrasing, of the
given determining the possible: Rebecca's solutions remained rooted in the
conceptual framework suggested by the product line. Mattel's given, Rebecca
implied, was also responsible for why she "always used to make [her] Barbies sluts": "I always made them wear short skirts and a tight shirt. They
were all legs. You don't have hippie Barbie or Barbie with Birkenstocks. All
she had was those pink hotpants." Barbie's "slut" features, like her ethnicity,

also led to some unpleasant interactions, including one incident involving nonconsensual sex representation, which occurred sometime before she was nine years old: "Someone came over—a guy—and he made Barbie and Ken do things that I was so embarrassed about, like taking off Barbie's clothes. Bad things like that. I used to say, 'You can't do that with Barbie,' and he did. I was offended." Mattel's given didn't, however, cause all her problems; the filled-Baggies waterbed her brother destroyed ("a trauma") she'd built herself.

Nor did it circumscribe her "possible" as much as the long list of hated features and bad scenes might suggest. To the contrary, Rebecca "loved" Barbie, her "best friend" during childhood and the genesis of her own identity as a writer: "I write, and that was like the beginning of my book writing because I'd have to premeditate what would happen, and it would have a beginning, a middle, and an end. My ends were very 'endful.' [Barbie usually killed herself or got killed.] I remember playing with Barbie every day, and it was never the same story." Despite Barbie's ethnic ill suitedness to the task, Rebecca did manage to narrate Barbie into her world: "I sort of fit her into my lifestyle." Rebecca never made Barbie a writer like herself— "I guess because I didn't have the Barbie word processor." But she gave her a bunch of matching narrative accessories. One was a "dysfunctional family," although without one-to-one correspondences between Barbie's cast and hers: "I come from such a dysfunctional family. It used to be that Barbie would get kicked out of her house, and she would live with Ken, and he would try to rape her, but she would say no. It was sick. She would have to wear his clothes because she didn't have clothes. She used to wear his shirt and a belt and that would be her Barbie outfit."[30]

More frequently, however, Barbie took on less troublesome aspects of Rebecca's life and family, sometimes enhanced through Barbie play, as when poverty became the more glamourized poverty of the "starving artist": "I liked Barbie to be poor, I guess because I was. Barbie was often a single mother because my mom was a single mother. I liked Barbie to be a starving artist. Sometimes I made Barbie young, like seventeen; other times she was thirty-five, and Skipper was her daughter. Barbie always had to have a pet because that was important in my life. I really transferred a lot of my ideals onto Barbie." Rebecca added that her desire to make Barbie a "single mom," which she reiterated frequently, was partly why she usually played with Barbie alone. Her friends and stepsister wanted Barbie to meet Ken and get married. Rebecca made Skipper Ken's date and Barbie "a loner" like herself, on this topic, too, giving Barbie a matching outfit.

Lisa Jones did not find Barbie so adaptable. Jones, who posits that a doll story is something every black journalist gets around to recording, remembers that, before black Barbie or Barbie's black friends, she wanted Barbie enough to buy two blond ones from girls at school with her Christmas money. She cut off their hair, dressed them in African-print fabric, and set them up to live with a black G.I. Joe she had bartered from neighbor boys. Then a racist incident made her sever her Barbie ties: "After an 'incident' at school (where all of the girls looked like Barbie and none of them looked like me), I galloped down the stairs with one Barbie, her blond head hitting each spoke of the banister, thud, thud, thud. And galloped up the stairs, thud, thud, thud, until her head popped off, lost to the graveyard behind the stairwell. Then I tore off each limb and sat on the stairs for a long time, twirling the torso like a baton."[31] African-print fabric was not enough to give Barbie a matching outfit; the skin she was in, and the skin Jones was in, consigned Barbie to the part of racist white girl.

Jones's story, I suspect, is the kind that many readers suspicious of Barbie expect to find here. Many, too, I imagine, will find it a source of political pleasure. It confirms the ill effects on individuals of social evils such as racism and of cultural products that reinforce these social evils for corporate profit. Yet, simultaneously, and equally satisfying, it presents the consumer as a heroic figure with agency and a capacity to resist the forces of oppression. On the surface, it's also intellectually reassuring. It suggests the value of a theoretical model that distributes the construction of meaning relatively straightforwardly among the producer, the consumer, and the social context: Mattel makes a white, blond doll; Jones recodes and then rejects it; white privilege affects both Mattel's production and Jones's consumption. Both the given and the possible seem identifiable, as does what constitutes resistance: giving Barbie African-print clothing and then killing her. Moreover, because the Barbie feature that troubled Jones really stands out in the product, her story also gives a boost to the explanatory power of content analysis. Since no artifact's consumers are fully accessible—given barriers of money, language, memory, and, with regard to objects from the past, mortality—it is quite reassuring to run across consumer testimony that confirms what content analysis would lead one to expect to find.

But Jones's story looks so easy access only if certain features are ignored. Who, for instance, were the African-print-clad Barbies meant to represent? White people less arrogantly centered on Euro-U.S. culture? African American adults (or women, teens, girls) in general? Particular people in Jones's family or social sphere? Jones as she imagined herself in the future? And, in the context of other consumer narratives, none of her reaction goes without saying, and both the given and the possible are much more difficult to identify. Georgia and Phyllis apparently didn't see a nonethnic given, although not, it seems, because of Barbie's skin color. Rebecca saw a similar given (Barbie was unfortunately white and blond) but a different possible: Barbie could still be a beloved catalyst for her fantasy. One can conclude from this array that white girls were much less likely to pay significant attention to Barbie's skin color; indeed, virtually no white women I talked to remembered noticing that Barbie was white. Still, the particulars of response remain somewhat unpredictable.

Yet there is certainly more to say about Barbie than that her meaning is wholly in the eye of the infinitely variable and mysterious beholder. While consumer interpretation of the given varies, the fact remains this particular given moved many, many consumers to undertake the construction of matching outfits, often with processes and products shared by others on a similar mission. So the question remains, what is it about Barbie that has generated so much memorable consumer activity and that has determined the content of consumer response?

Mattel spokespeople, of course, have always argued that there's something special "in" Barbie that makes her a prime candidate for child fantasy. In the early years, when Barbie's "more adult-like figure" distinguished her more in the market, much was attributed to it; later, her careers and "skins" received emphasis, as did, again, her biographical vagueness. Emphasized throughout was Barbie's beauty. As Nancy Zweirs, director of marketing at Mattel for the Barbie line, reiterated on an episode of "Phil Donahue" aired on 10 February 1993 devoted to adult Barbie collectors, "Little girls love Barbie because she's so beautiful. She allows them to dream about what it's like to be grown up."

Two messages underlie the corporate explanations. First, Barbie functions as an ideal fantasy catalyst because she is a desired and beloved commodity; that is, there is a connection between loving Barbie and fantasizing through her. As consumer testimony indicates, this is not always true. Many people who fantasized through Barbie seem to have had no particular fondness for the doll itself; some, like Bell, even hated her. (That Mattel's PR doesn't reflect this is hardly surprising; you don't have to be a marketing expert to figure out that "Barbie, the doll you can pretend with even if you hate her" does not make for a great commercial.) Second, something particular about Barbie—her body, her clothes, her beauty, her (lack of) story—make her a better fantasy catalyst than other dolls.

This second message, despite how much it sounds like corporate drivel when Mattel spokespeople utter it, also has a lot of credibility with Barbie watchers, pro and con. People often imply or state explicitly that Barbie is indeed the supreme fantasy catalyst and is so because of something in the product, the most popular. explanation being an unsanitized version of what Mattel says: Barbie stands apart as an adult doll whose large breasts turn children's minds toward sexuality. Many also assume that Barbie destruction and violence depend on something particular about Barbie as well, that people are, at least in part, reacting to something about this doll as opposed to other dolls.

From the evidence of consumer testimony, common wisdom on this topic is accurate to an extent. Official Barbie products affected actions and ideas partly through content that can be located "in" the objects. Barbie, looking (sort of) like an adult, often played an adult. Barbie's sexiness must be partly why she was the doll who figured in so many memorable doll-related sexual scenarios, of which I have recorded only a few here—at least three different women of ages ranging from twenty-five to forty told me that they made Barbie a prostitute. Ken's particular appearance sometimes mattered, too. Jessica, a white, heterosexual, middle-class woman, age twenty-nine in 1993, clearly saw Ken as the lumpless, unsexy guy Mattel intended him to be, although this didn't have the intended effect of failing to raise sexual thoughts. For Jessica, Ken's very existence meant that sex had to happen. His insufficiency signaled bad sex, not no sex: "With having a Ken doll and Barbie's anatomy there was a certain amount of sexual play required between the two of them. They had sex, but nothing seemed to work: Barbie's legs didn't open, Ken didn't have a penis. Of course, I was young to be figuring these things out, but at the same time there was something cold and distant about their sexual relationship. I worked out sexual dynamics with them because they were adult dolls."

Barbie's clothes and accessories also sometimes shaped play activities: Barbie had fashion shows, lived in her Dream House, etc. Consumers often described Barbie games as being caused by particular products: "I had the car, so she liked to drive in the car." "I had the swimming pool, and barbeque, and outdoor camping kit. Basically we played with these products. Barbie was living a life of luxury. . . . You get shoes and clothes with Barbie, so she would use those."[32] The last comment came from a heterosexual woman from Pakistan, age nineteen in 1993, who didn't, however, use everything she had—"I never liked to play with [Ken]; I'd always give him to a friend of mine." She also suggested that Barbie products functioned less to determine play activities than to confer social status: "Most of my friends had [Barbies] because their fathers would travel to the U.S. It was also novel to have a Barbie. It was like, 'Oh, she has a Barbie,' and the more you had. . . . They'd say, 'Oh, she has this many Barbies,' and it was better to go to her house and play with them. . . . I preferred to be playing outside, climbing a tree. I just said, 'I have a Barbie.' I collected these things, but I never really played with them. My friends and I would play outside, climb walls, but I had a Barbie." While few people indicated so explicitly that a big point of Barbie items was just to own them, the large number of people who happily remember owning items that they don't remember using supports a conclusion that this was often the big attraction.

As the comments above indicate, Mattel's particular offerings at any given time had a lot to do with consumer interpretation. So, too, it seems, did Mattel's presentation of what constituted a desirable array of Barbie goods. In the early years, Mattel wanted consumers to supplement their purchase of their first Barbie, not with more Barbies, but with outfits, accessories, and dolls in the category of friends and family. Mattel didn't promote "the new Twist 'N Turn Barbie" as a great second Barbie but as a desirable replacement; in fact, Mattel offered a trade-in whereby, in exchange for your old Barbie plus $1.50, you could get the new one.[33] Correspondingly, early consumers who thought about whether they had enough Barbie stuff generally seem to have judged this in terms of how many clothes and accessories they had: Georgia remembers wanting, not more Barbies, but more Mattel-made clothes; Phyllis, who had enough, had only one doll among her artifacts.

Consumers who encountered Barbie later, when Mattel was pushing each consumer to buy multiple Barbies, viewed the issue of having lots in terms of how many dolls named Barbie they had. It is especially consumers from later years, too, who encountered the conceptual problem of multiples: "I didn't know how one could be Barbie and then the other could be Barbie." This is interesting because children always, of course, saw more than one Barbie— rows on store shelves, dolls at a friend's house—and surely confronted other characters in multiple. As Michèle Barale remarked, Barbie is in this sense like Santa Claus, whom a child might encounter in multiple incarnation on shopping excursions in December: "There IS a Santa; there isn't A Santa." But, with Barbie, multiples seem to have become significantly problematic only after Mattel began to give the dolls, instead of the outfits, the marks of variation: by career, by color, and sometimes only by name and costume. And multiples became a problem in a way that underscores how much perceptions are shaped by both the objects perceived and ideas about race and class. Mattel's contradictory approach to Barbie diversity—Barbie comes in many colors, but only sometimes—seems to have led some consumers to a "solution" for what would seem to be one of the biggest illogics: Barbie being now white, now black, etc. Instead of seeing this as a problem, many simply didn't see that "other" Barbies existed (or existed as Barbie). Mattel, and life in a white-supremacist culture, erased the problem of racial multiples or transformed it into its opposite: Barbie is only white and blond. Harder to resolve was the problem, and sometimes the class contradictions, caused by Barbie's different careers. How could the same (white) person be a scientist and work in McDonald's? (Here is another way to look at Rebecca's repetition of multiples in renaming all her dolls Kayla: perhaps the problem was not so much that there were many dolls representing the same character, but that one character had an illogical class profile.)

But, while the actual products and advertising/explanations produced by Mattel clearly had an effect on what consumers wanted, saw, and did, Barbie consumption still looks quite different than the Barbie play on commercials. This is partly because Barbie play and interpretation often depended on a much more complicated relation between wanting and having than the one commercials showed. Commercials represent consumers who have what they want or whose only obstacle to acquisition is an understocked store—as in the Twist 'N Turn trade-in ads, which showed girls hurrying to the store to get Barbie "while supplies last at the low introductory price."[34] In real life, other obstacles, such as lack of money or parents' refusal, stood between desire and the acquisition of Barbie items, among other desired commodities, and the gap between wanting and getting affected Barbie attitudes and actions. Georgia's interaction with Barbie had everything to do with shame and anger about family finances. Eve's drama, too, was significantly about what was possible to acquire given her family's financial situation and also to her parents' refusal to let her deviate from the family style dictated from the top down.

Their stories suggest that the intensely felt gap between wanting and getting occurred especially in children from low-income families. The tale of Phyllis, whose family was well off, suggests by counterexample something similar. She did not perceive her lack of Mattel-made clothes as a source of shame; she had no reason to doubt that her handmade clothes were, as she was told, a sign of special love rather than an insufficient substitute like cheap go-go boots. But shame over inadequate Barbie supplies was not limited to poor children. Susan had a doll supply—and imagination—that betokened her white, upper-middle-class status: "My parents went on all these trips, and I had these little different black dolls from the Caribbean, so she [Barbie] adopted all these kids." However, her parents "weren't into" buying her much

Barbie stuff. She had one Barbie, some cheap, less desirable, imitations, no accessories, no Barbie property (she wanted the house with the little elevator), and, consequently, a humiliation like Georgia's, although Susan was poor in little besides Barbie goods: "I don't really remember taking Barbie anywhere; I just sort of played at home. It was kind of a jealousy thing—I remember not feeling good enough because I didn't have the stuff."[35]

Barbie play also differed from Mattel commercials and explanations because, as I suggested earlier, Mattel's blank-slate and discrete-personality models for how children construct Barbie identities are actually two among many and far from mutually exclusive. Barbie might be a cool teenager with a personality envisioned to derive from the doll and clothes, a representation of an imagined adult, and a composite of people in the child's life alternately or all at the same time: Barbie is and is not my mother, sometimes. One might want to be Barbie and yet put Barbie through experiences one did not want to have or had already had and did not want to repeat: I want to be Barbie, and I don't want to be Barbie, sometimes.

One more example will encapsulate the sources and habits of Barbie interpretation suggested thus far. Karina, who described herself as Hispanic, raised in a lower- or welfare-class family in Omaha, Nebraska, was seventeen years old when McCullough interviewed her in September 1993. Various features of her Barbie story will now be familiar. The tenure and content of her life with Barbie depended partly on her relation with her mother and her mother's understanding of gender-appropriate behavior. When Karina was eight, her mother got her "everything to do with Barbie"—including "the Ken," the horses, the McDonald's, the Dream House, "all the Barbie accessories"—because, while she knew Karina had outgrown baby dolls, she didn't want her to play with "male toys." Karina consequently played with Barbie up until junior high, which she considers longer than usual, because she didn't want her mother to feel bad that she was "dropping Barbie." Besides playing with Mattel-made products, she and her friends, who were "into" aliens, also added Alien Barbie to Mattel's line. Taking "the Barbies that cost ninety-nine" cents, they turned them into aliens by cutting out Barbie's limbs and sides and replacing them with swatches of fabric.

Karina identified with Skipper, a younger sister like herself, but wanted to look like Barbie: "I didn't want to be blond, but I did want to have a huge chest." She also wanted Barbie's feet:

> Barbie liked to buy shoes a lot. Barbie loved shoes because I was always entranced by Barbie's feet, because they were shaped so strangely. They weren't shaped like real feet. So I would always make my feet

look like that. I would walk around on my toes, I would make that big arch, because I thought that women's feet were that way naturally. It came as a big surprise to me—because my mom wore heels a lot—it surprised me that when my mom took off her shoes her feet didn't look like Barbie's. I thought that feet really looked that way when you were older, when you were a woman, and when you started to wear heels.

This is the inverse of a frequent misperception about Barbie's hair. A number of people remember cutting it off with the idea that it would grow back; Karina, in reverse, transferred a perceived biological attribute from Barbie to humans. Both cases suggest Barbie's ease in passing from representation to reality and back.

From all this imaginative and artifactual material—some purchased, some homemade—came Barbie scenarios:

> One [of my favorites] would be that the alien Barbies come to the Dream House because they need to eat some food. So Barbie brings them to the Barbie McDonald's, which I happened to have. They all eat food. They go back to the Barbie Dream House, and Ken comes home. Ken is very angry that Barbie is playing with alien Barbies because he feels that they are the downfall of the entire country. He says, "We've got to get these alien Barbies out of here." Then he starts hitting Barbie. [Karina recounted elsewhere that she and her friends always "had Barbie have a really dysfunctional relationship with Ken. There was a lot of battering and beating going on in the Barbie Dream House," with Ken usually the aggressor, although Barbie was occasionally one, too.] But the alien Barbies come to the rescue, and they go "Boop, boop, boop, boop, boop," and Ken falls out the third-story window. Then they'd still hang out in the Dream House. All of the other stories followed the same line. Barbie wasn't always the aggressor, but someone would come to Barbie's aid to overthrow Ken. Skipper was never really involved in this whole relationship between Barbie and Ken. Another story would be that Barbie and Ken would go out riding horses. I liked to have them riding horses because they would be really nice to each other. Skipper would . . . ride horses, too. Horses were fun.

Karina's narrative is typical in its idiosyncracy—no one else will tell exactly this one—and in other crucial ways. Her Barbie play depended in part on the particular material objects in her possession, including the Barbie McDonald's, the alien Barbies, and the Dream House, although what goes on in the

Dream House is hardly Mattel authorized. It also depended on others in her life (her mother, her friends) and on other cultural products and narratives (science fiction, McDonald's). And there seems to be a relation between, on the one hand, having, interpreting, and using Barbie artifacts and, on the other, childhood perception of family financial and social status. The relation is not simple since Karina was poor generally but rich in Barbie items. Still, there seem to be other marks of "have-not" status: the feeling of obligation to keep the toys her mother had payed for; the mutilation of the cheap Barbies only; perhaps the idea that different social relations obtain when Barbie and Ken are riding horses. Might there also be registered a recognition of ethnic marginalization in Ken's view that the aliens are the "downfall of the entire country," which, while appropriate dialogue for a science-fiction movie, sounds also like racist, anti-immigration rhetoric? It's likely the resonance here comes partly from the antiforeigner sentiment that had already been built into the genre of science fiction before Karina and her friends encountered it. Yet I can't help wondering whether, as a Hispanic child, she heard this "downfall of the entire country" line uttered by nonfictional characters about people like her. After all, as Bee Bell noted, what could be a better representation of the dual dominant discourses of xenophobia and (often shallow) multiculturalism than the dilemma, "Here are a bunch of aliens. Should we revile them or take them out to dinner?"[36]

What does gender, besides ethnicity and class, have to do with it? Surely something—but, again, nothing simple. What does it mean that women get together across species to overthrow Ken, which sounds like a feminist fantasy of female solidarity? Karina gives one possible explanation: "I did like Ken sometimes, but most of the time I didn't. It wasn't anything against Ken. It was just that he was the only male doll that I had. He was the one to take everything out on. Maybe it has do with me growing up in a divorced home; I lived with my mom since I was three." Is Ken representing an absent father, or everyone of his gender, or other men whom she encountered, real or fictional? Did he represent someone different when Ken and Barbie rode horses? Karina sometimes made direct correlations between people in her life and the Barbie world: "Unhappy things or times that I had in childhood I would project onto Barbie. When I got a spanking, someone would get a spanking at the Barbie household. It was usually Skipper." But clearly there was no consistent one-to-one correspondence since the dolls' characterizations changed from story to story and since many of her Barbie stories were collectively authored with friends, who must have contributed their own material, directly or indirectly—filtered through their own interpretations, suppressions, and silences, assuming that no one either knows all or tells all about family matters.

Karina's narrative is typical in that childhood experience of ethnicity, class, and gender must have affected her Barbie play and, typical, too, in that the precise effect is inaccessible. It cannot quite be extrapolated from her narratives. Even though the story about alien Barbies overthrowing the abusive, ethnic-chauvinist Ken invites simple correlation to the life of the teller, other features of Karina's Barbie memories indicate that, in both content and texture, such an explanation would belie the complexity of her own interpretive acts. It cannot be extrapolated from her Barbie objects since her narratives register only some features of them; Ken apparently mattered as male, but not as a bland blond hunk, etc. It cannot be extrapolated from the evidence of other consumers, which confirms that gender, ethnicity, and economic status matter here but gives no formula to determine how. It cannot be fully extrapolated from a longer or subsequent interview. Whether I ask twenty questions or two thousand, what I get is retrospective interpretation shaped according to the vagaries of memory and the use of dominant ideologies, narratives, and narrative styles. Although, interestingly, Karina did not tell her sister-from-another-planet story in the popular sister-from-another-planet narrative style, there is no doubt that her view and presentation style are equally informed and transformed by time and culture.

Typical, too, is that, even in its partially accessible form, the narrative cannot be mapped onto a conformity/resistance opposition or fixed at a particular place on a conformity-to-resistance continuum, whether the issue is conformity/resistance to social circumstances or conformity/resistance to Mattel. Barbie has a desirable, happy, nondysfunctional life when she and Ken go riding on official Mattel horses and when Barbie rides in her car: "I had a Barbie car, so Barbie liked to drive all over the place. . . . We'd have her meet other people. She liked to meet other people. Barbie was very outgoing." Here are Mattel products with the Mattel message about the beautiful life one can fantasize about entering. Conformity to Mattel? Yes, perhaps, but stay tuned for tomorrow's episode when Barbie and her alien friends throw xenophobic Ken out a third-story window. Is that conformity to Mattel? No, but it conforms to the dominant cultural narrative of the six o'clock news, which makes violence appear natural to "aliens" and exceptional among the horsey set, although the Dream House, with its memorable elevator, is hardly the expected "alien" habitation. Is it conformity to dominant social values? No, since women triumph in coalition activism over alienophobes. Yet Barbie "always forgave Ken when he had his little incidents. She knew more than him, so she was able to forgive him."

A conformity/resistance model is not undone by the existence of narratives in which some elements can be labeled conforming and others resisting. Assuming that, contrary to the belief of the woman who thought Barbie stole her sister, no one can actually stand outside culture and judge it unaffected, strategies of resistance never issue from someone, child or adult, who has shed all dominant values. My point here is that a conformity/resistance model does not quite work for three reasons.

1. A bunch of contradictory stances often exist simultaneously or in sequence. A child pretends that Barbie and Ken ride horses and have a cheery relationship while doing so. Cut and print: this belongs in a Mattel commercial for Barbie's four-footed accessories. From this standpoint, the consumer conforms. From another standpoint, the consumer, in conforming, resists: Does the vision of social activity unmarked by violence become disqualified as "resistance" unless Mattel is subverted in the process? (A related question: How does one characterize Barbie play by a child who does so against the wishes of her feminist mother—as resistance to an authority figure or as conformity to dominant ideology?)

2. We can label them one or the other or something in between only if we believe the fiction that we have full access to the consumer's past. What informed Karina's view that Barbie and Ken had different relations on horseback than at the Dream House? Who rides horses? The Ewing family on "Dallas"? Television outlaws? Cowboys and Indians? Her neighbor? Or is it about, instead, the country versus the city, or nature versus civilization, or home versus far away? My interpretation of how Karina conforms and resists here is based on having posited some associations that neither I nor, to a lesser extent, Karina can be absolutely sure of.

3. Consequently, the contradictions and insufficiencies mean that the model does not quite work in the sense of serving a theoretically or politically useful purpose. In order for mapping acts of consumption according to conformity and resistance to be worthwhile, something more must be acquired by doing it than the map itself. The map needs to be able to explain something or suggest guidelines for future actions and activism. But the frequent disjuncture between where particular narratives might lie on the register of conformity to Mattel and where they might lie on a register of social or ideological conformity suggests that both the descriptive and the prescriptive value of this opposition is limited. A Barbie game that suggests a stance of resistance to Mattel does not necessarily either predict a similar stance of resistance in the next day's Barbie game, correspond to a stance of resistance against the social values for which Barbie supposedly stands, or create a counterhegemonically posed adult in any direct or neat way. What then can be gained by

mapping acts of consumption as one or the other? Can we use the information to decide whether to give Barbie to children or to figure out how to plan effective counterhegemonic cultural activities?

These questions have no simple answers, and I defer further comment on them until later. It is worth noting here, however, that several consumers revealed their own skepticism about how much could be gleaned from their personal conformities or resistances. Although Karina had used Barbie in very non-Mattel ways and also thought that Barbie had made her feel more confident and helped her relate to other girls, she stated that, if she had a daughter, she would not give her Barbie: "I enjoyed it, but looking back on it I can see that why I enjoyed her is why I don't want Barbie to be a big factor in my daughter's life. The same with a son. I don't want him having a G.I. Joe or anything that demonstrates typical gender stereotypes that I don't think are healthy." Phyllis expressed similar concerns. She told me early in the interview that the big point she wanted to make about Barbie was that despite playing with Barbie she'd come out pretty androgynous, so she didn't think giving Barbie to girls was a problem. Later, however, she expressed a tiny bit of reserve about giving her daughter Cassie a Barbie, although she planned to do so (even though a close friend with a daughter Cassie's age would "kill her"): "If I felt totally comfortable today about my own appearance I wouldn't have any problems. But I don't. And I can't help wondering if Barbie has anything to do with it."

It's also worth acknowledging one of the <u>most cheering inadequac</u>ies of <u>the conformity/resistance model</u>: on one level, from the evidence of adult memory, <u>almost everyone seems to have been Barbie's queer accesso</u>ry. I do not mean *queer* here in the sense of nonheterosexual and/or unfixed gender: lesbian, gay, bisexual, transgender. While many of these stories indicate that gender identity and sexual identity do not come easily to anyone—is sex when you get hypnotized and serve refreshments on a tray?—relatively few actually deal with queerness in that sense. To throw a blanket sex/gender label *queer* over the whole of Barbie consumption would obscure both the amount of content that does not concern sex or gender and the undeniable presence of het Barbie in many stories that do. It would also obscure several key complexities of adult artifacts of memory, such as the way that the sexually queer content of the dyke destiny stories often unravels into gender content, so that sexually queer content is there and not there and there again rather than simply dominant content. What I mean to signify instead is that <u>oddness, idiosyncracy, non-Mattel generatedness in Barbie tales</u>—the way <u>that virtually every consumer seems to have queered Mattel's artistic inten</u>-

tion to some extent. Given the presence of queer moments in consumption in almost every Barbie story, I have wondered at times whether Mattel has any straight accessories or whether Barbie's human accessories are at most, to borrow a phrase from the personals . . .

Straight Acting

> I grew up on a farm, and I was very, very bored, and I didn't have any female role models. I mean we didn't during that point in the late six-ties. There were no models for me that I wanted to emulate. I didn't want to be a farmer's wife; I didn't want to work in a factory; I didn't want to be a teacher. So I took an inanimate object and gave it its own personality, and that's what I brought to life when I grew up.—Cynthia Jackson, "The Jenny Jones Show," 5 July 1993

One of the best indications of the many and complicated surface/depth relations of straightness and queerness is that the statement above came from the now-famous woman who underwent nineteen plastic surgeries in a $50,000 effort to look like Barbie. In terms of her childhood memories, Jackson is the straightest accessory I encountered, although a few come close. Michelle, for instance, primarily described games generated by Mattel accessories, a Barbie-and-Ken dating life suitable for Mattel commercials, and, when asked about Barbie's influence, an effect that would delight Ruth Handler: "Only for the fact that I played Barbie instead of hanging out on the street corner or seeing the wrong crowd." Yet Michelle also remembered thinking Barbie's hair and demeanor were fake: she was "too good to be true," not really virtuous.[37]

Jackson's account, in contrast, gives no hint of childhood deviation from either the letter or the spirit of Mattel's intention. It suggests a seamless fit with Mattel's PR and an appreciation of Barbie exactly as she and her ac-cessories rolled off the production line. Moreover, the plastic surgery aside, Jackson seems to have reaped exactly the benefits from Barbie that Mattel claims children will reap. Barbie expanded her sense of possibilities. When she grew up, she moved to London, conforming to the more sophisticated and jet-setting life that Barbie has had since the early 1960s. Then, changing with the times just like Barbie, she designed for herself a career that Barbie acquired in the 1980s—she's in a rock band—and, like Barbie, too, she took up a few more careers, including professional photography. She also wears clothes that match Barbie's outfits.

If not for the surgery and another professional sideline—she runs a cosmetic surgery information service for others who want to look like Barbie—Jackson could be a Mattel spokesmodel representing the infinite-possibility line incarnate. Her consumption of Barbie evolved with a healthy dose of imagination, which somehow also led her to embrace precisely those products Mattel offered; she invented a personality for Barbie that happened to be best expressed in outfits and accessories sold by Mattel. She promotes herself as the anti-bimboesque beauty Mattel claims Barbie to be: Jackson believes in "inner beauty" as well as superficial beauty and has a high enough IQ to be a member of Mensa. She also performs the corporate service of helping Mattel cast itself as the filler of needs rather than the creator of them (as in "I can't live another day without a refrigerator that has an automatic ice-cube maker"). Why does Jackson dress like Barbie? Because, she explained, she and Barbie tend to have the same taste in clothes. While this comment concerns the purchase of goods that Mattel did not create—adult clothes—it also reflects back on Mattel to reinforce the similar implication of her point that Barbie fulfilled her need for a role model. Both comments imply that her needs and tastes existed prior to Mattel's fulfillment and expression of them. But Jackson's real claim to fame disqualifies her from Mattel spokesmodel service. It suggests that, along with Mattel-authorized messages, Jackson bought the message that many critics accuse Barbie of promoting: In order to get the doors open to the glamourous life, you need to look like Barbie. At a time when Barbie comics are telling girls to love their bodies as they are, Jackson will not be making it onto Mattel's payroll.

So Jackson, it seems, is one of Barbie's queer accessories, in the broad sense. Her "Jenny Jones" episode, which concerned people who transformed their bodies in the service of fandom, implied by association that she was queer in the sex/gender sense, too. The other guests, all men, included, besides a man with $2,000 worth of Cher tattoos, Queer Donna, the "370 pound Madonna impersonator and fan," and two impersonators who'd had plastic surgery to better resemble their subjects: one did Cher, the other Joan Rivers. Although none self-identified on the show as gay (and although not all male cross-dressers are gay men), all but the tattooed man were highly queer acting—very campy. Several other queer moments involved Jackson herself, including Jones telling Jackson, "It's a good thing you weren't enamored of Ken; you could have wound up with a whole different set of operations," and Jackson telling Jones, in response to her question about whether she had met Ken, "I don't believe in fairy tales. . . . I don't think there's any such thing as the perfect man. I think there are plenty of pretty perfect women around, but men have got a long way to go yet." So why not trade in the boyfriend for a human Midge?

I am tempted to read Jackson in her queer "Jenny Jones" context as a consumer exemplar. Queerness below the surface, queerness in the next chair, queerness that will always emerge if you ask the right question or if you walk into your friend's bedroom at the very moment she is obsessively marking and fondling Barbie's breasts—or even merely changing Barbie's clothes, considering how much plastic-body contact is necessary, especially at the breasts, crotch, and ass, to get Barbie in and out of those tight outfits. Given how many people describe queer Barbie moments in the broadest sense of the term *queer,* given the fundamental queerness of a girl doll designed for girl children to admire and dress/undress, given Barbie's tendency to signal sex to consumers who often do not yet know much about it combined with my disbelief that people "naturally" construe sex as heterosexual at the moment when sex comes into their minds—given all these things, I can't help wanting to conclude that, at the straightest-appearing moments of Barbie consumption, consumers should be more properly called *straight acting.*

But I resist that temptation for three reasons. First, it's hard to make an exemplar out of Jackson. Even disregarding the nineteen surgeries, she's no typical consumer: few others testify to a Barbie consumption in which the purportedly free play of the imagination yielded Mattel's products so magically. Second, to use the term *straight acting* as it functions in personal ads—I look straight, but I'm really queer behind the clothes and between the sheets—is to lend queerness a unactedness, a fixed position beneath and outside the transformations of narrative convention and memory, that it shouldn't have. Although such a move would redress one injustice, by turning the tables to constitute straightness rather than queerness as the condition to be explained (away), it would perform another one. As the dyke destiny tales suggest, there are many consumer stories in which the teller is queer acting: the queer content, not the straight content, partly disintegrates on further scrutiny. Even if we could fully uncover childhood truths below fictionalized narratives constructed later, straightness and queerness would not always occupy the positions of above and below, respectively.

But we cannot do so, as the dyke destiny stories also show. Who are we to decide that the dykes in the conversation during which *butch dyke* turned out not to be the unifying signified were really sexually "straight" children? Although I argued that the dyke destiny wink is largely a function of reading gender-outlaw behavior as denoting sexual queerness rather than of remembering sexual desire for females, this is at most an argument about what the people in question remembered. What is it they don't remember (or aren't telling)? They might well have had sexually queer Barbie moments now lost to memory or experienced themselves sexually queerly apart from Barbie. All this is merely to reiterate that the archaeologist of truth is doomed never to find an artifact of meaning from which all layers of accumulated fiction have been dug away and dusted off.

Finally, I resist the temptation to make queerness the fundamental truth behind straight-seeming or queer-seeming narratives because I do not want to privilege queer moments in Barbie consumption in a way that erases what might be called the straightifying effects, that is, <u>Barbie's contribution</u> to <u>dominant ideolog</u>ies. It is crucial to recognize that queer moments appear in almost every account I presented: that the interpretive hijacking of cultural products is not performed only by people who actively identify as subcultural or who will identify as subcultural in the future (at age four I switched Barbie and Ken's heads; at age sixteen I dyed my hair green); that queer readings of Barbie should not be shunted to the margin or described as rare events that actually do mark a child as "different from the other girls."

Yet too much indicates that Barbie abets dominant ideologies to justify subordinating this effect in a paean to the delights of queer consumption. Barbie abets dominant ideology partly by the options that she doesn't come with officially, which matters even though consumers sometimes provide them. For example, many young people still describe having felt alone when they were coming out to themselves, often without anything but negative hearsay and sometimes without even a word to apply to it or knowledge that others like them existed. Things would be different if the ads during Saturday morning cartoons ever said, "Here's Barbie. She's getting dressed for a romantic date with Midge and choosing among her many wonderful outfits." I also want to take seriously the overall interpretation by people like Karina who felt that Barbie's promotion of dubious female ideals outweighed in effect Barbie's function as a catalyst or catharsis.

I also suspect that the wealth of queer moments that I culled from consumers is disproportionately large owing to consumer habits of memory and narrative. How did my own doll, which I don't even remember touching, get passed down to my sister so well worn? My interviews with others caution against presuming that my habits of play ordinarily or only involved straight, Mattel-friendly moments. Yet perhaps pretending that Barbie is having a fashion show is precisely the kind of thing that fades from memory, especially if it doesn't present itself as a memorable episode in a significant narrative. That "even back then" is the reigning interpretive point of so many Barbie narratives suggests that the even-back-thenness might well be the catalyst of memory and/or fabrication.

It may also be one of the catalysts for narrative. I have been arguing that narrative conventions contribute to the structure and content of Barbie stories: dyke destiny stories come partly from habits of looking into childhood for coming-out episodes; through sister-from-another-planet tales resonate tale tellings about other things described to be beyond our understanding. Another indication of the extent to which people construct Barbie narratives through already extant habits of cultural narration is the striking similarity between tales designated nonfiction by their tellers and those categorized as fiction. In Gary Fisher's "Storm," for instance, the sexual scenarios created by one girl puts her two playmates through a series of familiar changes:

> Jilly slowly lifted two naked dolls over her head, ritual-like, the way they made temples in Vacation Bible School. And one of the dolls was Bug's Christy. Tina gasped again but couldn't laugh, and Bug launched straight up. She flew for Jilly, then quickly thought better of it—like an angry sparrow banking, recalculating its chances against a hawk, and just in time. She sat back down, twitched, and stood back up. Tina said almost too casually: I think you should stop now, Jilly. Meanwhile Bug rummaged around for something large and heavy to throw.
>
> No one had ever noticed how black that black doll was until Jilly pressed it against Ken. Bug had always thought of color as something separating ball teams, or gangs, maybe white boys from black boys in the cafeteria, but never girls; and still it took a boy thing to bring it to her attention. She wanted to, yet couldn't blame Jilly; she knew that lovemaking had to be more than this uncaring, indifferent bending of body parts. Jilly's sex was just a rapid, lifeless thud, calculated for attention, not provocation, let alone inspiration.

The use of Barbie in an act of sexual quasi-terrorism, the interpretation of Barbie scenarios in terms of half-known "truths" about sex and race, Barbie's contribution to transforming those truths, the eruption of these sex scenes amid less troublesome ones where Barbie goes to a shopping center, all these have been seen in nonfictional accounts.

In Sandra Cisneros's short story "Barbie-Q," the speaker describes the thrill when she and her childhood friend came across Barbies, damaged in a warehouse fire, that they could purchase for cheap at a flea market, amplifying a meager supply described as follows:

Every time the same story. Your Barbie is roommates with my Barbie, and my Barbie's boyfriend comes over and your Barbie steals him, okay? Kiss, kiss, kiss. Then the two Barbies fight. You dumbbell! He's mine. Oh no he's not you stinky! Only Ken's invisible, right? Because we don't have money for a stupid-looking boy doll when we'd both rather ask for a new Barbie outfit next Christmas. We have to make do with your mean-eyed Barbie and my bubblehead Barbie and our one outfit apiece not including the sock dress.[38]

Many features of this story, too, appear regularly in nonfictional accounts: the same game played over and over with a mixture of real and imaginary props; the value placed on Mattel products and the slightly deviant-from-Mattel reading (mean eyes); the nonenthusiasm for Ken; the acute consciousness of economic status; and, elsewhere in the story, the ability to mention particular Barbies and outfits by their official names (Solo in the Spotlight, etc.).

Even "A Real Doll" by A. M. Homes, one of the most stupendously perverse Barbie fictions, which I mean as high compliment, has many incidents found in consumer tales. I've yet to encounter a male who, like the narrator, used his sister's Barbie and headless Ken as masturbation aids, explaining precisely, "I held Ken upside down above my dick and came inside of Ken like I never could in Barbie."[39] But I don't doubt that they're out there; his obsession with a sister's doll is common, as are now violent/now sexual expressions of it. The sister's acts also have "nonfictional" parallels: these acts, interspersed with some routine dress-up games using official Barbie outfits, include chewing off the feet, switching Barbie's and Ken's heads, cutting off Barbie's breasts, and burning up the body.

We can attribute the resemblance of these fictions to nonfictions partly to the fiction authors' ability to "capture" the texture and content of real life, which these do eloquently. The quote from "Storm" with which I began the chapter—Bug's future realization that "a truth's foundation could be eaten away by time and the little changes, the little slips in memory, the unconscious bits of self-preservation"—offers, I think, one of the best accounts of how memory erodes truth, an account no less valid because it occurs in a text labeled fiction. But the influence works in the other direction, too. It comes not only from the fiction writer's ability to capture truth but from the truth teller's sense of what makes a good story—here is a pivotal moment in my psychological development, here is an incident that economically reveals my characteristic habits of thought or my difference from the other girls my age. Queer moments, which seemingly mark the consumer's thought as individual rather than like everyone else's, are better candidates for character-development narratives.

As I suggested earlier, other narratives, too, inform the conventions of nonfictional Barbie narratives, and other agents of influence affect the stories people tell. I am another one. The many people who introduced into our conversations the topic of whether they had done something "weird" implies, perhaps, a presumption that I am looking for the bizarre and, perhaps, for the queer. But people certainly needn't know me to expect that weird Barbie play is the big object of interest. By now, weird Barbie stories and the debate about Barbie's effect on girls circulate widely in the media, and Mattel's claim that Barbie enables girls to fantasize about being adults and to work out their childhood difficulties—usually tamely described by Mattel in terms of girls whose parents are getting divorced playing that Barbie is getting divorced—has become relatively common knowledge.

Indeed, while I have been focusing on Mattel's apparent influence on my informants as children, what needs as much attention, perhaps, is Mattel's influence, direct and indirect, on my informants as adults. Why do so many people describe Barbie play as revelatory about their childhoods or seem to believe that Barbie actually does provide the supreme catalyst for childhood fantasies and workings out of childhood troubles? For one thing, the whole process of investing objects, organic or inorganic, with complicated meanings about sex, the body, money, labor, and other issues discussed above happens all the time. It is the phenomenon referred to as *fetishism,* which, as Emily Apter sums it up, "records the trajectory of an *idée fixe* or *noumen* in search of its materialist twin (god to idol, alienated labor to luxury item, phallus to shoe fetish, and so on." [40] Not everyone has fetishism in their day-to-day interpretive framework, either the *commodity fetish* (this object has more value, material and symbolic, than the cost of labor that went into it) or the *psychoanalytic fetish* (I'm upset that women don't, or my mother doesn't, have a penis, so I'm going to get turned on to high-heeled shoes that can stand in for the penis, thus creating the less anxious conditions needed for high pleasure—or to this eleven-and-a-half-inch-long plastic doll that's nearly twice as long as the proverbial six inches and never detumesces). [41] But many more people recognize the advertising trick of loading objects with meanings and functions that they don't directly fulfill: a fancy car will make you sexy. Most, I think, remember having invested objects other than Barbie with meaning—lucky socks, sexy leather, wedding rings, etc.—or having played "let's pretend" games with other toys. Barbie is hardly the only meaning-invested object.

Nor is she the first doll to get "the Barbie treatment." Dolls performed similar functions before Barbie existed. Beth Helsinger's indignation that the current rage for Barbie stories put her own pre-Barbie childhood imaginative life under erasure caused me to rethink my presumptions about Barbie's particular conduciveness to fantasy. So did her story of playing "tragedy" with her dolls, a game in which dolls wasted away from consumption or were left orphaned when their parents died of scarlet fever. This game was marked by the particular dolls and cultural narratives available to her. But it's not so different in imaginative content from Melanie's plane wrecks.

And, as Miriam Formanek-Brunell discusses in "Sugar and Spite: The Politics of Doll Play in Nineteenth-Century America," nineteenth-century doll play, no less than Barbie play, was also the occasion for subversion. While parental directives and books about dolls emphasized that doll play could help girls learn important social rituals, information about fashion and clothing, appropriate feminine submissiveness, and maternal devotion—with different types of doll play stressed at different times during the century—accounts of what children actually did often revealed quite different practices, including gleeful dismemberments that prefigure similar tales of Barbie destruction. They also reveal unsanctioned interpretations behind apparently conformist practices. For instance, adults apparently encouraged doll funeral rituals, which taught girls about an important aspect of feminine nurturing. Memoirs and questionnaires about doll play, however, indicate that the appeal of these games often lay in the opportunity to act out "aggressive feelings and hostile fantasies," sometimes changing the emphasis from "cathartic funerals to ritualized executions." Formanek-Brunell also notes that many girls simply rejected dolls for outdoor games or other toys; then as now, some girls rejected toys designed for their gender socialization.[42]

Mattel hardly created with Barbie the first doll that generated memorable and revelatory moments or even the first adult-like fashion doll, and dolls are hardly the only objects that generate imaginative play in children. Why does Barbie get so much attention? Why isn't there a corresponding subgenre of "here's what I fantasized about with my crayons" articles popping up in Sunday papers? I have no intention of discounting the common wisdom that Barbie's grown-up body impels children toward disturbing sexual matters and complex fantasies in a way that a baby doll or set of crayons might not. But I think that the predominance of Barbie stories must also be partly ascribed to Mattel's claim about Barbie's unique ability to serve the child's fantasy life and to those who publicize and validate this corporate claim through their own narratives (or books about Barbie). In other words, whether or not

Mattel has created a doll who is actually more suited than any other toy to engage the mental life of children in revelatory and complex ways, Mattel has certainly created one whom adults believe to be especially suited to perform this function. And, whether or not children use Barbie more than other toys to construct their narratives about their future adulthood, the inverse does seem to be true: many adults use Barbie more than other toys to construct their narratives about their past childhood.

To sum up my point about the effect of narrative conventions, tale-teller expectations, and Mattel's claims about Barbie on the huge percentage of queer moments in Barbie stories: all three contribute to it. This is not to argue that queer moments are few or marginal or that consumers who recount them invented them, consciously or not, to look more interesting and unique. But it is to suggest that, in the projects of remembering and telling Barbie stories, it is the straight stories, not the queer stories, that are more likely to wind up in the closet, just as untroubled moments are more likely to be closeted from memory or narrative than moments that disrupted understandings of the self, the context, and the artifact.

I have one other reason to distrust the predominance of queer moments, broadly described, in adult Barbie tales: the evidence provided by current children. When I witness contemporary Barbie play by children, I certainly see naked Barbies strewn around, Barbies fucking other Barbies, and Barbies trying to cross-dress. But I also see, in the same children, a huge reverence for Barbie and what she stands for. So, too, do many parents. Three friends recounted to me some version of the following conversation undertaken in a last-ditch effort to talk their children out of Barbie:

"Why do you want Barbie?"

"Because she's the most beautiful."

"Avi's beautiful, and she doesn't look like Barbie; Paula's beautiful, and she doesn't look like Barbie. Aren't they beautiful?"

"Yes."

"Then why do you want Barbie?"

"I want Barbie; she's so beautiful."

Even if the children were not merely assenting that their friends' moms are beautiful for strategic reasons, they certainly seemed to have bought some of Mattel's ideological line, despite, or alongside, heavy counterprogramming.

Now, there's no reason to interpret the phrase "Barbie is so beautiful" as transparent proof that children take what Mattel gives them. For some children, this statement camouflages a sexual fascination that Mattel takes pains not to encourage. I asked one six-year-old girl, for instance, to explain what was beautiful about Barbie. After she named Barbie's hair and clothes, she then pulled down Barbie's dress, touched her breast, saying, "And this," and then quickly pulled the dress back up. She then giggled, looking incredibly embarrassed, and turned away from me, so I didn't pursue the matter; ten minutes later, I noticed her covertly masturbating.[43] Children's statements, like adults', are often opaque. There is no reason to presume that a child who says, "I love Barbie because she is so beautiful," means only, "I love her physical appearance," or, "I believe that white, skinny, blond women are the best, and I want to trade on my looks to acquire luxury goods when I grow up."

But, while adult and child manifestations of Barbie interpretations may be equally opaque and equally likely to contain queer moments, there seems to be one major difference between them: adults who remember being anti-Barbie or Barbie deviants generally remember or describe themselves as being primarily that; children who manifest negative or deviant stances toward Barbie seem much more often to manifest their actions and criticisms as one set of tendencies embedded in a much more apparently pro-Barbie stance. Hannah certainly did. So, too, did my stepniece Kathryn, whom I interviewed by telephone at her grandparents' house after Grandma (my mother) called to tell me that Kathryn, on arrival, had immediately produced a bunch of Barbies and proceeded to put on a fashion show. Kathryn seemed to go with the Mattel flow in numerous ways. She had a collection with the reigning diversity spectrum: one of her Barbies had red hair, several were black, another "looked like a person from Korea," but most were blond. (She told me that the blond ones looked the same but had different outfits, thus registering a logic of acquisition in accord with Mattel's each-one-is-different marketing strategy, although simultaneously the underlying truth, as it were, is that they are all fundamentally the same.) She described commercial-worthy games in which dolls put on a concert or buy a new house and told me that Barbie was her favorite—in fact, "If you asked all the kids in America that are girls, they'd all probably say Barbie is their favorite. They wouldn't pick other dolls, like baby dolls." She affirmed the child's active role in defining Barbie's personality, which, she said, depended on what the girls who play with her think it is. And, although she described Barbie as having a personality only in order to humor me—"nice and caring . . . if you're asking me"—the one she ventured conforms exactly to the one in Barbie comics. But she also told me that playing with Barbie entailed forgetting about one big negative feature: "Barbie never looks like fat people, that's the bad part. . . .

The Barbie company is trying to make Barbie a role model, so if a fat person plays with Barbie, she might feel bad."

This mixture of love and criticism also shows up regularly in the letters column of Barbie comics. Twelve-year-old Jill Monkh combined praise for the "awesome fashions" with a request for a reality check: "I don't intend to be mean, but your comics aren't really based on the real world. . . . In other comics there are rivalries and disagreements." Barbie's response was as evasive as Monkh accused the comics of being: "It's true that the stories . . . do not usually revolve around conflict. We try to show solutions to problems and leave that as our focus. In that way, we hope that our readers will find helpful ways of dealing with problems they may face in their lives."[44] Emely Gonzalez, a "big fan" who wrote, "Can you do something with Barbie talking about prejudice and stereotypes?" registered her recognition that while the comics portray a "multi-ethnic environment," they never address racism. Barbie's answer indirectly admitted as much, although, unlike Emely, Barbie shied away from indelicate terms like *prejudice:* "A very good suggestion, Emely! The issue of how all of us from different races and backgrounds get along is certainly important. We'll pass your suggestion on to our writers, and see what they come up with!"[45] Problems without conflict and diversity without prejudice—exactly the fiction of Barbie comics, which never engage the conflict between Barbie's rightful place on top and the people she must step over to get there.

The examples above don't represent every Barbie pose. A few children I encountered simply rejected Barbie. (Evidence of this, unsurprisingly, never appears in the comics.[46]) Many others, I presume, have a love for Barbie untempered by criticism of Barbie's failures as a role model, paragon of beauty, or ambassador of multiethnicity. On the last matter, I wonder whether, given the consistent failure of white adults from the prediversity years to remember noticing that Barbie was white, there may be a corresponding blindness in white children of the "United Colors of Benetton" era about the shallow picture of diversity offered by Mattel and Marvel Comics today. An answer to this question awaits further research.

But preliminary research reveals two conclusions that I'm confident further research would sustain. The first, which backs up the conclusion suggested by adult testimony that virtually everybody seems to have been Barbie's queer accessory in one way or another, is simply that children in general *are* critics and that we condescend to children when we analyze Barbie's content and then presume that it passes untransformed into their minds, where, dwelling beneath beneath the control of consciousness or counterargument, it generates self-image, feelings, and other ideological constructs. I'm not arguing that children either escape the harmful effect of Barbie's dubious messages or function as omniscient critics. Barbie's skinniness still makes Kathryn feel bad, and recognition of this issue does not imply the recognition of other ones; equally important, however, is that she does view critically.

The second, which belies adult testimony that subversion, when it occurred, was the name of the predominant game, is that children's queer and critical moments occur frequently in the context of much straighter, more ordinary, "I love Barbie"–type play. When I look at children with Barbie today, I suspect that my sister must be right to attribute the well-worn condition of our family Barbie doll to me because the contrast between adults and children suggests that this is precisely the kind of forgetting that adults do. We remember deciding that Barbie was bad. We remember queer moments and subversions that made us "different from the other girls." We forget countless other unmemorable, and possibly quietly influential, hours of play.

Conclusion: Hegemonic Barbie, So What?

I argued in chapter 1 that Mattel's success at selling Barbie products for over thirty years depends largely on its utilization of hegemonic-discourse content and its increasing mastery of hegemonic-discourse strategies to mask limits, incorporate dominant definitions of freedom, and win the consent of reluctant consumers. Mattel does not actually sell products that abet the wide variety of life choices that they claim to encourage. Nor does it encourage anyone to question whether characteristic features of a just world include the ability of a few to achieve astounding career success or to amass a disproportionate amount of accessories. On capitalism, as on many other topics, Mattel toes the hegemonic-content line so that, when the "anything" that Mattel says we girls can do does not conform to dominant ideologies, Mattel can avoid appearing to have authored it. The line is designed to rope in everyone, progressive to reactionary; the products are designed to avoid challenging the status quo. Mattel's presentation of diversity does not boot blond, white Barbie from center stage. Nor does it address the hard issues—the "rivalries and disagreements" and "prejudice and stereotypes," in the words of Mattel's less euphemistic letter-writing critics—that must be addressed to make societies as just as they are multicolored. Yet, today more than ever, Barbie commentators are invoking Barbie's career freedom and multiethnicity as reasons to love her.

One more example of how well Mattel's line works, and of the contradictions and silences within it. On the "Phil Donahue" episode I mentioned earlier, Donahue kept berating the few anti-Barbie audience members by reminding them of Barbie's career choices and color diversity. At the end of the show, Phil and Mattel gave one embattled Barbie critic a gift, ostensibly to thank her for livening up the show, but also not so subtly to illustrate their point that Barbie represents equal opportunity for all people. The gift: an African American Desert Storm Barbie. Now, was it really a progressive move by Mattel—an artifactual vision of a rainbow future—to send a Barbie of color to the Gulf? Hardly. Unlike giving African American Barbie a doctor outfit, giving her army fatigues does not represent an affirmative-action move of sending her somewhere that too few people of color have been able to go before. It would have been a progressive move to have a *Barbie* comic in which Barbie questions why so many people of color were sent to fight this war, not to mention the racism of the whole endeavor and in the portrayal of the "enemy." But Mattel's discourse of diversity has no room for such contextual distinctions or contentious issues, and apparently it doesn't need to. It's hard to believe that Phil, liberal guy that he still prides himself on being, had heard no accusations of racism leveled against U.S. war conductors during this time. Yet, mesmerized by Barbie's diverse charms, he apparently missed the questionable progressiveness of this gift altogether.

The theory of hegemony, then, helps explain how so many Barbie products have moved from the toy shelves to the cash register and into the hands of millions of children. But what happens then? One might expect that a theoretical model so useful for understanding production and one feature of consumption—purchase—would also offer a model for understanding other features of consumption, such as consumer interpretation of the product. After all, if Mattel's line is hegemonic, shouldn't those consumer interpretations that reject Mattel's line be considered counterhegemonic? Shouldn't those acts and interpretations that seem to follow Mattel's directions—not the directions given in the infinite possibility line but the directions encoded in the actual array of products offered—be considered signs of Mattel's successful promotion of reigning hegemonies?

Only sometimes. The stance of a girl who recognizes Barbie to represent U.S. sanctioned ideal teenage girlhood, despises her for it, and throws her into the fireplace might well be termed *counterhegemonic*. The stance of a girl who loves Barbie, hates her own body, and diets excessively to achieve Barbie's weight might be considered testimony to Mattel's contribution to the maintenance of dominant ideologies. But many acts and artifacts of consumption cannot be so easily classified as one or the other. They cannot be classified at all without studying the consumer and the context of consumption, and they cannot be labeled conforming or resisting on the basis of whether they appear to follow or deviate from Mattel's artistic intention. One person may have put Ken's clothes on Barbie because it "looked funny," implying the underlying dominant presumption that boys should be boys and girls should be girls and that those who aren't should be ridiculed; another might have done so in defiance of precisely the same dominant idea. Similarly, "Barbie and Ken loved to ride horses together" cannot be understood without understanding what riding horses signified at the time to the consumer who utters this—which itself entails the sometimes if not always impossible task of reading the past or the present from the consumer's account of it. This statement cannot be prejudged conformist because Mattel makes horses to be ridden by blond Barbie in upper-crust outfits or because the girl put Barbie on the horse instead of setting up the horse to have sex with Barbie's puppy. Nor can it be presumed to represent the consumer's characteristic stance since killing antialien Ken may well have been the previous day's activity.

This opaqueness of artifacts of consumption—textual, discursive, pictorial, and artifactual—has some important theoretical implications for cultural criticism beyond issues of hegemony and resistance. Central among them is the impossibility of judging how and what cultural products signify by looking at the artifacts apart from the consumers and the (partial) context that they can provide. The relation of my own content analysis to the consumers I studied illustrates this well. From my content analysis could be hypothesized the existence of some consumer interpretations that I discussed, like Emely Gonzalez's sense that Barbie did not address racism, Lisa Jones's destruction of Barbie, and the perceptions of many that Barbie represented hot sex or dominant norms of ideal femininity. It did not predict, for instance, the interpretations of consumers who felt that they had to look elsewhere for models of nonethnicity at a time when Mattel was still trying to make sure Barbie didn't look "foreign."

Or did it? Is Barbie's contribution to Georgia's sense of class inferiority less important than Georgia's view that Tressie, not Barbie, had the nonethnic hair she longed to have? Georgia is one of many consumers who might alternately be labeled conforming or deviant with regard to the Barbie line. Two others among many are Cynthia Jackson, who had the nineteen plastic surgeries, and Karina, who varied between horseback riding and antialien smashing and who believed, despite the latter, that Barbie taught her to follow traditional gender roles.

As I argued earlier, there is both a justified thrill and a danger in focusing on deviant or queer Barbie readings. The justified thrill lies in the demarginal-ization of queer readings and the confirmation that people do not just absorb what is given them. This is crucial to recognize, not just because it autho-rizes the comforting thought that Barbie can't really steal your sister, but also because so many dubious censorship moves are justified by raising the specter of impressionable children who merely absorb what they see. (I'm contending, not that a subscription to *On Our Backs* is a suitable gift for a six-year-old, but that a false model of how children apprehend cultural prod-ucts underpins many censorship arguments, which also often use children to camouflage a different goal: to control what adults see and produce.)

The danger lies in the risk of letting the thrill or mere existence of queer instances obscure Mattel's contribution to reigning dominant ideologies or skew what might be overmathematically termed the straight/queer ratio. I suggested earlier that what people tell and remember may be distorted to privilege queer moments for many reasons. These reasons include their sense about what makes a good narrative or about what is called for in terms of Barbie memories—a sense gleaned from prevailing narrative conventions, from their understanding of me, or from the now widely publicized idea that many people do weird things with Barbie—and the likelihood that unusual or troubling Barbie moments are simply more memorable. There is evidence that such distortions occur (among, of course, many others since narratives are never mere transcripts of events)—evidence provided by adult narra-tives themselves and by the consumption of present children, which suggests by contrast that adults who primarily remember queer moments may be forgetting many more mundane other ones.

There is a danger, then, of overestimating the number of queer moments. More important, however, is a danger of overestimating their significance, and here I return to the subjects of hegemony and resistance. I argued above that hegemony/counterhegemony and conformity/resistance are of limited use partly because so many acts and interpretations cannot be determined to be one or the other or be fixed at some particular point in between. A bigger problem lies in the question of what we would glean from labeling acts of consumption in this way if we could do so. Incidents of anti-Mattel Barbie consumption do not even necessarily signal a consistently or thor-oughly resistant stance on the part of those consumers who describe them either toward Barbie or toward what (according to the consumer's percep-tion) she stands for. They reveal less about the adults those children will turn into. Childhood Barbie consumptions do not seem to predict adult cultural or political stances with much accuracy. A childhood Barbie fan once engaged in acquiring as many accessories as possible may now be resolutely and actively anticapitalist. And, if every consumer who cross-dressed Barbie or had queer fantasies about her were now ACT-ing UP, antigay initiatives with a good chance of being passed would not be on ballots all over the United States. To what extent, then, can the labels *resistant* or *counterhegemonic* describe or inform us about consumers in their past, present, or future roles as social beings, political activists, and cultural consumers?

Herein lies one question that politically motivated cultural criticism must address. Another question concerns how cultural activists can make use of other conclusions about Barbie consumption argued thus far. Does Barbie offer a particularly promising tool for subversive cultural activist creations given that queer Barbie has already had a relatively long sojourn, apparently, in the minds of many adults? Conversely, if the subversiveness of subversive artifacts depends on the ability of viewers or readers to understand what is being subverted, is Barbie ill suited to this purpose given Barbie's unstable and variable meaning? And does Mattel's at best only partial success at inscribing the meanings that it generates mean that Barbie subvertors, and cultural activists using other materials, have as little hope of getting subversive readings to adhere in circulation? I take up these questions in chapter 3.

Chapter 3

Barbie's Queer

Adult Accessories

Barbie has acquired many new adult accessories in recent years. A few have actually "played Barbie" by playing Barbie, either for love, like Cynthia Jackson, or for money, like Lori, from southern Indiana, who had little use for Barbie until the early 1980s ("I wasn't a prissy girl"), when she wound up supplementing her college money by impersonating Barbie for Mattel in local shopping-mall fashion shows. The job requirements included being tall with long blond hair, wearing a small size 8, "smiling a lot," and "somewhat even being clean-cut" as opposed to "pretty wild": "They didn't want a girl who looked great in the Barbie outfit, but when she took it off, the things that she liked to wear were short shorts and a tank top and a cigarette hanging out of her mouth."[1] Many more adult accessories, in ever increasing numbers, are Barbie collectors.

This chapter focuses on another burgeoning—but hardly new—subset of adult accessories: people who deliberately subvert, to recall Mattel's cease-and-desist letter, the "wholesome, positive, family-oriented image of BARBIE and Mattel . . . [that] Mattel has spent considerable funds and resources to develop." This subset intersects with that of Barbie collectors. Mark Ouelette, for instance, who chaired the 1993 annual collector's convention in Baltimore, generated a bit of hostility a few years ago when he drew an illustration for a collector's price guide that showed Barbie straddling Ken with his hands on her butt.[2] Ouelette protested that his drawings, while sometimes "kind of flirty," are "also innocent"; he might also have mentioned that they are nothing compared to the bisexual Skippers, drag-queen Kens, and queer sex scenes that other collectors produce. This subset also, I presume, includes some Barbie impersonators—although not Lori, who became one of Mattel's straighter accessories in the process of representing her. While retaining some doubts about Barbie's effect on girls' body image, Lori became enthusiastic enough about "the wholesome image" to take an active part in protecting it. By the time Mattel empowered her to hire her own backup models, she was willing to do some "snooping" to ensure that the applicants were really as wholesome as they claimed to be. She also rejected some outfits that she considered too immodest, thus making her a straighter accessory for Barbie than Mattel itself, which here, as on other occasions, was willing to contradict Barbie's official identity in order to sell products beyond what that identity appears to support.[3]

Among Barbie subvertors past and present number, too, people having other kinds of sustained adult relationships with Barbie: people within the ranks of Mattel, as I suggested in chapter 1, who slip cock rings onto the toy-store shelves and people in the ranks of reluctant bystanders who have verbally or artifactually intervened in the Barbie play of children. One is Rachel's mother, a freelance book designer who subverted Barbie's anatomical incorrectness in the late 1960s by painting nipples and pubic hair on Rachel's Barbies. Many other Barbie subvertors have no sustained adult contact with Barbie. Barbie is just one vehicle of subversion used only once or twice: today Barbie fucks Midge, tomorrow Marcia Brady fucks Laurie Partridge. Mary Patten, for instance, reproduced the Barbie-dildo photographs as one artifact among many in "My Courbet: A Beaver's Tale," her 1990 installation and video critique of lesbian invisibility in art history. This video, in turn, was one subversion among many: in 1989, she and Jeanne Kracher subverted yuppie/corporate lingo with their girl-eats-girl Power Breakfast T-shirt produced for ACT UP/Chicago; a current video in progress concerns the media coverage of Aileen Wournos, the so-called lesbian serial killer.

In considering Barbie's subversive adult accessories, I am particularly interested in the pedagogical and political issues that arose at the beginning of my own sustained adult encounter with Barbie when I tried to imagine teaching "Gals and Dolls." Can you wrest Barbie from Mattel and refunction her to challenge rather than abet dominant ideologies? How much can Barbie subvertors subvert—to what extent does the given determine the possible in both the making and the circulation of Barbie subversions? What insights do the possibilities and limits of Barbie subversion in particular offer regarding strategies of cultural activism in general? The first section discusses what might oversimplistically be termed the good news about Barbie's sub-vertibility and her potential as a political and pedagogical tool. Subsequent sections address what subversions, either in isolation or in circulation, often do not subvert and examines some key disjunctions between production and consumption, between intention and reception. Primary among these is the disparity between the huge number of Barbie subversions and the tendency to report them, both conversationally and in the media, as being one of a kind: how is it possible, for instance, to out Barbie 20 million times or to report each transgendering of Ken as if it had never happened before? From these issues larger questions emerge about outing and about deploying cultural studies pursued within academics on behalf of political/cultural activism undertaken outside academic contexts. I take these up at the end of the chapter.

Steal This Doll

Can you steal Barbie from Mattel for political and pedagogical gain? The following poem by Essex Hemphill suggests why at least part of the answer must be yes:

> Soft Targets
> (for Black girls)
>
> He was arrested and detained
> for nailing Barbie doll heads
> to telephone poles.
>
> He was beaten
> while in custody, accused
> of defacing public property.
>
> After healing, he resumed
> his irreverent campaign,
> this outlawed spook terrorist
> continued hammering horse nails
>
> through Barbie heads
> and setting them aflame.
>
> Barbie never told Black girls
> they are beautiful.

She never acknowledged
their breathtaking Negritude.

She never told them
to possess their own souls.

They were merely shadows
clutching the edges of her mirror.

Barbie never told Black girls
they are beautiful,

not in the ghetto evenings
after double dutch,

not in the integrated suburbs,
after ballet class.

"Soft Targets" displays Barbie as a great vehicle for social criticism. By jux-taposing two common race-specific occurrences—the enshrinement of white people in cultural products and institutionalized violence against blacks—Hemphill draws attention to the consequences of a racism that gives the white doll more value than black human beings. Mutilating Barbie is con-sidered a crime; police beating black men and Mattel perpetuating white superiority is not. He also implicates sexism in police action against black men, which is often perpetuated in the name of protecting white women. The phrase "defacing public property," which refers most obviously to the crime against telephone poles but also to the de-facement of Barbie, also invokes the dual status of Barbie's human referent, white women, as overcherished and yet underempowered ("property").

"Soft Targets" shows what you can do with Barbie by what Hemphill says—and by what he doesn't. He doesn't state who Barbie is or which Barbie he is talking about. He doesn't have to. The connection between the word *Barbie* and Mattel's doll is ubiquitous. Readers do not, for instance, have to get to the seventh stanza, when Hemphill first refers to Barbie as *she,* to realize that *Barbie* doesn't refer to Klaus Barbie, even though Klaus had his image backed up by police brutality, might justifiably be nailed in effigy to a telephone pole, and never, I presume, never told black girls that they are beautiful either. This misreading seems preposterous, but the point is worth making: reading *Barbie* and getting a mental picture of the doll requires the application of acquired knowledge. Most people have it, although their men-tal picture might deviate from what's out there. Note that Hemphill himself is another example of a Barbie observer who does not see, or see as significant or as successfully achieved, Barbie's recent and much-touted diversity.

People can also often call up something about Barbie's rep and the Barbie debates. Hemphill doesn't need to explain why "Barbie never taught Black girls / they are beautiful." As I argued in chapter 2, adult memories about childhood Barbie use testify to widespread familiarity with the debate over Barbie's fitness to serve as a role model: Does Barbie generate sex play in girls? Does she promote the superiority of beauty over brains or of skinny, white, blond, big-breasted women over every other female? So, too, does the widespread use of quickie references to Barbie in cultural products directed to very large audiences. Alison Sloane doesn't explain what she means by her comment in *Soap Opera Digest,* bought monthly by almost 1.5 million people, that most soap actors and actresses of the 1960s and 1970s "looked like they'd be more at home in Malibu Barbie's Beach House than in the fictional small towns where their characters lived."[4] Frank Coffey and Joe Layden, authors of *Thin Ice: The Complete, Uncensored Story of Tonya Harding, America's Bad Girl of Ice Skating,* which I bought at the supermarket, do not explain what Harding's former agent meant when he said, "Tonya Harding proves that you don't have to be a Barbie doll to succeed in this sport."[5]

There's a lot out there about Barbie, but that doesn't mean that she's not worth picking up again. Hemphill's poem shows otherwise, and my point is just the opposite. Common knowledge makes Barbie a great vehicle for social criticism. Like the U.S. flag, Barbie calls up for many people an image, a set of issues, and an understanding of the official and dominant raps: we know Barbie is supposed to stand for a female ideal just as we know the U.S. flag is supposed to stand for a U.S. commitment to freedom, democracy, and justice. As a result, Barbie is user friendly for the critic-producer, who can begin on covered ground and move on from there.

This is what Hemphill does, as do others who use Mattel's dolls for social criticism. In *Tongues Untied,* Marlon Riggs's 1989 video on black gay men, a monologuer uses "body by Nautilus, brains by Mattel" to describe a white bouncer at a racist gay club; he doesn't need to explain that through *Mattel* he alludes to Ken or that through Ken he alludes to ignorant, cut-from-the-mold, same-old-story racism. In the novel *Travels with Diana Hunter,* Regine Sands also works from common ground when she has her formerly anorexic lesbian character refer to her parents as Barbie and Ken: "All they wanted, for god's sake, they told one another, was to make her into a beautiful, cultured, selfish, rich elitist like themselves."[6]

The cultural producers discussed above all take advantage of common

16. Bedtime Barbie with the come-hither look on the cover of *Barbie: The Magazine for Girls,* March/April 1994.

knowledge about the Barbie debates. Many others take advantage of two even more widely known things about Barbie: clothes make the (plastic) woman, and each incarnation gets a name designating either (1) a leisure pastime (Rappin' Rockin' Barbie, Wet 'N Wild Barbie), (2) a geographic milieu called (*a*) home (Jamaican Barbie, "dressed in traditional Jamaican clothing . . . [that] truly captures the essence of the island, mon," to quote a Mattel Information Release from 1992), or (*b*) vacation hot spot (Island Fun Barbie), or (*c*) alternately both (Tropical Barbie looks either like the descendant of her colonizer-tourist *Hawaiian Holiday* self or like the colonized indigenous inhabitant depending on whether she comes in the skin color designating "white" or the skin color designating "tropical native"), (3) a play activity (Paint 'n Dazzle Barbie, which you paint on; Bedtime Barbie (fig. 16): "You'll have sweet dreams with Bedtime Barbie because she is so soft you can cuddle her all night long . . . make her eyes open or close for sleeptime fun!")[7], (4) a career (Doctor Barbie), (5) an event, "real" or fantasized (Wedding Fantasy Barbie), or, occasionally, (6) a vaguely referenced political stance (Animal Lovin' Barbie; Desert Storm Barbie of the Stars and Stripes line; the 1994 Doctor Barbie, which, in a few horrible manifestations, features an infant of color as one of white, blond Barbie's accessories. Aside from repeating the suggestion of much liberal white culture that the primary function of people of color is to enhance, by accessorizing, the self-image or leisure activities of white people—some of my best friends are black and/or I love having sex to an Afro beat—this particular combination reinforces both a dubious humanitarianism, in which charitable, enlightened white people bring the fruits of progress to the less light, and a justification for white supremacy: those people need our help.)

The naming device, the names, the ad copy, and the values encoded in the name/outfit/accessories combinations all make Barbie ripe for parody, and subvertors have made great use of them. The cover of *How-To '92: Model Actions for a Post-Columbian World,* a handbook for legal and illegal political/cultural actions, shows a detail from Jaune Quick-To-See Smith's 1991 series "Paper Dolls for a Post Columbian World with Ensembles Contributed by the U.S. Government" (fig. 17).[8] Quick-To-See Smith addresses precisely what the 1994 Doctor Barbie, continuing in Mattel's tradition of shallow diversity, would camouflage and fail to address several years later and, more important, what standard accounts of Columbus omit. In "Paper Dolls," the people who distribute the goods are not anxious to provide colonized Barbie and Ken, given the surname "Plenty Horses" in mocking imitation of white habits of stereotyping, with outfits, resources, and a power of self-determination just like theirs. Barbie comes with a maid's uniform for her, "for cleaning houses of white people after good education at Jesuit school or gov't school." There is also a "special outfit" for Ken, "for trading land with the U.S. government for whiskey with gunpowder in it." Barbie and Ken also get "matching smallpox suits for All Indian Families after U.S. gov't sent wagonloads of smallpox infected blankets to keep our families warm." Spreading the fruits of enlightenment is not the main goal here. Nor is there the benign intercultural give-and-take suggested by the world of Barbie, where white Barbie shares her doctor outfit with her friends and counterparts of color while blithely enjoying her boom box, and by the classroom tale of the first friendly Thanksgiving meal. Another accessory is a "flathead headdress collected by whites to decorate homes after priests banned cultural ways such as speaking Salish and drumming, singing or dancing. Sold at Sotheby's today for thousands of dollars to white collectors seeking Romance in their lives." Here, "sharing" appears as what, historically, it has often been: forced deculturation/reculturation imposed by the colonizer on the colonized and camouflaged as progress for the primitive. Appreciation is also represented in two of its

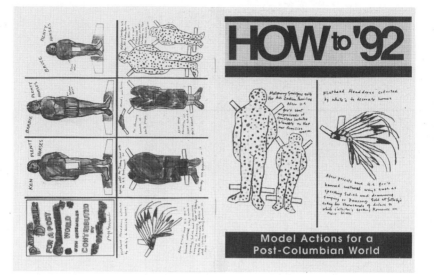

17. Cover of *How To '92: Model Actions for a Post-Columbian World,* showing a detail of "Paper Dolls for a Post-Columbian World with Ensembles Contributed by the U.S. Government" by Jaune Quick-To-See Smith, 1991. (Full series, 13 pieces, 11 × 17 in. each; watercolor and pencil on photocopy on paper.) Reproduced courtesy of Steinbaum Krauss Gallery, NYC.

most common manifestations, as theft and as its liberal descendant: appropriation undertaken without the consent of the appropriated for the benefit of the appropriator only.[9]

AIDS Barbie (fig. 18) from the 'zine *Diseased Pariah News* also addresses what Mattel never does.[10] In the interest of making Barbie look wholesome, Mattel makes silence about sex the rule and doesn't give its teens condoms for the same reason that most school boards don't: to avoid appearing to have authored or authorized sexual activity. *AIDS Barbie* addresses the consequences of maintaining that "nice girls don't use condoms" by parodying Mattel's theme-with-variations trope. It shows three AIDS Barbies, each accessorized with different "complications" far beyond those Barbie ever appears to contemplate—"And she thought that math class was tough!" Note, too, the new spin on Barbie's much debated lack of body fat: the Barbie "with Wasting Syndrome" seems to have undergone virtually no weight loss.

AIDS Barbie also alludes through its parody of Mattel to two other regimes of silence and corporate self-serving. The middle Barbie has "gynecological complications," which the Center for Disease Control (CDC) long refused to

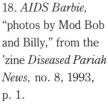

18. *AIDS Barbie,* "photos by Mod Bob and Billy," from the 'zine *Diseased Pariah News,* no. 8, 1993, p. 1.

recognize as symptoms of AIDS. As a result, the CDC underrepresented the number of women with AIDS or HIV and, in turn, contributed directly and indirectly to inadequate diagnosis, prevention, and treatment.[11] The trademark pseudoinformation at the bottom—"*Barbie is a registered trademark of Mattel, Inc. AIDS is a trademark of Burroughs Wellcome, Inc. All rights reserved."—reminds the viewer that the "rights" that now govern the testing, prescribing, pricing, and availability of drugs for people with HIV infection belong not to them but largely to patent-holding pharmaceutical companies. Burroughs Wellcome, which manufactures AZT, has a long history of putting profit over consumer access and well-being: AZT cost the consumer $12,000 a year before ACT UP protests forced Burroughs Wellcome to reduce prices and to reveal the information (held back for a year by Wellcome and the FDA) that half the recommended dose of this toxic, expensive drug was no less effective. The indirect reference to AZT also implicates the medical establishment and the U.S. government, which protected Burroughs Wellcome by underreporting AZT's side effects and by overfunding research on AZT, thereby neglecting other potentially more effective drugs and also alternative treatments that offer no payoff to pharmaceutical companies.[12]

Paper Dolls and *AIDS Barbie* both play off the gaps and camouflages in Mattel's Barbie line to deal with gaps and camouflages in the dominant ideological lines, the hegemonic-discourse content, from which Mattel crafts its own: the discourse of diversity that never addresses the difference between sending African American Barbie to the Gulf and sending her to med school; the deliberate eye closing to teen sexuality when attention would imply authorship; the masking of profit motive as benevolent concern (we manufacture Barbie for the benefit of girls; we sponsor medical research for the benefit of the ill; we bring you our culture and take yours in the name of cultural exchange only). Another often-filled gap in Mattel's line concerns Barbie's sexual orientation. The 'zine *P.C. Casualties* economically slams what's missing from Mattel's line in a list of identities that Barbie, like many other cultural characters, never gets: "LESBIAN BARBIE: Invisible." (Other dolls include "SM BARBIE—Comes with leather restraints, paddles, and three tribal tattoos. All models complete with genitals"; "NATIVE AMERICAN BARBIE—No longer available, since white Barbies have pushed her on the floor, stolen her belongings and killed her. Offensive white Barbies celebrate holiday in honor of this"; and "BATTERED BARBIE—Burdened with small children. No marketable skills and no assets. Self-esteem sold separately.") [13]

But despite, and because of, Mattel's refusal to author Lesbian Barbie, Barbie's been outed all over the place in the past few years. Since the 1989 *On Our Backs,* Barbie's been sighted in porn produced in North Carolina, the Netherlands, and Australia. In 1991, Barbie and friends got outed in Chicago in *Barbie the Fantasies,* a 1991 play produced by Poison Nut Productions that consisted of eight unrelated scenes "skewering the perfect All-American images of Barbie and her friends." As one reviewer described,

> In the first scene G.I. Joe . . . does an illegal cable hook-up so that he and Ken . . . can watch the big fight on ESPN; Barbie . . . protests until she discovers the wonders of the cable home shopping network. The behavior quickly descends from slightly immoral to crude and tawdry—scene two finds a lecherous Mr. Mattel . . . proposing a three-way with Barbie and Midge . . . , and following scenes deal with adultery, stereotypical images of homosexuality (Ken's a flaming queen and Barbie's a bulldyke wearing combat boots), prostitution, oral sex between Ken and G.I. Joe, and violent homicide (lots of violent homicide).

The audience also saw video shorts: among them, footage of Barbie the actress offering a sneak preview at the Chicago gay pride march during the previous June, riding in a limo and "guzzling beer in a manner blatantly unfit for the favorite toy of millions of little girls." [14]

In 1993, Barbie and Ken came out a few times, and did other nonmainstream things, in *Mondo Barbie,* an anthology of Barbie fiction and poetry. Besides reprinting Ken's appearance as a sex toy for a human male in A. M. Homes's "A Real Doll," the anthology also includes Rebecca Brown's "Barbie Comes Out," in which a narrator meets Barbie (now calling herself Barbara) in a dyke bar and listens to her horrible life story of being shuttled around and abused—"She remembered having her limbs yanked out and crammed back in. . . . She tells me about the scissors and the needles and the matches, glue and dirt. The places where they put her hands. The holes they put her head in"—and of having only one constant friend. This friend, now her lover, is Ken, now the pre-op transsexual Kendra, who, as several nonfictional adults remember suspecting, turned out to be "a dyke trapped in the body of a dream boat." [15]

In 1993, too, Barbie appeared on a holiday card announcing Totally Out Barbie. A parody of two big sellers of that year, Totally Hair Barbie and Teen Talk Barbie, she wears a leather jacket, freedom rings, pink triangle, and a woman-symbol earring, highly visible given her short hair. She is also "makeup resistant," "comes with her own Magic Toolbox," although "Grrl-friends and Dream Hog sold separately," and is shown uttering "Clit power": "Press her button to hear more radical phrases." [16] Barbie got transgendered by the Barbie Liberation Organization (BLO), which bought a bunch of Teen Talk Barbies and Talking Duke G.I. Joe dolls in late 1993 and switched their voice boxes. The result, according to a *New York Times* article that reinforces, albeit somewhat tongue in cheek, the gender stereotyping the BLO set out to attack: "A mutant colony of Barbies-on-steroids who roar things like 'Attack!' 'Vengeance is mine!' and 'Eat lead, Cobra!' The emasculated G.I. Joe's, meanwhile, twitter, 'Will we ever have enough clothes?' and 'Let's plan our dream wedding!' " [17] The BLO then returned them to the shelves with the phone numbers of local television stations included in each box to encourage the unwitting purchasers to publicize what they'd picked up. It worked. The BLO got national coverage.

The examples above, which represent only a fraction of queer Barbies, have all received substantial circulation; mainstream, subcultural, or both. There are far more that haven't. Bee Bell, for instance, who had Barbie say "Goodbye fuckers, I'm going to hell" twenty years ago, dragged Barbie into transgender and genderfuck dykehood in 1993 with Passing Butch Glenn (fig. 19). A transformation of Skipper's friend Kevin, Glenn reads Leslie Feinberg's *Stone Butch Blues* and comes with Queer Nation–inspired jacket stickers saying "MASS-PRODUCE MY FIST" (a takeoff of "Assimilate my fist" stickers, which protest against the assimilation-

19. Bee Bell, *Passing Butch Glenn*, 1993. Photo: Jay York.

ist give-us-civil-rights-because-we're-just-like-you-and-we'll-be-very-polite-when-we-ask-for-them brand of activism), "YES, I KNOW IT'S THE WOMEN'S BATHROOM," "FUCK YOUR GENDER," "FUCK *MY* GENDER," and "QUEER GIRLS MAKE ME HARD."

Bell's subversion is just one among countless others produced for a solo audience. I've encountered many others, some produced in material form, some generated in conversation, including the many adult assessments of Barbie's effect on girls recounted in chapter 2. Sheer numbers, perhaps, provide the most important testimony to Barbie's ability to serve critics and subvertors. They show that, unlike its anatomically incorrect doll, Mattel's ideological line has highly visible cracks and holes. Lots of people notice the contradiction between Mattel's silence about sex and constant signaling of sexual possibilities and notice what goes unarticulated in Mattel's portrayal of diversity and of the everything we girls can do. This, along with Barbie's fame, gives cultural producers who produce for circulation an easy-access, consumer friendly vehicle to work with—a crucial feature of any cultural production designed to abet social change by challenging dominant ideologies. Simply put, a lot of people will get it, or at least part of it. At least as important, a lot of people will do it themselves or will already have done so. If we measure cultural interventions and strategies of resistance by whether they catalyze big social changes by themselves and fast, Barbie subversions, like most, will not past the test: you can't shoot down an antigay referendum by wheatpasting Subversive Barbie all over the state of Oregon, or get all the school boards in the United States to distribute condoms in schools, or get everyone to think about when so-called cultural exchange is really cultural theft or land theft. You can't use Barbie to stop making everyone who doesn't look like her feel bad; you may not even be able to make yourself stop feeling bad. But, if we measure resistance and ideological transformation in smaller increments, Barbie's subvertability and visible cracks matter a lot. It matters that lots of people recognize and think about Mattel's silences, camouflages, and dubious claims and come prepared to a Barbie subversion that uses Mattel's line to expose social injustice by drawing connections that they might not have considered before.

From this standpoint, Barbie is a great vehicle for criticism and subversion and also a great teaching tool. Barbie subversion is also worth doing simply for the pleasures of recognition, self-affirmation, and transgression that Subversive Barbies give to makers and viewers who are already antiheterosexist, antiracist, anticapitalist, anti-imperialist, etc. But this assessment is based mostly on an assessment of production, on the meanings that you can give Barbie. As I argued in chapter 2, however, and as Subversive Barbies themselves show—since they, too, are artifacts of consumption—consumers don't necessarily take out the meanings that producers put in. Subsequent sections reconsider Barbie's subvertability from the standpoint of circulation: nonsubversive meanings that do, or seem likely to, get put into circulation alongside intended subversive meanings. First, however, I consider a counterexample that problematizes the equation theft = resistance, which the examples above seem to validate but which is actually as problematic as equating divergence from Mattel in childhood with resistance to social injustice.

Steal This Profit

Some Barbie collectors are in the business of subverting Barbie's ideological profile; others aren't. But, from one angle, Barbie collectors, both queer accessories and straight, are the biggest Mattel subvertors around. No matter what else they have done to Barbie, collectors have, in fact, embraced an alternative, Mattel-unfriendly set of criteria for Barbie's economic value, which primarily they, not Mattel, cash in on. While many collectors do stock up on future collectibles at the Walls of Pink, most collector dollars, not insubstantial in amount, pass independently of Mattel within a collector's economy with its own vocabulary, culture of knowledge, and system of value ascription: "*NUMBER FOUR BARBIE*: RED LIPS, S/S [swimsuit], WHAT A FACE! REALLY STUNNING, COULD EVEN BE A #3 FACE, NM [near mint] $395."; "*BLACK [hair] 1961 B.C.* [bubble cut]: RED LIPS WITH TINY LIP RUB, B/W, S/S, EC [bendable waist, swimsuit, excellent condition] $95"; "*NUMBER THREE*: BLONDE WITH BROWN EYELINER AND BIG RED FULL LIPS. SHE COMES IN A PINK R SILHOUETTE BOX DRESSED IN '*EVENING SPLENDOR*' WITH TM STAND. SHE IS REALLY SPECIAL, MIB [mint in box, i.e., all sealed packaging remains sealed] $3200." [18]

And Mattel has little control over the situation. It can't put a stop to this diversion of Barbie money. It can't really catch every copyright infringement or Barbie-image violator. Barbie collector culture is too huge to monitor, although Mattel might well want to do so since collectors' conceptions of Barbie do not always conform to Mattel's. I've already mentioned the controversy over Barbie getting straddled. Another conference organizer suggested to one of my researchers two possible conference souvenirs for a Barbie convention in Maine (suggested title "Barbie's Merry-Go-Round in Maine"): Clam Digger Barbie and Garage Sale Barbie (with the theme "Now Barbie's entering our world"), whose feet are killing her as she waits for a cab. Now, aside from the cab, these are hardly costumes that would issue from Mattel, which gives Barbie far more upscale careers and costumes and depends on her love of the new: Barbie buys every new fashion that comes along; she doesn't paw over cheap used stuff. But is scrutinizing every convention souvenir worth Mattel's time? Or worth its own image? How would Mattel look if it went after people whose infractions seem minor in comparison to the great free publicity they give Barbie?

Mattel is left with few options. It can flex its legal muscle and collect due

homage; handouts for the 1992 Barbie Nevada Round-Up, for instance, duti-
fully indicate "BARBIE trademark used with permission of Mattel, Inc." It can
work with collectors to generate goodwill toward the corporation—thus, beginning in 1994, the new monthly *Barbie Bazaar* column "From Mattel." It can
collaborate with convention hosts to ensure that convention souvenirs meet
its criteria, as it did for the first time in 1993. The 650 registered participants
at the annual, national scale Barbie Doll Convention received a doll with a
unique head manufactured by Mattel according to the specifications of the
convention hosts, the Baltimore Barbie Collectors Club of Maryland. Club
members designed, produced, and attached the rest. The result, according
to *Barbie Bazaar,* was "a black-haired beauty wearing a pink satin coat over
a metallic silver dress, complete with hat, sunglasses, a special wrist tag
and certificate of authenticity." [19] But Mattel can't jump into collaborations for
every Round-Up around. Nor does it; regional conference organizers often
cannot even get a visit from a Mattel spokesperson.

This isn't surprising. It's hardly cost or time effective for Mattel to put
resources into an edition of 650 that might otherwise be spent on a product
that could be sold by the hundreds of thousands. Like legal action, conference
surveillance and souvenir collaboration are poor financial investments for
Mattel: they work toward protecting assets but promise virtually no financial
return. Mattel's other collector-management strategy offers a bigger payoff:
finding ways to tap into the market for rare Barbies. This strategy, like the
infinite possibility strategy, involves both product design and rhetoric manipulation. On the low end, Mattel expanded a practice begun in the 1960s of
offering some large stores product exclusives. (The Sears and J.C. Penney's
1969 catalogs both showed Talking Barbie saying, "I have a date tonight," but
only Penney's had the Talking Barbie Pink Premier Gift Set.) [20] According
to Mandeville, Mattel retooled this practice for the collector's market after
discovering in 1988 that people were rushing all over to grab Happy Holidays
Barbie, which Mattel had issued with some trepidation about the price, almost $40: "Mattel got the message loud and clear. The collector, and even
parents would gladly pay more money for quality. Thus began the neverend-
ing parade of store specials that drive us all crazy today!" [21] And it's quite
a parade. In a 1993 article on these "limited edition custom Barbie dolls,"
Barbie Bazaar reported that FAO Schwartz, which was still selling its special
and much-publicized Madison Avenue Barbie first issued in 1992, had a new
Barbie Rockette. Toys R Us had Moonlight Magic and Police Officer Barbie,
Service Merchandise had Sparkling Splendor, "various supermarket chains"
had Holiday Hostess, and "wholesale clubs" had Festiva Mexican Barbie.

(The spin-control police must have been napping when they sent Mexican Barbie, the only "ethnic" special mentioned here, although Mattel has produced others, to the discount clubs, and during the debate over NAFTA no less.)[22] The Home Shopping Club also had a Barbie exclusive that year, which was touted as coming with the first-ever numbered certificate of authenticity produced by Mattel.

On the high end, Mattel now makes limited edition dolls costing about $175, advertised most noticeably in Sunday magazine sections in full page ads with headlines like "The Limited Edition Platinum Barbie. Barbie beauty and Bob Mackie glamour together again for a limited time" and with texts emphasizing the rareness of both the doll and the opportunity to buy it. About Platinum Barbie we read: "Her formfitting dress shimmers with the reflected light of over 8,000 handsewn sequins and beads. The plunging neckline is encrusted in Mackie's signature bugle beads . . . please order soon, because she's part of a special limited edition that's sure to sell out quickly." Chrystal Rhapsody Barbie similarly (but, of course, uniquely) has a dress that "shimmers with the reflected light of over 75 Swarovski chrystal rhinestones" from Austria and must be ordered early because "production is limited and no orders over the amount produced can be honored"; she is also the "first Barbie with contemporary, hand crafted porcelain sculpting." Gold Sensation Barbie, instead of shimmering with reflected light, has a "dazzling gown that shines like liquid gold" and "authentic 22 kt. gold electroplated jewelry [that] is a first in Barbie history"; "this very special Barbie is not available in stores and can only be purchased through direct subscription."[23]

All in all, a marketing masterpiece with Mattel's signature concepts: lots of variations on the same physical property (many ways to produce and describe "shiny") and creative suppression of the concept *replication* and of what makes these Barbies no different than the mass-produced ones. After all, it is always the case that "production is limited and no orders over the amount produced can be honored." Mattel will not manufacture you a Rappin' Rockin' Barbie if you missed picking one up when they were in stores any more than it will send Festiva Mexican Barbie to FAO Schwartz if you don't want to buy wholesale. Rappin' Rockin' Barbie is in this sense a limited edition, too, and is heralded as such under a different marketing banner, Mattel's familiar claim that Barbie "changes with the times." Besides, it's not clear how much more limited the officially named limited editions are. Except for the Home Shopping Club, which told viewers that "only" 50,000 dolls would be available, the ads for these dolls are like the ads for Elvis plates, baby dolls, and all the other limited editions being mass-marketed these days. Ads never indicate the number of dolls available, suggesting that it will be limited to the number of people who order them, which, in turn, cannot be small or Mattel would not front the cost of advertising nationally with full-page ads. As the discourse of infinite possibility masks considerable limits, the discourse of rarity and limits masks a considerable absence of limits.

Although the operative strategy here is actually the discourse of *non-*infinite possibility, Mattel's entry into the collector's world of limited editions and rare finds provides another example of Mattel's "hegemonic smarts." Mattel can't profit from collectors' desires for Barbies that are rare because old, so they found another way to denote and produce "rare," just as they managed to denote and produce "feminist" without ever having Barbie think about reproductive rights. Mattel reappropriated some Barbie dollars by attracting collectors of old dolls and, according to Mandeville, created in the process a new kind of collector whose primary interest was these new rareties: "New collectors joined the ranks. New 'dealers' came out of nowhere, and men signed up for Barbie Fan Clubs like they were registering for Selective Service." He also reports, however, that people weaned on the new are starting to buy the older ones, which means a redirection of money away from Mattel; Mattel also, of course, never sees the money that dealers take from markup.[24] Yet it profits far more than it did when "rare" designated only a Barbie that sold for three dollars thirty years ago. Sharing profits with Barbie promoters has been a successful part of Mattel's moneymaking endeavors since it started authorizing licensed products in the early 1960s, and Mattel's move can well be described as having drawn at least some dealers, formerly acting as free agents, into a licensor-type position.

Mattel's interaction with collectors shows its hegemonic smarts. It also, however, provides another example of the limited value of a theoretical framework that locates resistance in counterhegemonic practices. In the abstract, the collector traffic in Barbie can well be described as counterhegemonic. Collectors redescribed Barbie so that her utmost value depends on criteria for rareness that Mattel cannot produce or cash in on and from which only collectors benefit. Old rare still costs more than new rare. A 1994 price guide in *Barbie Bazaar* lists a "Sears Exclusive Red Fantastic (1967)" for $795–$895, MIB, and $495–$575, MNP (mint, no package), up to twenty times the cost of today's store specials and five times the price of Chrystal Rhapsody Barbie. Not a dime of this will go to Mattel, nor will any profits from the resale of the 1988 Holiday Barbie, which now goes for $335–$385, MIB.[25] In this case, Mattel has not quite succeeded, to recall Stuart Hall's formulation, "in *framing* all competing definitions *within their range*," although it has managed to reap some significant profits of its own.

Yet would one really want to call every Barbie collector who buys from a dealer or sells for personal profit either counterhegemonic or resistant, even though each has gotten Mattel where it really hurts—the corporate Barbie pocketbook? No. Surely, some dealers and collectors must be thinking, "Ha ha ha, Mattel isn't getting this Barbie money," and many collectors display their collections in much queerer scenarios than *Barbie Bazaar*'s "Meet a Collector" column would suggest. But many aren't out to wrest money from the corporate giant, to tarnish Barbie's image, or to resist attempts from above to cash in on and dilute their subculturally generated values. Unlike the feminists who look with scorn on Barbie's pink briefcase, the leather dykes who aren't thrilled to see their black leather jackets in Blooming-dales, and everybody who hates Vanilla Ice, the crowd at the 1993 Barbie convention, according to *Barbie Bazaar*'s reporter, responded to the Mattel-made souvenir doll with an ovation that "shook the rafters" and "gasps of delight."[26] (*Barbie Bazaar* is filled with these textual hints that Barbie gives you orgasms no matter where you stick her.) They could not all have been gasping because the "metallic silver dress" matched their little Barbie hand-cuffs. The reporter seemed genuinely honored by Mattel's contribution, and *Barbie Bazaar* in general, along with numerous other sources, indicates that many collectors love Barbie with little thought of subverting her or Mattel. A few, like the magazine's reviewer of *Mondo Barbie,* work actively to protect her; he made no mention of sex/gender queerings, save for an oblique com-ment about the "rigid gender roles adults enforce."[27] For those collectors who are nonsubversive and antisubversive in stance, buying from a dealer rather than from Mattel, or defining untouched as MIB rather than virginal, might well be described as accidentally subversive.

I make this point because it calls into question a frequently used mea-sure of resistance. When we want to ascertain whether hegemonies main-tain power, whether ideologies continue to hold sway, whether apparently counterhegemonic practices are indeed so, whether subversive strategies remain cutting edge or have been declawed and incorporated by dominant culture, or whether political strategies are working, the answer is often, and often rightly, I think, considered to reside in the answer to the question, Who really benefits? Who really benefits from the idea that democracy flour-ishes only under capitalism or that women need to be protected by men? Who really benefits from the "discovery" of rhythm-and-blues by the Rolling Stones, or graffiti artists by East Village gallery owners, or Native American spirituality by Anglo new agers? Who really benefits when teachers in visible heterosexual unions identify as queer? The teachers themselves, who get the rebel aura of queerdom and the ability to provide health insurance for their spouses at the same time? Queer activists, who get more allies? Institutions, who get to hire queer studies with a built-in "don't worry" response for nervous parents? (In this case, I think, all three.)

I'm a big fan of these questions myself, but it's important to recognize their limitations, which the matter of Barbie collector culture highlights. The traffic in old, rare Barbies certainly benefits the traffickers (and you can certainly use these diverted-from-Mattel gains to underwrite a lot of wheatpasting materials or to staff grassroots organizing projects). But collector theft from Mattel is often beside the point, just as Barbie's ideological influence is beside the point of much collector queering of Barbie's meaning and value. The terms *pristine, unused,* and *untouched* may have different or additional connotations when collectors utter them than they did when Mattel tried to forestall (adult concerns about) child sexual fantasy by making Ken lumpless. Yet the culture of collecting does as much as Mattel to keep "Barbie is so beautiful and the more you have the better" circulating in Barbie's world. This is not to argue that ideological subversion and nonsubversion, straightness and queerness, never stem from the same person—that a collector who buys a fabulous Barbie outfit is never wearing a dress just like hers on his own dates with human Ken or Kendra. Nor is it to imply that you can read someone's politics or even taste from the objects they like. (I'd hate to have my politics inferred via my favorite television show, "Silk Stalkings," and I'm still mystified by why I absolutely had to own a pincushion made to look like a wide-brimmed, flowered hat even though I don't like sewing, ruffles, hats, or flowered material.) It is simply to say that subcultural theft, like childhood deviations from Mattel's line, does not necessarily signal subversive intent or effect and that answers to the question, Who benefits? do not always provide a measure of resistance either. Theft doesn't always equal resistance. The next sections look at a different subversion/nonsubversion mix: the conflicting effects that often occur in the production and circulation of deliberate subversions.

You Can Take Barbie out of the Mainstream, But . . .

I begin with a 1993 "Hard Copy" report about a Barbie slasher who induced police in a small Ohio town to "call in the FBI" after they found twenty-four mutilated Barbies, slashed in the breasts and crotch, and to worry that "whoever is doing it could move on to real life Barbies": "The investigation began the day after New Year's. Workers in this Hills store found a horrible massacre with 12 Barbie doll victims. At first it looked like simple vandalism. But then there came reports from 3 other stores. . . . Twelve more tiny victims, all mutilated in the exact same fashion." The report then cuts to black-and-white footage from an early commercial with the commercial's female voice-over singing the "Beautiful Barbie" song. Simultaneously, a louder male "Hard Copy" voice-over repeats Mattel's story that Barbie was the first doll to "look like a young woman" and obligingly performs for Mattel the standard promotional move of implying that corporate profit matters less than corporate giving: "Since she was introduced 33 years ago, . . . millions have been sold and collected and treasured. Last year alone, Barbie sales were estimated at a billion dollars. But Barbie has been more than a gold mine. Since her introduction Barbie has grown with America. . . . She's been the ideal for young girls across America, . . . a fashion plate, a friend, a role model." The piece then cuts back to contemporary color footage and continues, "Some feel it's only a prank, while others feel it's their own daughters who have been violated. Police are truly worried they have a sick person on their hands. Meanwhile, the slashed dolls are under examination at the FBI's Cleveland office. 'I have an assistant' [comments Detective Timothy McClung of the Perkins Township Police] 'who has been doing a psychological profile on the type of person who would be involved in this type of activity.'"[28]

This is pure "Hard Copy," a lurid melodrama made more so by sleazy elision and name-dropping. You have to be paying attention to realize that we get no evidence of the FBI seriously pursuing the case; it's actually an assistant to a small-town police detective who's been working up a "psychological profile." Pure "Hard Copy," but not purely "Hard Copy." Most sickeningly not unique to "Hard Copy" is the reported-without-question logic used by police personnel. If they were prone to associating plastic women with human ones, then why did they dismiss twelve mutilated dolls as "merely vandalism"? Why did it take twenty-four dolls and the concept *repeat offender* to make the case worthy of investigation and prosecution? Given the number of violent acts against women that are habitually dismissed as routine, this high threshold of tolerance is all too familiar. So, too, is the implication that the massacre is particularly terrible because Barbie is particularly cherishable and that Barbie is particularly cherishable because of the features suggested through the sweet-old-fashioned-girl footage from prediversity times past. Just as violence against some people (white, rich, famous) makes news, generates police action, and raises public outcry more than does violence against others (nonwhite, poor), violence against Barbie (white, rich, famous) constitutes a bigger crime and causes supreme distress (some people feel that their daughters have been violated).

Yet were Perkins Township police personnel totally off base in reading the slashed Barbies as a sign of the slasher's desire to perpetrate violence against women? There's something a bit nauseating, at least to me, in the thought of someone slashing Barbie's breasts and crotch over and over, precisely because it is not ludicrous for "Hard Copy" to suggest that someone out there might be getting ready to slash up real women and girls. Real women and girls get slashed up all the time. Nor is it ludicrous to suggest that representations of violence against women come sometimes from the desire to act violently against women or that they make some contribution to the perpetuation of it. Is the frequent representation of women meaning yes when they say no really unrelated to the still common belief that women who say no really do mean yes?

I hesitate to make this point because I think that violence against representations of people certainly has its place—like in "Soft Targets"—and I don't want to validate the actions that such connections between representation and reality have often generated. The reasoning used by the Perkins Township Police to deem twenty-four mutilated Barbies an occasion for FBI intervention puts them in some bad company. It puts them in the company of the many censorship advocates who draw facile connections between what happens in representations and what happens to people. The notion that if you slash Barbie you might well slash women is not so different than the idea that if you see women "objectified" in pornography you will treat women as objects or that if you make pornography you disrespect women. It also puts them in the company of people who censure such sexual practices as S/M on the basis of similarly underfounded connections between one arena and another. There is lots of evidence that a person might find a conquest narrative appealing in fantasy, or in highly controlled sex games based on the consent of all involved, without having any desire to find herself there in "real life"; the move from fantasy to sex play, or from either of these to other arenas, is no more predestined than the move from mutilating Barbies to mutilating people.

I don't endorse censoring representations or punishing violence against representations. When we endorse censorship, we advocate a control mechanism that, recent history tells us, is most likely to be deployed by the overempowered against the underempowered: against Mapplethorpe or *On Our Backs* rather than the het stuff; against, not all *Playboy* readers, but just those who lack enough disposable cash for a subscription if it's banned from convenience stores. If representing violence against people were a crime, the people who tortured a George Bush puppet at the 1991 ACT UP demonstration in Kennebunkport, Maine, on Labor Day weekend—which had 500 law-enforcement people on hand, one for every three demonstrators— would probably have been arrested in a flash, while violent television episodes and movies appeared on screens across the country under no threat of legal action against their producers. We spend our time better, I believe, in working, not to censor representations of violence against women, but to transform the economic, social, and ideological conditions that perpetuate it and in making counterrepresentations and then working to get them into wide circulation: representations, for instance, that help people figure out what actually constitutes saying yes or saying no.

I'd never want to censor or prosecute Barbie slashings, but they sometimes disturb me. Even when slashers clearly signal that their intended target is the ideology that Barbie represents, the result is still a representation of violence against women that circulates in a culture in which too many people consider violence against women acceptable partly because of how frequently it circulates in representation. Judy Edelstein had a related reaction to the giant Barbie doll heads turned tissue dispensers in the massage parlor where she worked, drawing a smaller-scale connection between representation and her reality: "The doll heads were the owner's idea, but Pat and I hate them. Pat says that pulling out a kleenex is like pulling a little bit of brains out of the doll's head. . . . I think much the same about myself sometimes. I feel this job eating at me until I wonder if I'm all hollow inside." [29]

Of course, it's highly likely that neither the Ohio slashings or the tissue dispensers were made with a challenge to dominant ideologies in mind. Similar issues, however, come up with deliberate subversions. Kelly Harmon reacted to the play *Barbie the Fantasies,* which she reviewed for the *Windy City Times,* one of Chicago's gay papers, much as I did to the Barbie slasher. Harmon liked much of the play and appreciated its subversions because they both gave her pleasure and challenged "unconscious assumptions" left over from childhood: "All of my dolls were straight because I didn't know the concept of lesbianism when I was little. It never occurred to me that women might become romantically involved with each other"; "perhaps that's why I find it refreshing to see two finalists in the Miss Vagina Pageant [from another play considered in her review] fall madly in love with each other, and to see Barbie the Bulldyke wreaking havoc at a corporate board meeting." Yet one feature of the production diminished Harmon's pleasure: the video interviews with people about their Barbie views and memories. She was disturbed that "men and boys almost uniformly talk about disrobing and dismembering their sisters' dolls," especially when she found out from the director, Steven Milford, that the portion of Barbie abuse in the clips corresponded to the portion in the footage that he shot. Moving Barbie from dominant straight culture to queer subculture (Barbie the Bulldyke), and moving queerness from the margin to the center of power (Mattel's boardroom), could not provide an interpretive context in which violence against Barbie didn't look like an expression of "garden-variety" hostility toward women.

I find this a lot with Barbie subversions, that they perpetuate as much as subvert crummy ideologies. Put more simply, they do something that really bugs me. Dyke Barbies generally bug me for the same reason that I grew to hate my collection of dyke destiny narratives: as a group they perpetuate fem invisibility. When I first saw "Gals and Dolls," I wondered whether, given her pointy feet, Barbie was inevitably fem; I later discovered that subversive dyke Barbies are almost invariably butch, at least when they come solo. They all seem to have short hair, and I can't blame their producers: if I wanted to make a Dyke Barbie easily readable as such, I'd probably butch out her hair, too. I'd make myself invisible in other ways for the sake of increasing the audience who would "get it." I'd put Georgia O'Keeffe posters on the walls of her Dream House and the Indigo Girls in her tape box, even though I like neither, because they signal "dyke taste" more than does my own, which runs more to Prince. I could probably get myself in there somehow—perhaps some miniature books by Joan Nestle to signal "fem Jewish dyke." But I'm left with the choice of either relegating myself to a far more hidden code than butched-out hair or emphasizing less easy-access features—since more people listen to the Indigo Girls than read Joan Nestle. General readability is purchased at a cost. Many people, dyke and otherwise, can recognize Totally Out Barbie as signaling *dyke,* but most dykes simply don't look like her; using the most readable images perpetuates the invisibility of those who don't conform to them.

I had a related problem about perpetuating dubious stereotypes in the process of trying to subvert other ones with my own with my first Subversive Barbie: *Barbie's Dream Loft* (fig. 20). Nadine McGann designed the environment for me in 1989, with its then ultrachic artsy/postmodern furnishings. An additional doll, more accessories, and some reposings were later provided by other female accessories.[30] The current scenario, a top/bottom dyke sex scene staged by me, has a white, blond Barbie "bottom," dressed in a strapless number with thigh-high stockings, who is bent over a chair. Topping her is the Western Fun Nia I recieved for my birthday, the "American Indian" doll I misidentified and still think of as Chicana Barbie. Wearing only a vest and cowboy boots, she stands bent over blond Barbie with a hand on blond Bar-

20. *Barbie's Dream Loft.* Environment by Nadine McGann. Additional dolls, objects, and reposings provided by the following female accessories: Karen Corrie, Cheryl Daly, Susan Hill, Laurence Kucinkas, Erica Rand. Photo: Jay York. 1989–.

bie's butt, a hand moved now and then to suggest alternately spanking, anal penetration, and the more run-of-the-mill hand-to-vagina activity generically known as finger-fucking.

I love this subversive Barbie because it makes Mattel complicit in sexing up and queering out the scene. The risqué lingerie, of a type quite popular these days among all those dykes who cruise (at) the racks of Victoria's Secret, is official Barbie lingerie. Also from Mattel are Chicana Barbie's quintessential queer accessories, the vest and boots—although, I admit, this costume had something of a different flavor before I discarded the perky cowgirl dress that was part of the original outfit. I love this piece, too, for its parody of "we are the world" diversity scenarios, for its send-up, complete with "I shop therefore I am" Barbara Kruger postcard, of postmodern radical chic and for its charming figuration of bad-girl sex.

But I couldn't turn it into something I could love without reservation. Among other problems, I struggled with how to assign roles to my two Barbies. Putting Chicana Barbie on top reinforces racial stereotypes of the dark brute overpowering the less animalistic white girl; the hair contrast alone places my *Dream Loft* firmly within the hetero-generated tradition of lesbian representation, which often features an aggressive, dark-haired vixen seducing a blond innocent. Putting blond Barbie on top would have subverted these stereotypes but performed white supremacy. In terms of race, there was no way out of dominant discourse.

I turned blond Barbie over because it seemed like the lesser of two evils. I also rationalized, according to currently popular lesbian ideology, that, since power play "in bed" needn't reflect or determine power relations "out of bed," I was not destining Bottom Barbie to political "bottomness." Besides, Top Barbie was probably about to be flipped anyway—that is, blond Barbie and Chicana Barbie would soon be trading places. In other words, I constructed a discursive frame to redeem the Barbie bottom. Through this frame, Bottom Barbie could be construed to fit the requirements stipulated by the writer of a personals ad I recently read who was looking for someone "fem but functional." What more could you want to find or to be?

Well, of course, you could want a lot. Most of all, I think, you could want to live in a world without racist dark-brute stereotypes to risk reproducing, where the sex acts depicted here do not connote sick, disgusting, immoral, and perverse to the many people who think lesbians and perversity are bad, and where putting Chicana Barbie on top does not represent a subversion of predominant distributions of power. You could also want to find the ability to inscribe your carefully crafted discursive frame in the minds of every potential viewer of your piece. I doubt that I could circulate the *Dream Loft* without doing more for many viewers than reinforcing homophobic and racist stereotypes, although part of the problem here lies in production rather than context of circulation. As Charles Nero suggested, for instance, I could have turned it into two photographs, one with Chicana Barbie on top, one with Anglo Barbie on top. I'd still have a product that repeats racist configurations, but I'd also be suggesting a more progressive sharing or alternating of power. (I don't mean to imply here that tops or bottoms in sex are less progressive than switchers, just that the extrasexual resonances would be better.) I could also have done more with the *Dream Loft* to signal that viewers ought to be revaluing racism, lesbians, or perversity; it's not clear where the author stands.

In other words, few of the limits to Barbie subversion come from the artifact itself. You can make combat boots to camouflage her pointy feet and padded clothes to pull her out of the running for queen of the eating-disorder prom. You can make your own position clear in relation to the stereotypes that you manipulate. It's quite clear where Quick-To-See Smith stands from her explicit naming of the bad guys involved in "Paper Dolls for a Postcolumbian World"; we don't wonder if she wants Native Americans to get more smallpox-infected blankets. I could have used her strategy with my *Dream Loft* or my hypothetical Dyke Barbie—by adding, for instance, a poster, sticker, or button saying "Jewish Dyke with Long Hair Who Hates the Indigo Girls: Deal with It."

Yet even more explicit messages come with no guarantee that they will stick in circulation. The viewer's contribution to the production of meaning precludes certainty of message. And, since, as I have argued, it is impossible fully to predict viewer interpretation, producers cannot hope to anticipate every response that they would want to forestall or every message that they need to be explicit about. With my *Dream Loft,* for instance, there was one issue I never thought about until my lecture at Wayne State, when Lisa Roberts, a student there, asked me if I thought it might be a bit suspect to use an artifact I had made myself as the vehicle for my own conclusions about Barbie subversion in general; listeners might conclude that I had crafted the object to suit my conclusion.[31] This possibility had never occurred to me, partly because the sequence of mental events was different: first I made the *Dream Loft,* then I worried about it, then I wrote about it. But now it's rather hard to believe that, for all my agonizing over how people would interpret my piece, I never anticipated this problem.

I've been reminded over and over during the past few years, beginning with my first attempt to circulate a Subversive Barbie, that neither putting explicit meanings in objects nor circulating objects with a carefully crafted discursive frame gives you total control over your audience. As I explained in the introduction, I asked around for advice about whether to teach "Gals and Dolls." After getting some opinions and thinking through the risks to me and dyke students of teaching Barbie porn, I decided on a compromise designed to introduce the material while protecting myself somewhat and semiforestalling lesbian discomfort: I presented the discursive frame instead of the pictures. With a factual introduction about having received the photographs from a friend in San Francisco who knew I was interested in pop culture— thus distancing myself a bit from the images—I described both the images and my struggle over whether to show them, using the incident to introduce a paper topic on how images' meanings change in circulation. Initially, my strategy seemed to work. I left class with the little thrill that calculated risk, the illusion of discursive control, and a good class discussion can bring. This euphoria lasted until the next class, when a student asked me to clarify: "I don't understand the point of that story. What is it that you like to do with

Barbie dolls?" Clearly, when using a Barbie dildo to stick it to Mattel, I could not guarantee that I would not actually be sticking it to myself.

Similar problems recurred frequently, especially with "Gals and Dolls." Two years later, I sent an essay, with these photos included, to our secretarial department for copying. I got it back with only the text copied because the secretary found the pictures disturbing. I discovered during the subsequent havoc that I could have been prosecuted for sexual harassment, despite my lack of intention to harass anyone, because our sexual harassment rules, like most around today, define effect alone as sufficient cause for prosecution—a situation, of which I discuss the legal and political ramifications elsewhere, that should give anyone pause who teaches sexually explicit material.[32] Another time, I was on a panel during which, unbeknownst to me, two other female professors on the panel turned ashen when I mentioned these images, creating, apparently, the most riveting spectacle of the evening. There were other instances in which, according to reports from friends, I circulated in representational afterlife at places I'd given lectures in ways different from what I would have desired: "I've heard of her. Isn't she the person who uses Barbie as a dildo?"

These incidents can hardly be used to generalize about circulating all Barbie subversions, although it's worth noting that some of these unwanted interpretations reproduce an effect generated by Mattel. Mattel made Barbie—the famous teenage fashion model who can also be you or your friend—to move easily between representation and reality, fiction and autobiography. As adult memories testify, she moved this way for many consumers. She moved this way under my authorship, too, particularly in the cases where people remembered Barbie as my sex toy rather than as a sex toy used by a woman in a picture or, more precisely, as a doll being represented as a sex toy in a picture—after all, it's certainly possible that the producers of "Gals and Dolls" took off Barbie's easily detachable legs and merely posed her as if she were being inserted, which would have spared the insertee the discomfort of Barbie's pointy feet or the work of taping the legs together.

Still, these reactions probably have more to do with the shockingness of bad-girl sex—or just sexual explicitness at all—getting play in an academic setting than with anything emanating from Barbie or Mattel, except that her preciousness and Mattel-made good-girl rep makes the already scandalous dildo even more scandalous in its hefty eleven-and-a-half-inch model. I know all too well that, when the subject is sex, people often think you do what you write, lecture, or teach about or present in other ways. So do lots of other people—hence all those interviews with actors about whether they worry that playing a gay character will make people think they're gay. Yet these reactions also point to the same issues raised by anti-Barbie violence. Interpretations of Barbie subversions depend partly on what's in the mainstream. "Gals and Dolls" would not have a shock value that overshadows everything and everyone around it if talking about sex in academic settings were a daily occurrence and if using sex toys were not considered outside, as Gayle Rubin puts it, the "charmed circle" of acceptable sexual practices.[33] If mainstream advice about preventing HIV infection emphasized sexual practices that involve absolutely no more exchange of fluids than the much promoted abstinence, dildos simply would not be scandalous. In a better world, they'd be in high school curricula and public service announcements.

Context, then, both lends nonsubversive meanings to subversion-directed objects and limits what producers of objects and discursive frames can expect to have stick in circulation. The next section considers some more contextual limits.

Too White, Too Easy, Too Center Stage, Too All about Barbie

Why Hemphill's poem "Soft Targets" belongs in this book is obvious; it's a great Barbie subversion. What isn't so obvious is whether there is any way to put it here without abetting the racism that the poem condemns. I stated earlier that understanding the poem depends on a general familiarity with Barbie. Yet understanding it in the richness of its referents requires knowing more than Barbie. Charles Nero pointed out to me that Hemphill's poem takes up a common theme in African American literature and criticism: the effect on African Americans of living in a culture that does not reflect their beauty back to them. He referred me to several other examples, including the poem "No Images," written by Waring Cuney in 1926, about a woman whose does know the beauty of her brown body:

> If she could dance
> Naked,
> Under palm trees
> And see her image in the river
> She would know.
>
> But there are no palm trees
> On the street
> And dish water gives back no images.[34]

To categorize or value Hemphill's poem as a Barbie subversion is to subordinate the poem's African American specificities, as Mattel does with its
young black man into rock and roll, and to make multicultural respect and
intercommunication look as falsely easy as Mattel makes it look. White people
cannot fully "get" this poem merely by knowing about Barbie; we need to
do the work of studying African American culture. As Gloria Anzaldúa and
Cherríe Moraga write in *This Bridge Called My Back: Writings By Radical
Women of Color,* it is a common white liberal presumption that people of color
should be doing all the cultural work in the "multicultural and multiethnic environment" that Barbie surveys with pleasure after a trip to the museum: that
people of color need both to study white cultural heritage in schools (which
don't put theirs in the lesson plan) and to explain their ethnically specific culture to white people; white people don't have to do anything but hire speakers
of color now and then to come and tell us about it.[35] To imply that Hemphill is
particularly important for his ability to understand white-generated cultural
products is to validate these presumptions.

It is also to disrespect and "disappear" Hemphill himself, whose cultural
production is not primarily "about" Barbie and is, in my opinion, far more
compelling than that of Mattel. Consider his poem "Homocide (for Ronald
Gibson)":

Grief is not apparel.
Not like a dress, a wig
or my sister's high-heeled shoes.
It is darker than the man I love
who in my dark fantasies comes for me
in a silver, six-cylinder chariot.
I walk the waterfront/curbsides
in my sister's high-heeled shoes.
Dreaming of him, his name
still unknown to my tongue.
While I wait
for my prince to come
from every other man
I demand pay for my kisses.
I buy paint for my lips.
Stockings for my legs.
My own high-heeled slippers
and dresses that become me.
When he comes,

I know I must be beautiful.
I will know how to love his body.
Standing out here
on the waterfront/curbsides
I have learned to please
a man.
He will bring me flowers.
He will bring me silk
and jewels, I know.
While I wait,
I'm the only man who loves me.
They call me "Star"
because I listen
to their dreams and wishes.
But grief is darker.
It is a wig
that does not rest gently
on my head.[36]

I can justify including this poem in its entirety for the same reason I in-cluded "Soft Targets": it certainly bears on the topic of Barbie. Hemphill's portrayal of a gay drag queen, who three times invokes Barbie's most notori-ous accessory, high-heeled shoes, offers a perspective on the meaning and use of women's clothes and accessories without which any account of Barbie is misleadingly straight. "Homocide" also evokes the gaps, insufficiencies, and bad fits that run throughout consumer accounts of Barbie—the desires and griefs and needs that cannot be managed or described through formfit-ting outfits, mental or physical, through "dresses that become me." But I really included "Homocide" because I don't want readers to leave this book thinking that Hemphill's import lies primarily in his ability to explicate Barbie or Barbie consumers. I want readers to think, "I want to read *Ceremonies* cover to cover because of the immense pleasures of reading that it will pro-vide me as well as insights about many people and issues that deserve my respect, attention, thought, and activism much more than does Barbie." So I included the poem that induced me to read *Ceremonies* and that concerns a subject central to Hemphill's identity, activism, and writing: black gay men.

Hemphill is only one Barbie subvertor whose cultural and political work get dubiously distorted when their Barbie subversions are given center stage and categorized as such. *Shocking Pink,* the "radical magazine done by young women for young women," has a nice slam on Mattel's search for a Barbie model and the bogusness of its claim that Barbie is a woman of the nineties. But Barbie bashing is the least of what this issue does. It also contains contact information for numerous lesbian, youth, and activist groups and features on the National Union of Eritrean Women, the safe and erotic use of dental dams, racism in fashion, and the torture of Palestinians in Kuwait in the so-called aftermath of the Gulf War.[37] Quick-To-See Smith, whose work is also misrepresented by a solo focus on her Barbie subversion, shows what's missing in Mattel's diversity rap through "Paper Dolls for a Post Columbian World." But its political project is undermined by categorizing it so as to suggest that the action it should generate is more thinking about Barbie. "Paper Dolls" demands a move, not from one Barbie to another, but from Barbie outward to activism on other many fronts and against many other targets, both artifactual and human. So, too, with *AIDS Barbie.*

To summarize, categorizing Barbie subversions as such performs a violence in the act of recontextualization that is not unlike the violence enacted by the "translation" of consumer accounts into academic vernacular: the context, the cultural agent (as consumer or producer), and sometimes the product get erased, disrespected, and distorted. In the case of subculturally generated Barbie subversions, something else happens, too: white, straight, blond Barbie gets returned to the center stage that Mattel has put her on. I do not raise this issue to indulge in self-flagellation, white guilt, or some virtuoso rhetoric designed to make my recognition of a problem absolve me from culpability in perpetuating it. I'd be perpetuating it more by excluding these subversions, which show well why Barbie in general and white Barbie in particular do not deserve top billing. Besides, I'd white out and straighten up Barbie subversion. My goal might be different than changing Barbie's eyes to blue so that she won't look "too foreign," but the effect is the same. And I'd give up the chance to back up with evidence the following hot tip: if you find a great Barbie subversion, check out its source because it's probably coming from a producer and subcultural context that are well worth your attention.

My point isn't that I shouldn't have put them here but that, owing to the broader context in which subversive Barbies circulate, the very same things that make Barbie so subvertor friendly—easy access and already present interest—often work against subversive effect. Some of this context can be blamed on Mattel. Circulating *Shocking Pink* and "Soft Targets" puts plastic, white Barbie on center stage partly because it is white, blond Barbie that they subvert, which they do, in turn, partly because Mattel privileges this Barbie among all others. *Shocking Pink* might not be warning readers to avoid being tempted by "the evil Mattel" into "growing your hair long [and] bleaching it a straw colour" had Mattel not advertised for a blond woman to represent Barbie. Hemphill might have written his poem differently were Mattel making more than a superficial effort to tell black girls that they are beautiful.

Yet the burden of blame can hardly be dumped entirely on Mattel's shoulders. It belongs on the culture of cultural consumption, white supremacy, and antiqueerness that gives Barbie more currency and value than the other cultural referents in Barbie subversions—a culture that Mattel benefits from and perpetuates but did not, in fact, create. *Ceremonies* costs about $10.00, slightly less than Totally Hair Barbie, but we can't say that the millions of people who bought Barbie in 1992 would have spent the money on *Ceremonies* if Barbie weren't there. It's not wholly Mattel's fault that people are more likely to read Sandra Cisneros's "Barbie-Q" in *Mondo Barbie,* sold in many bookstores, than in *Woman Hollering Creek,* the Cisneros anthology, sold in fewer bookstores, from which *Mondo Barbie* reproduced it—that "the vibrant and varied life on both sides of the Mexican border" attracts fewer sellers and buyers than "all that misplaced Barbie angst of our youth," to quote the two books' cover blurbs.[38]

Barbie is a great tool for social criticism and subversion because, as a widely debated cultural icon, she provides an easy-access hook into issues besides Barbie. But Barbie threatens to overshadow those other issues, to remain center stage, and to obscure the work that communication and activism entail precisely because of what makes her easy access: she starts out with too much of the spotlight. This context also puts some limits on what Barbie subvertors can make for wide circulation. How many people, for instance, would get the AZT reference in *AIDS Barbie?* On one level, this doesn't matter. *Diseased Pariah News* readers are likely to get it, and one might well argue that the piece is all the better for it; there's much to be said for the pleasures provided by subcultural coding that makes the knowledge of the marginalized central for a change. Besides, it's hardly the job of the dominated to make themselves or their products an easy read for the dominating; the work of communication needs to go both ways. It's the context, not the artifact, that's all the worse because not enough people can connect Burroughs Wellcome to AZT or have the knowledge to understand "all rights reserved."

These limits of production matter only when the subvertor has a larger audience in mind than those people who will understand the crucial referents. One such subvertor is Barbara Sjogren, who made *Vedda's Return* (1994), a found-objects construction in a roomlike box. On one side, Barbie stands naked, pressed up against and facing the wall, with a Walkman speaker wire wrapped around her body. Ken lies splayed, tied by the strap of a zebra-skin purse. Standing at the front as the "guardian of the closet" is a wood Sri Lankan sculpture of a (male) Vedda, draped in a mink stole or cape. Sjogren's acquisition of the Vedda, a tourist curio representing the aboriginal inhabitants of Sri Lanka, testifies to the complexity of cultural interchange. It is one of two she and her husband received during two one-year sojourns in Sri Lanka as gifts from Sri Lankans who presumed that white visitors would love them. She speculates that neither gift giver, one their "driver," the other an academic colleague, owned one himself. The Sri Lankan homes she visited rarely did; they more often had a miniature *Venus de Milo,* also made in Sri Lanka.

Sjogren's intention in the piece is to address this complexity of cultural interchange and to expose the injustices of which the objects, in circulation, are both symptom and symbol. To oversimplify, Barbie and Ken are supposed to represent consumerism, sexism, and that pornography that circulates for "greed" rather than "communication." The Vedda critiques at once consumerism (since it represents a pre-Barbie, preconsumerist society), primitivism (since it represents early times by embodying the stereotype of the dark native), and the disappearance of a preconsumerist society (since it is actually an object for purchase that, like Barbie and the piece's big toy gun, cashes in on dubious values). The mink stole and zebra-skin purse reference exploitation and extinction—so, too, does the Vedda since the survival of the human Vedda into the twentieth century remains a matter of scholarly debate. The "closet" door, made from a beach-shack door, refers to homelessness and through it to uprootedness and displacement, topics with personal resonance for Sjogren. She's a white woman born in Tanzania to U.S. medical missionaries who moved to Nebraska in 1953 when she was four and, after several other stops, including Chicago, wound up in Maine. Her sojourns in Sri Lanka magnified divergent facets of her relation to the concept *home:* she felt at home there because the climate resembled that of her birthplace, but never at home because her skin color made her an exotic object of scrutiny although it also conferred privileges such as facility getting through roadblocks.[39]

Sjogren's personal history is like Karina's alien-Barbie-and-the-horsey-set narrative in that it is both unique to her and typical in its complications. While her geographic history may be idiosyncratic in detail and more complicated than average, it can stand for the idiosyncrasy and complexity of each person's travels, far ranging or not. It suggests how much more complicated is individual identity than is implied either by Barbie's identity-through-accessory or by categorization according to class, race, nationality, and gender—all these being perceived from particular experiences and creating particular mental collections of referents. Both Sjogren and I are white middle-class women living mostly in the United States during the 1970s and 1980s, but our pool of referents is quite different. When we were discussing potential misreadings of her piece, I told her that the dark brown Vedda in fur reminded me of the stereotypical black pimp portrayed in blaxploitation films of the 1970s; perhaps people would think that he, not consumerism, had tied up Barbie and Ken and that he was ready to have his way with them. She'd never heard of such films. We also had different ideas about whether "tied up" would signal "bad porn" to most people and about what, if anything, constituted "bad porn," owing to different experiences with porn material and the porn debates and, more simply, to different tastes.

These complications also suggest that the question, How far can a subversion circulate as readable? must be approached like the question of whether a subversion can be classified as resistance. There is no object that can circulate to everyone with meaning intact, just as none will incite a revolution for social justice. Both matters need to be approached, and objects need to made, with limited and audience-specific expectations. Nonetheless, it is important to recognize that the possibilities for inscribing subversive readings are also limited by unfortunate features in the context in which they circulate and that these features often undermine subversive intent. Barbie subversions exemplify this problem: since they circulate in a culture where knowledge about Barbie is common currency and knowledge about Veddas, Burroughs Wellcome, and African American literary history isn't, subvertors who want to take their message on the road through Barbie risk having Barbie, as it were, take over the steering wheel.

Sjogren also typifies many adults in that she formed her adult stance toward Barbie somewhat independently of her own childhood use. Shogren doesn't remember being either negatively or passively transformed by Barbie. To the contrary, Barbie catalyzed her creativity: in the early 1960s, at the age of eleven or twelve, she designed clothes for Barbie, packaging them with her own logo and selling them for a dollar apiece. But she refused to let her daughter have a Barbie—because, she told her, Barbie promotes sexism and consumerism. She also has confidence that viewers of *Vedda's Return* will recognize these features. The next section considers disparities between common knowledge about Barbie's subvertability and perceptions of fixed meaning encoded in both Barbie subversions and reactions to them.

Mattel Rules, or the Etiquette of Originality

The promotion by "Hard Copy" of the idea that Barbie bashing is harmful to the public is less purely "Hard Copy" in its extremist flourish than one might think. Joanne Oppenheim, for instance, president of the Oppenheim Toy Portfolio, "a quarterly publication that reviews toys, books and videos for children and is opposed to war products," reacted far from mildly when the BLO switched Barbie and G.I. Joe's voice boxes, although one might expect otherwise given her opposition to war toys: "I've got a very strong negative feeling about terrorist acts against children, no matter how noble the motives. . . . It's a cheap shot, and it's unfair to the kids."[40] Terrorism? It's hard to imagine children being traumatized by getting the altered dolls. To my knowledge no one was. One boy, it seems, simply changed his G.I. Joe narrative to accommodate the new voice. He pretended that G.I. Joe was on a spy mission that required a disguise, a testimony at once to the unfortunate fixity of gender stereotypes, since talking like a girl could only be a costume donned only in dire situations, and to the unreasonableness of many claims about what children cannot handle.

Much more common in Barbie circulation than associating Barbie bashers with rapists and terrorists are the other favors performed by "Hard Copy" for Mattel. As I argued earlier, the obliging perpetuation of Barbie myths and the avowal of Barbie's service to girlhood are widespread. The story of Ruth Handler, mom, and Mattel's rap about how Barbie embodies how all we girls can do anything would be nowhere without the help of uninvestigative reporters and cheerleaders like Phil. But Mattel rules also in Barbie subversions, in accounts of them, and in Barbie criticisms, which, ironically, usually imply that Mattel rules as a meaning maker. Despite the widespread common knowledge that many children do things with Barbie that Mattel would not reenact in a commercial and thus contribute greatly to the production of Barbie's meaning, most Barbie underminings suggest to the contrary that Barbie has a relatively fixed meaning created by Mattel alone.

A rare exception here are the exposés on Earring Magic Ken with his gaywear and cock ring, which virtually always present Ken's queerness as a collective accident by all involved (although, as I suggested previously, this is hard to imagine). Mattel looks clueless for having produced it and is put in the position of having cluelessness as its only "defense." Mattel either must confess to having intentionally made a gay Ken who uses sex toys or protest that the gay connotations were totally unintentional. Mattel also looks a bit out of (spin) control in every accusation that Barbie remains a bad role model despite the company's attempt to redeem her with careers and color variety. These accusations imply that Mattel either can't redeem Barbie or can't effectively pretend to have done so.

Yet what underlies virtually all these accusations, and is often the reason for uttering them, is the assumption that Mattel rules its consumers (except for the utterers, who can see through them)—that Mattel has created a product with a relatively fixed meaning that circulates with meaning intact. To say that Mattel wants Barbie to mean x but that she really means y, or that Mattel knows that Barbie means y but unsuccessfully tries to make Barbie appear to mean x, is still to imply that Barbie means and conveys y. This assumption of fixed meaning also underlies most Barbie trashings and subversions. When they use Barbie for social criticism, their ability to do so depends on it, and the criticisms often imply it. "Barbie never told Black girls / they are beautiful" implies that Barbie "tells" black girls something contained in Barbie. When they are meant to be funny, their humor usually depends on it: Dyke Barbie is funny because Mattel made Barbie heterosexual.

And people often assess the stability in circulation of Mattel-generated meanings independently of evidence of its instability. Bee Bell sent Barbie to hell twenty years ago and created Passing Butch Glenn in 1993. Yet for her this has nothing to do with Barbie's function as a symbol. As she told me, everyone knows what you mean when you call someone a Barbie doll: she's a blond bimbo. You don't mean that she is a person who might be on the way to hell or a dyke bar. Bell, of course, is right. Barbie's eminent subvertability *is* largely irrelevant to her ability to function as a commonly understood symbol. This is a significant way that childhood interpretation of Barbie does not generate or determine adult interpretation and a characteristic that is not unique to the consumption of Barbie. Even if we associate the U.S. flag with imperialism rather than freedom, we know that subversions of the flag are subverting its intended meaning, not what it means to us. But Barbie subversions, trashings, and exposés often carry much more of an implication that the meaning of the object in question is otherwise stable in circulation. This is due to another feature of the culture of Barbie subversion that makes the "Hard Copy" coverage of the Barbie slasher more typical than idiosyncratic: the etiquette of originality.

In "The Size 10 Dress," readers learn the etiquette of originality in the culture of mass production. They learn to respect each other's "natural" desire to look unique, to avoid copying someone else's look, and to look and describe with an eye to originality—so that two girls who have accessorized the same dress differently look "as different as night and day."[41] This is, of course, a discourse and habit of seeing that Mattel encourages, so that two Barbies in slightly different outfits look different enough to make both worthy of purchase. It permeates the culture of Barbie subversion as well. Here, again, "Hard Copy" is typical at its apparently most "Hard Copy"–esque. Its report implies that it has uncovered a never-before-heard-of phenomenon produced by a uniquely sick mind. It offers no precedents for Barbie slashing or tampering. It doesn't mention the guy from Lexington, Massachusetts, who put pornographic pictures and literature in boxes containing Barbie, Midge, and G.I. Joe in 1991 or the store clerk in Tampa who redressed Ken in Barbie's clothes and returned him to the toy-store shelves in 1990, to be dubbed "Kinky Ken" by the press.[42] The *New York Times* article on the BLO doesn't mention these incidents either, even though one would expect a newspaper that prides itself on its serious, nonscandalous, and in-depth reporting to discuss precedents in an article deemed to merit a third of a page. They wouldn't have been hard to find; Kinky Ken made headlines around the country.

You'd think from surveying either of these reports, and almost all the reports they don't reference, that Barbie tampering was a once-in-a-doll's-lifetime occurrence. Through tone and omission, each incident is presented as unique. Each circulates as national news, even though examples appear relatively often in the media, and even though it has also made the news relatively frequently that unorthodox Barbie play, including lots of mutilation, happens in homes "across America." The same is true for Subversive Barbies circulated less publicly. They often appear to the people who see them as highly unique when, in fact, they aren't.

This happens in academe, too. Originality has become a highly suspect concept in recent years, deemed by many, as Rosalind Krauss well terms it, a largely fraudulent "modernist myth" that is perpetuated through a repression of repetition much like Mattel's.[43] Just as Mattel asks us to think of Moonlight Magic Barbie as a Toys R Us exclusive—rather than as one of many Barbies in one of many mostly black evening gowns with one type of gold lamé accent among many (here it's the gold lamé overskirt as opposed to the gold lamé bolero jacket on the J.C. Penney Golden Winter exclusive)—we are asked by many texts to think of artworks and artists as one of a kind also. Each of Cezanne's paintings of Mont St. Victoire is described as an "original" although he painted over a hundred and was the first neither to paint this landscape nor to paint landscapes with his characteristic disregard for the illusion of three-dimensionality. Picasso's disrespect for the integrity of the female form in *Les Desmoiselles d'Avignon* is often described as a mark of his uniqueness, originality, and genius, although performing primitivizing pictorial violence on prostitutes is thoroughly of his time in subject and attitude.[44]

Many critics have pointed out that originality is often overattributed to artists and objects. Many, too, have pointed to the hegemonic horrors that the enshrinement of originality serves. One among many is that, when artists deemed great are described as great because original, the conditions of their success are mystified. Professional success appears to be in no way an effect of access to training, commissions, reviewers, etc. or of a class status, gender, or skin color that facilitated this access; it seems instead to be the just reward bestowed on a genius whose original ideas issued forth from within.[45]

This is by now old critical news. Although originality has proved to be a relatively resilient concept, almost all the numerous texts and courses that addresses gender, class, race, and sexual orientation presume that, far from being originals generated from nothing in an original artist's mind, many features of artworks represent ideas, images, and social formations that have originated elsewhere. I've been surprised, then, by how many colleagues viewed my own Barbie work with a more Mattelesque eye for originality. The same people who would never have thought of suggesting that I should stop writing on Denis Diderot, an earlier topic, because there already exist a journal, countless articles, and many books devoted entirely to Diderot studies would approach me quite differently about Barbie: "I don't know how to tell you this, but I heard of someone else writing on Barbie." When I replied, "How many people write on Picasso?" they were often pretty surprised at themselves for not thinking of my object-of-study repetition in this context. As with other Subversive Barbies, my textual subversion circulated as if Mattel had decreed that Barbie was never allowed to come without the aura of originality of one of her accessories—without that "never before seen just like this" flair.

As if, but, of course, not because. The etiquette of originality, like the sister-from-another-planet narrative, has sources and causes besides Mattel. It preceded Mattel and exists apart from it. Every fashion trend that signals uniqueness or "being different," from wearing black or Doc Martens to shaving one's head, requires the etiquette of originality to be legible. Even when applied to Barbie subversions, the etiquette of originality may serve a function little related to Mattel. As Marjorie Garber points out, the fascination with cross-dressed Ken is part of a general fascination with, and "cultural anxiety" about, cross-dressing and gender ambiguity. From this angle, repressing the nonuniqueness of "Kinky Ken" can be seen as a repression of the widespread nature of genderfuck more than of Mattel subversions.[46]

There is also some justification in seeing Barbie scholarship and subversions as somewhat rare. More people do write about Diderot than about Barbie, which only recently became an object of major scholarly interest, and writing about pop culture still, unfortunately, is frequently judged somewhat renegade; writing about Barbie is news the way writing about Madonna was news in the late 1980s. And Barbie subversions are older news to me than to many. I don't just come across Barbie news; it gets brought to me and by people who don't transmit their queer Barbie sightings to everyone they know. So I've seen more dyked-out Barbies in little biker jackets than most; others, not surprisingly, are more surprised and delighted. They will be less surprised and delighted, I presume, as the trend continues to pick up. Yet now, as earlier, the attribution of originality is in excess of what available information justifies. Subversive Barbies, and narratives of weird childhood Barbie games, are popping up all over the place. But the etiquette of originality has diminished little; it has only become increasingly remarkable. And, as with the sister-from-another-planet narratives, it is no surprise that Barbie finds herself enshrined by it even if Barbie is not its only subject or sole cause since the convention echoes what it subverts.

It also has the effect of reenshrining and stabilizing what it subverts. One of the more ironic effects of the transfer of the discourse of one-of-a-kinds from Mattel to Mattel subversions is that Barbie goes straight every time she goes queer: the purported uniqueness and scandalousness of each Biker Dyke Barbie make the object subverted seem otherwise far more stable in meaning. Or at least she shuts the closet door on all her queer sisters, who don't seem to exist when she's around. The world of Barbie looks like the classic image of the small town described by its inhabitants as straight except for the spinster "sisters" who live down the lane. If each Biker Dyke Barbie circulated as one in the Lesbo Barbie Line, the world of Barbie would look much more like what that small town would look like if every queer in it came out: a place where queerness exists not only in the house down the lane but in many houses, town squares, government offices, and schools. Instead, each Biker Dyke Barbie gets a one-of-a-kind treatment that represses the existence of others before and beside it. In this sense, circulation undoes the message of production. The production of so much in the Subversive Barbie line suggests that Barbie is highly stealable from Mattel. The circulation of individual subversions as scandalous one-of-a-kinds suggests, to the contrary, that Mattel rules, just as the ring of scandal and shock value in human outings suggests often that heterosexuality is the rule.

Another standard feature of many Barbie (and human) outings seems to contradict the down-the-lane message: the aura of "the real truth." Mattel doesn't want you to know this, but Barbie's really a dyke and/or makes your daughter do dyke things. But this convention has its own problems, aside from the obvious one of implying that some knowledge totally transcends subjectivity. It minimizes the extent to which Mattel contributes to the perpetuation of compulsory heterosexuality. The real truth isn't actually that Barbie primarily is or makes you queer. It also gives queerness a fixed bedrock location that it shouldn't have. As I argued in chapter 2, heterosexuality is not bedrock either: many childhood Barbie narratives do suggest that, at her most seemingly straight, Barbie is really only "straight acting." Others, however, suggest that Barbie is, on occasion, queer acting; it's the queer content that unravels on scrutiny. We do an injustice to the mobility and scope of queerness by locating it in only one place: underneath. It is also on top, around, and in between.

The contradiction in the mass production of Barbie outings—the problem, otherwise put, of how Barbie (unlike, say, k. d. lang) can get outed 20 million times without ever being considered "out"—foregrounds some problematic features of outings in general. It also raises a crucial issue concerning the disparity between academically generated knowledge and the word on the street as well as the crucial question, What should we do about it? A logical answer seems to be, Spread the news. In the case of Barbie, shake up Mattel's rule by demystifying its hold on consumers and pointing out the frequency of subversion. But I'm not sure that this would work. Relevant information already circulates widely. The *New York Times* writer on the BLO could have found "Kinky Ken" without much trouble (like the "Ruth Handler, mom" writers could have found her corporate title), and many people see their first Biker Dyke Barbie with the knowledge that children, perhaps even themselves, have done nonmainstream things with Barbie. But people frequently don't bring this information to bear on the adult products. They may be moved to make a connection between Dyke Barbie and their own childhood—"if you think this is weird, wait til you hear what I did with Barbie." Yet thinking that this connection signifies Barbie's general mutability, or queer Barbie's nonscandalousness, is much rarer, partly because, as I argued in chapter 2, people often view their own history with an eye toward originality, too: my Barbie story shows what is special about me, how different I was from the other girls, etc.

But the bigger question than whether we can spread the word about Barbie concerns what would be gained by undertaking such a project and whether spreading the word should necessarily be the first or primary goal in cases where the insights produced by academic work—such as collecting more Barbie anecdotes and subversions than the average person will ever see—contradict and, perhaps, seem more liberating than common knowledge. As critics and activists have been increasingly arguing lately, we cannot presume that liberatory readings serve liberatory causes. As Janet Halley points out, for instance, textual criticism has advanced the dismantling of a "hetero/homo hierarchy" by showing up these identity constructions to be "incoherent and multiple"; since heterosexuality and homosexuality are neither clearly bound nor mutually exclusive, the hierarchy cannot stand either. Yet definitional incoherence has actually worked in the legal arena to enforce, not dismantle, hierarchy. The definitions used to "form and police the class of heterosexuals," which, in turn, are used to police the people excluded from this category, have precisely the incoherence that seems liberating to recognize in other contexts. (For instance, judges in *Bowers v. Hardwick* embraced the definition of *felonious sodomy* as "the behavior that defines the class of homosexuals" even though, in states where sodomy is illegal regardless of participants' genders, this means that all heterosexuals could be potentially classed as homosexuals.) We can't, then, merely expose the fiction of rigid categorization; we need to analyze "the ways in which concrete exertions of power intervene to determine whether consolidations or dispersals of identity will, in a particular time or place, be liberating or oppressive." [47]

Cindy Patton makes a similar point about what you can neither learn nor do without studying identity definition in use:

> Despite the excellent accounts of differences within "gay identity," until we stop insisting that identity per se is essentialist, the uses "ordinary gay people" make of these (and other—white, female, Southern) identities will remain untheorized, unknown, unavailable to thoughtful strategies of intervention. . . . Quotidian uses of identities must be understood in the context of a struggle to control the uses of identity construction. The plainly essentializing logics within this field must be viewed as options deployed within a deadly game of queer survival, not as "foundations" for "identity." [48]

In other words, the phrase "I'm a dyke" does not always mean that the utterer believes her (or occasionally his) sexual identity to be essential—part of her nature—or believes dykeness to be fixed in content; it might, instead, be uttered because it serves in a particular context. Antiessentialist political activists, then, should not necessarily be working to get the utterer to stop uttering this phrase; rather, they should be working to figure out whether uttering it works, politically and otherwise. We should also be working to bring these "quotidian uses" back to the definitions that we started with. As Maxine Wolfe suggests, the opposition between fixed and fluid identity categories, as well as the whole essentialist-constructionist opposition that has defined the terms of much debate about queer identity—Are you born that way, or does society make you that way?—does not begin to account for how people live their lives. Many, she notes, "live their lives as Lesbians or Gay men; there is a materiality to their identity and for most it is not 'fluid' or 'categoriless,' but neither is it essentialist." [49] At the same time, however, as Wolfe's comments also suggest, the fruit of bringing daily uses back to definitions is not final definitions refined for good—a permanent answer to questions like, What is identity? or, What constitutes resistance?—but working definitions that need instead to be refined in and for particular contexts.

These points can be brought back to bear on the matter of Barbie's own unstable meaning, eminent subvertability, and mass outing. They suggest that, despite the insights to be gained by noticing the repetition of outings and "I'm different" stories, it's less important to bust them as mass produced and ordinary than to see how repressions of repetition and mutability function in circulation, which they do, like the namings of fixed identity discussed above, to both negative and positive effect. On the one hand, they make Barbie circulate as straight and queerness circulate as scandal. On the other, they also create the very conditions for subversion and social criticism: Dyke Barbie and "Soft Targets" depend on the widespread perception of fixed meaning or, more precisely, on the ability of subvertors and viewers to call up a fixed meaning that Barbie is supposed to have, to repress unfixed meaning at least temporarily.

From this angle, a statement or implication that "Barbie means x" needs to be considered just as statements like "I'm a dyke" do. "Barbie means x" does not necessarily mean that the utterer believes this or doesn't recognize counterevidence. Often, as I have argued, it does. But sometimes, instead, it serves as part of a strategy to use Barbie as a vehicle to address racism, sexism, or heterosexism or simply for the pleasures that subcultural subversions provide. Subvertors do well, then, to work from an assumption of fixed meaning. They are tapping into the conceptual framework of the many potential viewers who do think that Barbie comes with meanings attached. They are equally addressing consumers who can suspend knowledge to the contrary in order to get the point. Most people, I think, fit into one of those two categories.

There's a lesson here for Barbie subvertors: you need to subvert what's out there, the perceptions that people have or can conjure up. But this is not the big point, even though, as I've suggested, Barbie is a great object to subvert—if, indeed, *subversion* is the right word to describe the products or the project. Michael Moon suggests that it isn't, that *subversion,* rendered flat from overuse and, perhaps, "theory bound" from its now comfortable home in academic writing, has become rhetorically inadequate to the task of describing many of the products, effects, and goals at issue here.[50] He suggests, borrowing from the journal *Race Traitor,*[51] that *treason* is more appropriate and that acts against Barbie need to be situated and undertaken among a set of practices—product related and otherwise, designed for audiences of one or of many and undertaken whenever, wherever, and however possible—to demolish the categories and presumptions that underpin social injustice. Barbie "subversions" often work toward this goal, as reactions to them, ranging from "terrorists acts against children" to surprise at seeing Barbie deheterosexualized, attest. They also suggest both how entrenched are regimes of normalcy, power, and privilege and how crucial it is to take on the project of denaturalizing and dismantling them. People both inside and outside categories that confer privilege and power need to enact disloyalty and to show up these categories as constructed frauds. In other words, we need, as Adrian Piper argues, "to blast the simplistic categories we impose on people."[52] *Treason,* perhaps, does better invoke the goals, the stakes, the big project, the field of action, and what we are up against, which the term *regime,* unfortunately, does not overstate.

But, precisely because it now has a more modest reach, *subversion* is better suited to keeping something else in focus: no matter what we call acts against Barbie, and no matter what the context of acts in which we situate them, they remain the merest fraction of what we need to be doing in cultural activism, which in turn is only a fraction of what we need to be doing in our fight for the redistribution of power and resources on which the survival of oppressed peoples depends. Much more important than the insights about circulating Barbie that can be gleaned from the disparity between academic and common knowledge is the general point for activists that this Barbie disparity backs up. We can't design any activist strategies without figuring out first how queerness, among other things, is understood by both allies and foes in the actual political arenas in which we operate. This is absolutely *not* to argue that we need to accept dominant perceptions; our rights, our dignity, and our survival depend on changing them. Nor is it to argue that we should use anything that works for the moment without attention to long-term goals and to both immediate and enduring costs of putting particular images into circulation or strategies into practice. Some strategies are simply unacceptable, such as the assimilationist strategy, used all too frequently during gay rights voter battles in Lewiston and elsewhere, of putting a straight face forward and queer activists in the closet—a strategy that, besides being unsuccessful at the ballot box anyway, trashes our dignity and actually works against civil rights for anyone who isn't straight acting.[53]

Yet we need to make sure that we're operating in political arenas with a clear sense of the representations that are out there. Otherwise, besides being arrogant jerks, we risk major failures in communication and coalition building, thwarting our political effectiveness on other levels as well. At a time when it is politically imperative to forge the alliances that we need to fight what is generally termed the *radical Right,* coalition activism and the work of communication that it requires are crucial. And we need to figure out what's "out there" by being out there. As the particulars of Barbie outings in circulation underscore—in contrast both to other outings and to other frequently repeated subversions like flag burnings that, unlike dyke Barbies, circulate as acts with a history—we can get only so far by looking at representations apart from their circulation or by trying to apply insights gleaned about one cultural practice to another one.

Conclusion:

On Our Backs,

in Our Hands,

on Our Broadsides

It doesn't take (the representation of) vaginal insertion to insert Barbie into the sexual arena. The Handlers, it will be remembered, pulled her out of a sexual arena in the first place and kept her there even after the Barbie-hating mothers in their first market study confirmed that sex was the big message. Mattel's later spin control on this issue was never designed to unsex Barbie, which would have been a bad move since Barbie's appeal depends so much on it. A dorky boyfriend is a boyfriend nonetheless. Summer flirtations with men of mixed race still represent sexual possibilities beyond the comfort zone of most white parents in the 1960s even if Barbie exits them with virginity intact. And Barbie eventually acquired skintight clothes that made at least one Barbie model blush.

Mattel's spin control was, however, designed to circulate another interpretation enough to open the purse strings: Barbie as a good girl and, later, as paragon of feminism and diversity in their most widely palatable, and co-opted, forms. Mattel pushed this interpretation so successfully that Barbie needs to be understood as a cultural artifact who causes much of her own meaning if for no other reason than that, besides thwarting future projects of subversion, to argue otherwise would be fundamentally to disrespect consumer testimony. Most consumer-made narratives and objects, both re-actions and subversions, bear witness to the widespread belief that Barbie comes with meanings attached. Many of these also indicate that this belief is not misguided. As I argued in chapter 2, the given does to some extent determine the possible; consumers often took out much of what Mattel put in. But, equally as often, they took out less and added more themselves than common wisdom would suggest. They gave Barbie queer accessories, and they acted as Barbie's queer accessories to the crime of abetting her escape from the straight context of meaning that Mattel spent millions of dollars to give her.

At the same time, however, queerness does not really stand in relation to straightness in Barbie consumption as the underlying truth to be unearthed, as the most formfitting underwear of the straight acting, or as the terminal point at which interpretations always arrive, even if one truth suggested by Barbie in circulation is that queerness operates in the center as well as at the margins of cultural consumption. Many of Barbie's queer accessories are Mattel's queer accessories in the sense of unlikely allies. Self-identified queers bent on queering Barbie imply her straightness in the act of subverting it and generate, sometimes inadvertently, the perception that Barbie is much straighter than consumer testimony suggests her to be. Barbie queerers make subversions that get repeatedly interpreted as one-of-a-kinds rather than as yet another manifestation of Barbie's queerness or queerability. And they marshal unlikely allies to Mattel's defense, like the woman against war toys who saw giving G.I. Joe Barbie's voice box as a terrorist act against children. Overall, as I argued in the previous chapter, it's just not so easy to dispense with the artifactual and interpretive accessories that Mattel has given Barbie, many of which are designed to make Barbie as straight as they come. Subvertors can't just chuck them at will. They will always face limited audiences and antisubversive readings until Barbie's real-life social and cultural contexts, both mainstream and subcultural, get reaccessorized and refashioned for justice. It's easy to turn Barbie into Fem Barbie. The difficulty of making Fem Barbie visible as such has more to do with heterosexual presumption in dominant culture and antifem prejudice among dykes than with the artifact—or its producers, who perpetuate both but invented neither. And no amount of demystification, queer accessorizing, or subversion can erase the dubious ideological effect of Barbie. Even if you know that no one could really grow up to look like her, Barbie might still make you feel bad about being fat. Barbie's queer accessories, however, can do much to show up this effect as partial and subvertable.

The title *queer accessory* does not belong only to Barbie consumers either. It has also at times belonged to Mattel and not just at those moments when Barbie's queer accessories on the inside pulled a fast one on the spin police.

The bottom line is that Mattel made a female doll for girls to dress, undress, fondle, and obsess over and unsexed her only halfheartedly, thus making her good-girl rep somewhat laughable and making Barbie easy fodder for any girl with a queer *Dream Loft* in mind.

This also makes Barbie a great political and pedagogical tool. One thing I learned from talking to people about Barbie is that we need to be very humble about our own ability to inscribe meaning in objects, to discern the meanings that others attribute to them, or to transfer conclusions about resistance, subversion, and hegemony from person to person, object to object, context to context. But I also learned something else. Surprisingly often, the stories I heard were about how Barbie turned people into cultural critics and political activists—about how seeing activist queer Barbies, or remembering their own Barbie queerings, or hearing about my Barbie work, induced them to move from Barbie anecdotes to thinking about cultural politics, ideology, oppression, and resistance, and sometimes to political plotting and practice. When I hear these stories, I am reminded anew that, while I don't think that our world is better because Barbie inhabits it, she certainly hits a nerve well worth locating and tweaking—in the classroom, in the bedroom, and on the political stage.

Notes

Introduction: On Our Backs, in Our Attics, on Our Minds

1 "Gals and Dolls" (photo-essay), *On Our Backs,* March/April 1989, 32–34. The credit line states, "Photos and models: Evans, Brill, Smith."

2 In contrast, many lesbian publications are explicitly designated for lesbians only.

3 Joseph Fairchild Beam, "Making Ourselves from Scratch," in *Brother to Brother: New Writings by Black Gay Men,* ed. Essex Hemphill (Boston: Alyson, 1991), 261–62.

4 For a good critique of the "rebel" image that now circulates in the media, see Paul Rudnick, "Can a Rebel Have a Housekeeper and a Car Phone?" *Spy,* March 1992, 52–58.

5 Hayley Spicer quoted in "The World According to Mr Punch," *Punch,* 12 February 1991, 5.

6 Iain Chambers, *Popular Culture: The Metropolitan Experience,* Studies in Communication (London: Methuen, 1986), 43.

7 These decisions, and, of course, all the material that follows, have also been informed by the work of many writers in the intersecting areas of cultural, feminist, and gay/lesbian/queer studies, whose studies, particularly of audience, subculture, hegemony, and resistance, I brought to my encounter with Hannah as well as other Barbie material. Although I do not undertake here an extensive review of previous scholarship in these areas, my debt to it is enormous, too much so to be articulated through a short list of texts and authors. Such a list, however, would include, besides the texts cited in later notes, the following: Louis Althusser, "Ideology and Ideological State Apparatuses," in *Lenin and Philosophy and Other Essays,* trans. B. Brewster (New York: Random House, 1971); Pierre Bordieu, *The Love of Art: European Museums and Their Public,* trans. C. Beattie and N. Merriman (Cambridge: Polity Press, 1990), and *The Field of Cultural Production: Essays on Art and Literature,* ed. Randal Johnson (New York: Columbia University Press, 1993); Michel de

Certeau, *The Practice of Everyday Life* (Berkeley and Los Angeles: University of California Press, 1984); Lynn Hunt, *Politics, Culture, and Class in the French Revolution* (Berkeley and Los Angeles: University of California Press, 1984); Cindy Patton, "Safe Sex and the Pornographic Vernacular," in *How Do I Look*, ed. Bad Object-Choices (Seattle: Bay, 1991); Janice A. Radway, *Reading the Romance: Women, Patriarchy, and Popular Literature* (Chapel Hill: University of North Carolina Press, 1984); Joanna Russ, "Pornography for Women, by Women, with Love," in *Magic Mommas, Trembling Sisters, Puritans and Perverts: Feminist Essays* (Trumansburg,' N.Y.: Crossing, 1985); Joan Wallach Scott, "The Evidence of Experience," *Critical Inquiry* 17 (Summer 1991): 773–97, reprinted in *The Gay and Lesbian Studies Reader*, ed. Henry Abelove, Michèle Aine Barale, and David M. Halperin (New York: Routledge, 1993). *The Gay and Lesbian Studies Reader* provides an invaluable resource overall, as do the anthologies *Pleasure and Danger*, ed. Carole Vance (Boston: Routledge, 1984), and *Cultural Studies*, ed. Lawrence Grossberg, Cary Nelson, and Paula Treichler (New York: Routledge, 1992). The latter contains a superb bibliography; see also the editors' introduction (p. 15, n. 1) for a bibliography covering the historiography and field of cultural studies.

8   Deborah Bright, "Dream Girls," in *Stolen Glances: Lesbians Take Photographs*, ed. Tessa Boffin and Jean Fraser (London: Pandora, 1991), 151–52.

9   As Georgia Nigro, a child psychologist who conducted some preliminary exploration for a study of the psychology of doll play, explains, this is one reason for the paucity of such studies. It is virtually impossible to set up an experimental environment that can approximate sufficiently the context in which doll play ordinarily occurs outside the experimental context for each subject: in particular architectural spaces, surrounded by particular objects, with particular individuals, etc. (conversation, June 1992).

10   On the basis of fourteen play sessions with one child over the course of a year, Diana Kelly-Byrne argues that children construct play scenarios more revealing of inner concerns as the relationship between adult and child grows stronger. The progression of my Barbie interactions with Hannah, especially in contrast to my discussions with children I don't know as well, supports Kelly-Byrne's conclusion (*A Child's Play Life: An Ethnographic Study* [New York: Teacher's College Press, 1989], 227).

11   For instance, the writing of Vivian Gussin Paley on the imaginative play of one of her kindergarten classes suggests that the contrast between Hannah's beach tale and our less emotionally complicated Birthday Barbie conversation one year later may be partly a function of a different developmental stage. In her experience, four-year-olds are more likely to display their troubles close to the surface: e.g., "Once upon a time a father moved out of my house and took his radio." Later, they learn to mask their concerns: "The king found a new palace, and the princess lived with him and made him a prince" (*Boys and Girls: Superheroes in the Doll Corner* [Chicago: University of Chicago Press, 1984], 110–111). This is only one of the topics that an ethnography of children's Barbie play needs to consider.

12   Conversation with the artist, 22 December 1991. Jessica's parents, unfortunately, would not allow these photographs to be published.

13   I have not left out insider stories owing to some idea of keeping my mind "pure"—to keep what consumers couldn't have seen from creeping into my analysis. Nor do I claim to be able to re-create through this strategy the exact source material seen by any given consumer. I can hardly presume that Barbie consumers of 1965 saw every Barbie product or ad produced during that year or that they saw in them then what I see in them now. Moreover,

what I see in a Barbie product or printed text about Barbie is marked by my own artifactual context—how many people reading an article on Barbie's thirtieth birthday have already read a hundred others? My decision is based more on priority than purity; studying consumers requires a focus on what they saw. For an account based on interviews with Mattel people, see M. G. Lord, *Forever Barbie: The Unauthorized Biography of a Real Doll* (New York: Morrow, 1994).

Chapter 1. Making Barbie

1 Eben Shapiro, " 'Totally Hot, Totally Cool,' Long-Haired Barbie Is a Hit," *New York Times*, 22 June 1992, sec. D, p. 9.

2 Dick Hebdige, *Subculture: The Meaning of Style* (London: Methuen, 1979), 15–16. Hebdige is quoting Stuart Hall, "Culture, the Media, and the 'Ideological Effect,' " in *Mass Communication and Society*, ed. James Curran, Michael Gurevitch, and Janet Woollacott (London: Edward Arnold, 1977), 332–33.

3 Lisa Tickner, *The Spectacle of Women: Imagery of the Suffrage Campaign, 1907–1914* (Chicago: University of Chicago Press, 1988), 161.

4 Hall, "The 'Ideological Effect,' " 333.

5 Denise Gellene, "Fame Dogs 'Real' Barbie, Ken," *Los Angeles Times*, 29 January 1989, sec. 4, p. 4; Ian Gillespie, "What a Doll," *London (Ontario) Free Press*, 18 February 1989, sec. C, p. 1.

6 Gellene, "Fame Dogs 'Real' Barbie, Ken," sec. 4, p. 1.

7 Sydney Ladensohn Stern and Ted Schoenhaus, *Toyland: The High-Stakes Game of the Toy Industry* (Chicago: Contemporary, 1990), 50–52, 59.

8 Ibid., 66.

9 Richard Warren Lewis, "Jack Ryan and Zsa Zsa: A Millionaire Inventor and His Living Doll," *People*, 14 July 1975, 61–62.

10 Ibid., 61. See also "Jack Ryan Dies at 65; Inventor of Barbie Doll," *New York Times*, 21 August 1991, sec. B, p. 13.

11 Stern and Schoenhaus, *Toyland*, 71–76; Joan Tortorici Ruppert, "The Rise and Fall and Rise of Ruth Handler," *Barbie Bazaar* 5 (January/February 1993): 26–27.

12 Cy Schneider, *Children's Television* (Lincolnwood, Ill.: NTC Business, 1987), 26.

13 Sybil DeWein and Joan Ashabraner, *The Collectors Encyclopedia of Barbie Dolls, and the New Theatre of Fashion* (Paducah, Ky.: Collector, 1977; reprinted with updated values in 1992); Billy Boy, *Barbie: Her Life and Times* (New York: Crown, 1987).

14 Compare Jenny Vogt, "Barbie and G.I. Joe," *Palm Beach Post*, 19 February 1989, sec. C, p. 1.

15 "The Barbie, G.I. Joe File," *Pensacola News-Journal*, 12 February 1989.

16 Ibid., 26.

17 Billy Boy, *Barbie*, 10.

18 Ibid., 19.

19 Ibid., 19, 22.

20 Helmut Jahn, "The Fashion Magazine 5:56," 4 (July/August 1992): 47 (first ellipses in original).

21 Sumiko Watanabe, "Javanese Lilli," *Barbie Bazaar* 4 (November/December 1992): 48–60.

22 Ibid., 48.

23   Ruppert, "The Rise and Fall and Rise of Ruth Handler," 26.

24   Patricia Leighton, "The White Peril and *L'art nègre:* Picasso, Primitivism, and Anticolonialism," *Art Bulletin* 72 (December 1990): 609–30.

25   A. Glenn Mandeville, "The Many Cases of Barbie," *Barbie Bazaar* 2 (January/February 1990): 12.

26   Quoted in Billy Boy, *Barbie,* 18.

27   Mandeville, "The Many Cases of Barbie," 13.

28   A. Glenn Mandeville, "Barbie's Vinyl Ventures," *Barbie Bazaar* 3 (January/February 1991): 29.

29   A. Glenn Mandeville, "And Then . . . I Met Ken," *Barbie Bazaar* 2 (March/April 1990): 24.

30   Schneider, *Children's Television,* 30.

31   Ibid., 29; Mandeville, "I Met Ken," 24.

32   Schneider, *Children's Television,* 29–30.

33   Ibid.

34   Ibid., 29.

35   Thanks to Robert Branham for a conversation that triggered this connection.

36   Betty Lou Maybee, "Mirror Mirror, Chrystal Ball," in *Here's Barbie,* Cynthia Lawrence and Betty Lou Maybee (New York: Random House, 1962), 131–53.

37   Cynthia Lawrence, "The Size 10 Dress," in *Here's Barbie,* 78, 96, 99–100.

38   Ibid., 81.

39   Betty Lou Maybee, *Barbie's Fashion Success* (New York: Random House, 1962). Cynthia Lawrence, *Barbie's New York Summer* (New York: Random House, 1962), and *Barbie Solves a Mystery* (New York: Random House, 1963).

40   Lawrence, *Barbie Solves a Mystery,* 16.

41   Maybee, *Barbie's Fashion Success,* 6.

42   Betty Lou Maybee, "Captain Hooten's Return," in *Here's Barbie,* 165, and "Barbie's Big Prom," in ibid.

43   Cynthia Lawrence, "Barbie, Be My Valentine," in *Here's Barbie,* 4.

44   Maybee, *Barbie's Fashion Success,* 38.

45   Lawrence, "Barbie, Be My Valentine," 8–9. Suzanne Weyn, *The Phantom of Shrieking Pond,* Adventures with Barbie, vol. 5 (Los Angeles: Price Stern Sloan, 1992), 55.

46   Betty Lou Maybee, *Barbie's Hawaiian Holiday* (New York: Random House, 1963), 13, 23, 19, 133–47, 66.

47   Ibid., 63 (ellipses in original).

48   Ibid., 39.

49   Much has been written on the construction of "the other" against, and as a way to define, the norm that constructors perceive themselves as occupying. See especially two groundbreaking texts, Franz Fanon's *Black Skin, White Masks* (New York: Grove, 1967) and Albert Memmi's *The Colonizer and the Colonized* (Boston: Beacon, 1965).

50   David Roediger, *The Wages of Whiteness: Race and the Making of the American Working Class* (London: Verso, 1993), 95.

51   For excellent studies of this multiple identity formation in the nineteenth-century United States, see ibid.; and Eric Lott, *Love and Theft: Blackface Minstrelsy and the American Working Class* (Oxford: Oxford University Press, 1993).

52   In a subplot of *Barbie's Hawaiian Holiday,* Barbie helps the Hawes' thirteen-year-old son Gerald get his parents to accept his own passion for surfing, another instance of the positive

valuation of the pleasures Apaki stands for, and another suggestion that it is only Barbie, and only people of her particular class and race, who have the proper attitude toward the place of pleasure.

53 Letters column, *Barbie Fashion,* December 1993, 31. In response to Allison Reddington's letter, which criticized the story for glamourizing homelessness with a carpeted shelter, fashionably dressed inhabitants, and the implication of imminent job prospects, Hildy Slate, who wrote "The Volunteers," explained that Mattel had forced her to change her story so that it wouldn't "scare" very young children.

54 William K. Zinsser, "Barbie Is a Million-Dollar Doll," *Saturday Evening Post,* 12 December 1964, 72–73.

55 Eve Kosofsky Sedgwick, *Epistomology of the Closet* (Berkeley and Los Angeles: University of California Press, 1990), 136.

56 Don Richard Cox, "Barbie and Her Playmates, *Journal of Popular Culture,* no. 2 (Fall 1977): 305–6.

57 Leah Rosch, "The Brains behind Barbie," *Working Woman,* May 1990, 90.

58 Kim Masters, "It's How You Play the Game," *Working Woman,* May 1990, 90. On Barad, see also Nancy Rivera Brooks, "Barbie's Doting Sister," *Los Angeles Times,* sec. D, pp. 1–2.

59 Rosch, "Brains behind Barbie," 90.

60 "Barbie Doll's Careers," Mattel Information Release, 1992.

61 Karen Harrison, "The Glamourous Gourmet," *Barbie* 2 (Fall 1985): 26–29.

62 Judith Graham, "Mattel Hopes for Help from Barbie's Friends," *Advertising Age,* 21 March 1988, 2; Kim Foltz, "Mattel's Shift on Barbie Ads," *New York Times,* 17 July 1990, sec. D.

63 Lisa Jones, "A Doll Is Born," *Village Voice,* 26 March 1991, 36.

64 "Mattel Unveils New African American Dolls," Mattel Information Release, 11 February 1991. On the hair and color of these dolls, see Jones, "A Doll Is Born," 36.

65 "Shani: A Character Sketch," Mattel Information Release, 1991.

66 Mattel, Inc., *Girls Toys, 1992,* 74–76.

67 *Barbie Fashion,* August 1993, 31.

68 "Letters to Barbie," *Barbie Fashion,* November 1993, 32.

69 Ibid.

70 "All That Jazz," *Barbie Fashion,* September 1993, 2–13.

71 "Barbie Doesn't Like Math," *Portland Press Herald,* 1 October 1992, sec. D, p. 10.

72 Mattel, Inc., *1991 Annual Report,* 1992, 26, 28.

73 Ramon R. Isberto, "4000 Filipinos Lose Jobs after Barbie Takes a Walk," *Los Angeles Times,* sec. 5, pp. 2, 6. According to a slide show on women in the Philippines produced by the Philippine Solidarity Network (PSN), Mattel's abuses in the Philippines' Bataan Export Processing Zone were not limited to low wages. "We call our company 'Motel,'" says a worker at Mattel, "because we are often told to lay down or be laid off." According to the PSN, Mattel also offered prizes to workers for undergoing sterilization, thus avoiding the issue of maternity benefits, and expelled striking workers by force during a 1981 strike. (Annette Fuentes and Barbara Ehrenreich, *Women in the Global Factory,* INC Pamphlet no. 2 [Boston: South End, 1983], 23, 13, 46–47. Thanks to Margot Hostie and Laura Mytels for this reference.)

74 Mattel, Inc., *1990 Annual Report,* 1991, 14–15.

75 Ben and Jerry's Foundation, description of funding criteria, 1992. The company also funds

"Partnershops," franchises donated to nonprofit groups without initial start-up fees (*Ben and Jerry's Chunk Mail*, vol. 2, no. 1 [1993]: 1).

76 Karen Caviale, "Barbie Continues Goodwill Mission," *Barbie Bazaar* 2 (July/August 1990): 6.

77 Steve Lohr, "And See to It That Ken Composts," *New York Times*, 8 May 1992, sec. D, p. 4.

78 Caviale, "Goodwill Mission," 6.

79 "Mattel Sues Ken, Barbie," *Chicago Sun Times*, 11 May 1990, 14.

80 "Letters to Barbie," *Barbie Fashion*, June 1993, 31.

81 "Role Model, or Too Thin to Be In," *Barbie Fashion*, 27 March 1993, 2–12.

82 Peter Bowen, "A New Toxic Avenger," *Outweek*, 17 April 1991, 56.

83 Letter to Barbara Bell from Judy A. Willis, 24 March 1993, reproduced in Marsha McLaughlin, "Tapping the Collectible Unconscious: Barbie Psychic Barbara Bell," *Barbie Bazaar* 5 (September/October 1993): 45.

84 *Barbie Channeling Newsletter* and letter to Bell, both reproduced in ibid., 43–44.

85 Denise Gellene, "Forever Young: After Thirty Years Barbie Has More Clothes, Friends, and Fans than Ever," *Los Angeles Times*, 29 January 1989, sec. 4, p. 4.

86 Zinsser, "Million Dollar Doll," 73.

87 Stephanie St. Pierre, *Wildlife Rescue*, Adventures with Barbie, vol. 3 (Los Angeles: Price Stern Sloan, 1991).

88 Lisa Trusiani, quoted in Marsha McLaughlin, "An Interview with the Staff of *Barbie* and *Barbie Fashion* Comics," *Barbie Bazaar* 5 (March/April 1993): 25.

89 Martha Groves, "Loggers Want Barbie to Play a Different Tune," *Los Angeles Times*, 19 December 1990, sec. D, p. 1, 4.

90 Cartoon in *Lesbian Contradiction: A Journal of Irreverent Feminism*, no. 9 (Winter 1984–85): 5.

91 "Dr. Darlene Powell-Hopson," Mattel Information Release, 1990.

92 Barbara Manning, "Cana Cockrell: She'll Be Your Barbie Doll," *Los Angeles Magazine*, June 1987, 16.

93 "The Heart of Art," *Barbie Fashion*, 28 April 1993, 2–29; "The Case of the Disappearing Diamonds," *Barbie*, 27 March 1993, 21–30.

94 Barbara Slate, "The Memory Book, Part Two," *Barbie Fashion*, 31 July 1993, 3–9.

95 "Letters to Barbie," *Barbie*, 27 March 1993, 31.

96 "The Heart of Art," 8.

97 Mattel did experiment with a different body and face for the Japanese market but returned to the norm in 1991 after market testing in Japan revealed that consumers were ready for the Western version and that a doll unlike other dolls sold in Japan might well garner Mattel a bigger share of the doll market than the relatively unsuccessful "Moba Barbie" (David Kilburn and Julie Skur Hill, "Western Barbie: Mattel Makes Japan Push with Revamped Doll," *Advertising Age*, 7 October 1991, 94).

98 Quoted in Alison Dembner, "35 and Still a Doll," *Boston Globe*, 9 March 1994, 16.

99 Lin Poyer, "Barbie: The Quintessential Bimbo?" *Christian Science Monitor*, 14 April 1989, 19.

100 Ibid.

101 Carol Lawson, "Stereotypes Unravel, But Not too Quickly, in New Toys for 1993," *New York Times*, 11 February 1993, sec. B, pp. 1, 4.

102 "Has Ken Come Out?" *People,* 11 October 1993, 66.

103 Dan Savage, "Ken Comes Out," *Chicago Reader,* 23 July 1993, sec. 1, p. 8.

104 "Making Earring Magic," *Barbie Magazine,* no. 37 (1993): 19. In an interesting plotline, Barbie and friends are distressed to discover the collection labeled "BAD" by critics. "BAD," however, turns out to be good: it's an acronym for the "Best Accessory Design" award.

105 Candace Irving in William E. Geist, "At 25 Barbie is Healthy, Wealthy, and Celebrated," *New York Times,* 25 February 1984, sec. B, p. 3; Jill Barad in Rosch, "Brains behind Barbie," 90.

106 Beverly Beyette, "A Dress-Up Job: Barbie's Principal Designer Scales Down Glamour and Plays Up Fantasy," *Los Angeles Times,* 6 February 1991, sec. E, p. 5.

107 Mattel also sold Midge into matrimony in 1991; Barbie was a bridesmaid.

108 The cards, which are sold individually and in a postcard book, each have on the back: "Barbie is a trademark owned by and used under license from Mattel, Inc."

Chapter 2. Older Heads on Younger Bodies

1 Gary Fisher, "Storm," 1992, typescript.

2 Conversation with Joleen, July 1993.

3 Conversation with Lise, 30 July 1993.

4 Sybil Dewein and Joan Ashabraner, *The Collectors Encyclopedia of Barbie Dolls* (Paducah, Ky.: Collector, 1977, 1992), 257, 301.

5 Conversation with Georgia, 9 August 1993.

6 One of the two dresses with rickrack shown by Sarah Sink Eames in *Barbie Fashion,* vol. 1, *1959–67* (Padukah, Ky.: Collector, 1990) is the 1965 Brunch Time, remarketed the next year as Coffee's On, which came with casserole dishes and a matching coffeepot (pp. 133, 170).

7 Carole Nicksin, "Barbie and Tammy: The Real Story!" *Semotext[e],* (1987): 286 (ellipses in original).

8 Toni Morrison, *The Bluest Eye* (New York: Pocket, 1972), 20–22.

9 Nicksin, "Barbie and Tammy," 287.

10 Conversation with Cheryl, spring 1991.

11 Conversation with Elspeth, Portland, Maine, June 1991.

12 Telephone conversation with Teresa Ortega, from Chapel Hill, N.C., spring 1991.

13 Conversation with Lisa, Greene, Maine, summer 1991.

14 Conversation, Detroit, 13 March 1993.

15 Eve Kosofsky Sedgwick, *Epistemology of the Closet* (Berkeley and Los Angeles: University of California Press, 1990), 22.

16 Conversation with William Pope.L, summer 1993, whom I thank for many insightful conversations on the material for this chapter.

17 James Clifford, introduction to *Writing Culture: The Poetics and Politics of Ethnography,* ed. James Clifford and George Marcus (Berkeley and Los Angeles: Univ. of California Press) 1986, 7.

18 Penny Lorio, "Uncloseting Barbie: Get over It, Ken, It's a New Age," *Washington Post,* 2 May 1993, sec. C, p. 5.

19 Conversation with Sue, Auburn, Maine, August 1993.

20 Lorio, "Uncloseting Barbie," 5.

21　Joan Nestle, "The Femme Question," in *The Persistent Desire: A Femme-Butch Reader,* ed. Joan Nestle (Boston: Alyson, 1992), 142–43. Both *fem* and *femme* are current in contemporary spelling. I prefer the spelling *fem* because the location of foreignness on one side of the butch/fem configuration discomforts me.

22　On the particular construction of butch/fem's "erotic charge" during the last ten years, see Kath Weston, "Do Clothes ·Make the Woman? Gender, Performance Theory, and Lesbian Eroticism," *Genders,* no. 17 (Fall 1993): 14–17.

23　Letter from Margaret, 8 August 1992.

24　Joan Nestle, "Flamboyance and Fortitude: An Introduction," in *The Persistent Desire,* 16.

25　Men also recount being punished, emotionally and physically, for crossing gender lines to play with Barbie. Kirk remembers being "ruthlessly tortured" in the early 1960s by male peers when, despite his best efforts to hide, he got caught playing with Barbie; his brother, he recounts, spent the next fifteen years reminding him of his supposed "faggotry." More recently, a local news story about a woman convicted of child abuse listed the following among the acts against her children detailed by the district attorney: "She held her son's hand over the flames of a stove because she did not want him to play with Barbie" (*Lewiston-Auburn (Maine) Sun Journal,* 4 February 1994, 36).

26　Conversation with Cynthia, July 1993.

27　Sigmund Freud, *Leonardo da Vinci: A Study in Psychosexuality,* trans. A. A. Brill (New York: Random House, 1947), 35–36.

28　Conversations with Bee Bell, autumn 1992 and summer 1993.

29　Conversation with Eve, August 1993.

30　Interview with Rebecca by Kelly McCullough, September 1993.

31　Lisa Jones, "A Doll Is Born," *Village Voice,* 26 March 1991, 36.

32　Interview with Michelle by Kelly McCullough, October 1993; interview by Kelly McCullough with a nineteen-year-old woman from Pakistan, October 1993.

33　Cy Schneider, *Children's Television* (Lincolnwood, Ill.: NTC Business, 1987), 36. According to Schneider, the campaign was highly successful; despite blizzards and the like, the new Barbie sold out in three weeks in the two test markets.

34　Quoted in ibid.

35　Interview with Kelly McCullough, September 1993.

36　Bell suggested that this question also accorded with recent trends in science-fiction movies, in which human characters often show ambivalence about what the proper relationship to aliens should be—as opposed to earlier ones, in which people knew immediately once they had seen aliens that they had to be destroyed.

37　Interview with Kelly McCullough.

38　Sandra Cisneros, "Barbie-Q," in *Woman Hollering Creek* (New York: Vintage, 1991), 14–15.

39　A. M. Homes, *The Safety of Objects* (New York: Norton, 1990), 168, 151–73. This story and "Barbie-Q" are both reprinted in *Mondo Barbie,* ed. Lucinda Ebersole and Richard Peabody (New York: St. Martin's, 1993).

40　Emily Apter, introduction to *Fetishism as Cultural Discourse,* ed. Emily Apter and William Pietz (Ithaca, N.Y.: Cornell University Press, 1993), 4.

41　How Barbie functions as each of these is a highly interesting topic. I did not pursue it here because I am less interested in whether Barbie is, e.g., a cathected phallus than in the meanings invested in her once such a cathexis, if there is one, has been made and in how such cathexes are understood in circulation. They are not generally understood in psychoanalytic-fetish terms.

42   Miriam Formanek-Brunell, "Sugar and Spite: The Politics of Doll Play in Nineteenth-Century America," in *Small Worlds: Children and Adolescents in America, 1850–1950* (Kansas: University Press of Kansas, 1992), 115–21.

43   Other adults offer testimony of Barbie's sexual content to children. Vivian Gussin Paley noted that Barbie's sexual taboo status was well known among the girls in her kindergarten class (*Boys and Girls: Superheroes in the Doll Corner* [Chicago: University of Chicago Press, 1984], 11). Carol A. Queen suggests something similar about slightly older children's fascination with Madonna: "Who responds to eroticism more viscerally—and unconsciously—than a pubescent girl? When I ask my young [ten-year-old] friend and her pals what they like about Madonna, they chorus, 'She's pretty!'" ("Talking about *Sex*," in *Madonnarama: Essays on Sex and Popular Culture*, ed. Lisa Frank and Paul Smith [Pittsburgh and San Francisco: Cleis, 1993], 148).

44   "Letters to Barbie," *Barbie,* December 1993, 32.

45   "Letters to Barbie," *Barbie,* April 1993, 30.

46   These columns, of course, cannot be used to measure the extent to which children are critical of Barbie since they are edited by people working for Mattel with an eye to emphasizing Barbie's appeal. The combination of letters in any given issue makes this obvious. A typical column contains primarily fan letters, with some, such as letters from teenage boys or from readers from other continents, designed to indicate the scope of Barbie's popularity. That the one or two critical letters are always "I love Barbie, but" letters reveals less about predominant habits of Barbie criticism than about the editorial strategy, which is clearly not to give proportionate time to every perspective but to give the impression of antitotalitarian editing. (This is another arena in which Mattel presents itself as the affirming agent of a seemingly infinite range of consumer interpretations while in practice validating primarily those that serve its own interests.) But the critical letters do provide a fascinating look at what some children don't buy about Barbie.

Chapter 3. Barbie's Queer Adult Accessories

1   Telephone interview by Kelly McCullough, 15 October 1982. Interestingly, for a brief time Lori also played She-Ra; despite She-Ra's different work profile, the human referent, at least in this context, was the same.

2   Gordon Young, "Pop Culture Princess," *San Jose Metro,* 21–27 April 1994, 16.

3   Lori's refusal to wear the leotard or bathing suit had less to do with considering them inappropriate for Barbie than inappropriate for a Barbie model: it was "more than what should have been on a real human being going in front of children." But the point still holds. Mattel's concern to sell the doll products mattered more than protecting the Barbie impersonator's innocent look, just as Mattel has been willing to resort to some convoluted spins to give Barbie a nurse's outfit when she was still only a model or a wedding dress after marriage became forbidden. It's also worth noting that Lori credits Barbie with being her accessory. Playing Barbie, like (Mattel's account of) playing with Barbie, enabled her to imagine herself as and then to transform herself into the confident and successful woman she considered Barbie to be: "Especially when you had the outfit on: you were Barbie, and Barbie could do no wrong."

4   Alison Sloane, "Funny, You Don't Look like a Soap Star!" *Soap Opera Digest,* 18 January 1994, 54. I base the 1.5 million circulation figure, which represents both subscription and

over-the-counter sales, on a survey of the "Statement of Ownership, Management, and Circulation" notices that appear in each issue.

5 Frank Coffey and Joe Layden, *Thin Ice: The Complete, Uncensored Story of Tonya Harding, America's Bad Girl of Ice Skating* (New York: Pinnacle, 1994), 175.

6 Essex Hemphill, "Soft Targets," in *Ceremonies* (New York: Plume, 1992), 122–23; Regine Sands, *Travels with Diana Hunter* (Denver: Lace, 1986), 72–78; Marlon Riggs, *Tongues Untied,* 1989, film.

7 Blurb on the cover illustration for the March/April 1994 issue of *Barbie: The Magazine for Girls,* 3.

8 *How-To '92: Model Actions for a Post-Columbian World,* produced by the Alliance for Cultural Democracy (PO Box 7591, Minneapolis, MN 55407; tel. 612-724-6795). It also has two great texts: a "Introdictment" on Columbus and an account of linkages between his colonial offenses and later injustices.

9 I'm arguing, not that intercultural exchange and appropriation are always bad, but that they need to be pursued and described with attention to relations of power between the people involved. On the issue of cultural mixing, see Lucy Lippard, *Mixed Blessings: New Art in a Multicultural America* (New York: Pantheon, 1990), esp. chap. 4.

10 *AIDS Barbie,* ("photo by Mod Bob and Billy"), *Diseased Pariah News,* no. 8 (1993): 1.

11 For a comprehensive account of the history and current situation of the CDC's classification system and its effect on women with HIV in terms of diagnosis, treatment, and access to clinical drug trials, see ACT UP's *Treatment and Research Agenda for Women with HIV Infection,* first circulated in 1990 and still in progress.

12 George M. Carter, *ACT UP, the AIDS War, and Activism,* rev. ed., Open Magazine Pamphlet Series, no. 15 (Westfield, N.J., 1992). See also *Voices from the Front,* a 1991 documentary on AIDS activism produced by the Testing the Limits Collective.

13 *P.C. Casualties* (Spring 1991), quoted in Bryn Austin with Pam Greer, "A Freak among Freaks: The 'Zine Scene,'" in *Sisters, Sexperts, Queers: Beyond the Lesbian Nation,* ed. Arlene Stein (Harmondsworth: Penguin, Plume, 1993), 93.

14 Kelly Harmon, "Plastic Values and Perversity," *Windy City Times,* 29 August 1991, 19.

15 *Mondo Barbie,* ed. Lucinda Ebersole and Richard Peabody (New York: St. Martin's, 1993), 160, 164.

16 Produced by "E.M.R."

17 David Firestone, "As Barbie Talks Tough, Ken Goes Shopping," *New York Times,* 31 December 1993, sec. A, p. 12.

18 Quoted from the 1992 catalog newsletter ("39th list") of the Florida collector Marl Davidson.

19 Joan Tortorici Ruppert, "You've Come a Long Way, Barbie," *Barbie Bazaar* 5 (November/December 1993): 30–32. To give a sense of the scope of collector fandom, at least five thousand more people tried to register after hearing about the conference on "Donahue," but even the waiting list had been closed, at eight hundred, eight months before the conference. These numbers, of course, represent merely the fraction of collectors who tried to attend the conference.

20 *Mattel and Christmas Catalog Reprints, 1969–1972,* a special edition of *Barbie Bazaar* (1992), pp. 29, 32.

21 A. Glenn Mandeville, "Barbie Gears Up for Collectors," *Barbie Bazaar* 5 (July/August 1993): 32.

22 Bob Gardner, "Custom Barbies Sparkle and Shine," *Barbie Bazaar* 5 (November/December 1993): 17–18.

23 Ads in *Parade Magazine,* 18 October 1992, 21; USA *Weekend,* 28–30 August 1992, 11; USA *Weekend,* 2–4 July 1993, 3.

24 Mandeville, "Barbie Gears Up," 33.

25 "Price Guide," *Barbie Bazaar* 6 (January/February 1994): 7, 4 (pages of this section numbered independently of the rest of the issue).

26 Author's comment and photo caption in Ruppert, "You've Come a Long Way, Barbie," 32, 31.

27 Scott Arend, review of *Mondo Barbie, Barbie Bazaar* 6 (March/April 1994): 51. His list of Barbie's roles is equally evasive: "victim, super-achiever, confidante, enemy, bimbo, beauty, rebel and mentor." It's certainly possible that the editors rather than the reviewer made the closet decision, and it's certainly important that *Barbie Bazaar* chose to review this book at all. In the final review product, however, Barbie's straight rep is protected.

28 "Hard Copy," 13 January 1993.

29 Judy Edelstein, "In the Massage Parlor," in *Sex Work: Writings by Women in the Sex Industry,* ed. Frédérique Delacoste and Priscilla Alexander (Pittsburgh: Cleis, 1987), 67.

30 *Barbie's Dream Loft,* environment by Nadine McGann, additional accessories and reposings by Susan Hill, Karen Corrie, Laurence Kucinkas, Cheryl Daly, and Erica Rand. 1989–.

31 13 March 1993. I identify Roberts as a student not to pull rank or subtly to mark her insight "precocious," thus perpetuating the condescending and false notion that student insights are rare, but because her name is not uncommon—I know of one other myself—and I want acknowledge her as specifically as possible.

32 See my "Doing It in Class: On the Perils and Payoffs of Teaching Sexually Explicit Queer Images," *Radical Teacher,* no. 49 (1994), 29–32.

33 Gayle S. Rubin, "Thinking Sex: Notes for a Radical Theory of the Politics of Sexuality," in *The Lesbian and Gay Studies Reader,* ed. Henry Abelove, Michèle Aina Barale, and David M. Halperin (New York: Routledge, 1993), 13.

34 Waring Cuney, "No Images," in *The Negro Caravan: Writings by American Negroes* (1941), ed. Sterling A. Brown, Arthur P. Davis, and Ulysses S. Lee (reprint, New York: Arno, 1969), 375.

35 Gloria Anzalduá and Cherríe Moraga, eds., *This Bridge Called My Back: Writings by Radical Women of Color* (Watertown, Mass.: Persephone, 1981). I refer here to their introduction, but the point is made eloquently throughout the anthology.

36 Hemphill, *Ceremonies,* 144–45.

37 *Shocking Pink,* no. 2 (ca. 1992) (136 Mayall Road, London, SE24 OPH, Great Britain; tel. 071-274-3150).

38 Sandra Cisneros, *Woman Hollering Creek* (New York: Vintage, 1991).

39 Conversation with the artist, May 1994.

40 David Firestone, "As Barbie Talks Tough, Ken Goes Shopping," *New York Times,* 31 December 1993, sec. A, p. 12.

41 Cynthia Lawrence, "The Size 10 Dress," in *Here's Barbie,* ed. Cynthia Lawrence and Betty Lou Maybee (New York: Random House, 1962), 99–100.

42 "Be on Lookout for Porn in Toy Packages," *Lewiston-Auburn* (Maine) *Sun-Journal,* 25 November 1991, 6; "Way to Go, Ken!" *Fortune,* 27 August 1990, 14.

43 Rosalind E. Krauss, *The Originality of the Avant-Garde and Other Modernist Myths* (Cambridge, Mass.: MIT Press, 1985).

44 Arguments about the nonoriginality of these artists are made by, among others, Richard Shiff, *Cezanne and the End of Impressionism: A Study of the Theory, Technique, and Critical*

Evaluation of Modern Art (Chicago: University of Chicago Press, 1984); and Carol Duncan, "Virility and Domination in Early Twentieth-Century Vanguard Painting" (1973), revised in *Feminism and Art History: Questioning the Litany,* ed. Norma Broude and Mary D. Garrard (New York: Harper & Row, 1982).

45   On this particular point, see, esp. Rozsica Parker and Griselda Pollock, *Old Mistresses: Women, Art, and Ideology* (New York: Pantheon, 1981); and Griselda Pollock, *Vision and Difference: Femininity, Feminism, and the Histories of Art* (New York: Routledge, 1988).

46   Marjorie Garber, *Vested Interests: Cross-Dressing and Cultural Anxiety* (New York: Routledge, 1992), 2.

47   Janet Halley, "The Construction of Heterosexuality," in *Fear of a Queer Planet,* ed. Michael Warner (Minneapolis: University of Minnesota Press, 1993), 98, 90.

48   Cindy Patton, "Tremble, Hetero Swine!" in ibid., 166–67.

49   Letter to the author, April 1994. Wolfe also points out that the essentialism vs. constructionism debate is also problematic because it doesn't deal with gender differences in articulation. To argue for one or the other, or for one mix in general, does not address why gay men frequently say that they knew they were gay from the moment of consciousness while lesbians often say otherwise.

50   Letter to the author, July 1994.

51   *Race Traitor* is available at PO Box 603, Cambridge, MA 02140.

52   Maurice Berger, "The Critique of Pure Racism: An Interview with Adrian Piper," *Afterimage* 18 (October 1990): 9.

53   On the bad politics of this strategy in civil rights activism, see "Why I Hated the March on Washington," a 1993 broadside produced by QUASH (Queers United against Straight-Acting Homophobes); Marla Erlien, "Up against Hate: Lessons from Oregon's Measure Nine Campaign: An Interview with Suzanne Pharr," *Gay Community News* (March on Washington issue), April 1993, 3, 11; and my "We're Not David Koresh—and We Don't Play Him on TV Either," *Apex* (Portland, Maine), December 1993, 3, 9, 11. For an account of the horrifying arguments used by lawyers trying to overturn Colorado's antigay amendment, see Donna Minkowitz, "Trial by Science," *Village Voice,* 30 November 1993, 27–29.

Index

Academic knowledge, 20–21; and activism, 5–10, 20–21, 151, 188–192

ACT UP, 148, 150, 157, 169

Adult consumers: on Barbie as "Sister From Another Planet," 102–105, 127–130; on Barbie's ethnicity, 118–122; on Barbie's hair, 118–120, 128; on Barbie's race, 100, 122–123; on Barbie's sexuality, 100, 114, 116, 121, 124, 205 n. 43; on body image, 132; and class status, 97, 116–118, 121, 126–129; as gender outlaws, 106; on gender stereotypes, 132; as interpreters and theorists, 128–130

Amerman, John, 71–73

Apter, Emily, 139

Artistic intention: and creation of meaning, 8; and cultural producers, 38–39; in "high art," 38–39, 45; of Mattel, 38–40, 44–45, 63, 86, 88–92. See also Construction of meaning

Ashabraner, Joan, 33

Authenticity: homemade vs. store-bought clothes, 96–97, 116–119, 126; and Mattel tag, 96–97; real vs. imitation Barbies, 96–98

Barad, Jill, 24, 66–67, 73

Barale, Michèle, 125

Barbie: age of, 24, 52; and anatomical correctness, 45–46; as blank slate, 40, 59, 63–66, 85, 92, 99, 127; as blond, 14–17, 78; breasts of, 29, 46, 58, 66, 123–124; contested value of, 98; cultural capital of, 51; invention of, 24–38; last name of, 24, 49, 65, 82; meaning located in, 98; measurements of, 22–26; myths of origin, 1, 24, 29–38; as "other," 54–55; parents of, 49, 52; and pro-military patriotism, 6, 8, 55, 76; as role model, 17, 27–29, 42, 66, 98, 114, 149–150; sexuality of, 58, 87, 193; as status symbol, 96, 124–127; uncontroversial politics of, 6, 74–77, 87, 154; and weight, 142, 153. See also Diversity; Ethnicity; Race

Barbie Bazaar, 21, 35–37, 40, 42

Barbie Children's Summit, 6, 73–77

Barbie clothes: consumers on, 117–119; homemade vs. store-bought, 96–97, 116–119, 126. See also Authenticity

Barbie comics: children's critique of, 143, 205 n. 46; and dieting advice, 75–76; people

Erica Rand is a dyke activist and member of
ACT UP/Portland, Maine. She is Assistant Professor of Art
History at Bates College.

Library of Congress Cataloging-in-Publication Data
Rand, Erica, 1958–
Barbie's queer accessories / Erica Rand.
p.   cm. — (Series Q)
Includes bibliographical references and index.
ISBN 0-8223-1604-8. — ISBN 0-8223-1620-X (pbk.)
1. Sexual orientation—United States—Miscellanea.
2. Homosexuality—United States—Miscellanea.   3. Barbie
dolls—Social aspects.   4. Barbie dolls—Marketing.
5. Popular culture—United States—Miscellanea.   I. Title.
II. Series.
HQ23.R36   1995
306.76—dc20   94-38509 CIP